What I Think

Also by Herbert Stein

THE FISCAL REVOLUTION IN AMERICA: POLITICS IN PURSUIT OF REALITY,
second revised edition (AEI 1996)

ON THE OTHER HAND: ESSAYS ON ECONOMICS, ECONOMISTS, AND
POLITICS (AEI 1995)

THE NEW ILLUSTRATED GUIDE TO THE AMERICAN ECONOMY (with
Murray Foss, AEI 1995)

PRESIDENTIAL ECONOMICS: THE MAKING OF ECONOMIC POLICY FROM
ROOSEVELT TO CLINTON, third revised edition (AEI 1994)

AN ILLUSTRATED GUIDE TO THE AMERICAN ECONOMY: A HUNDRED KEY
ISSUES (with Murray Foss, AEI 1992)

GOVERNING THE $5 TRILLION ECONOMY (1989)

WASHINGTON BEDTIME STORIES (1986)

What I Think

Essays on Economics, Politics, and Life

Herbert Stein

The AEI Press

Publisher for the American Enterprise Institute
WASHINGTON, D.C.

1998

Available in the United States from the AEI Press, c/o Publisher Resources Inc., 1224 Heil Quaker Blvd., P.O. Box 7001, La Vergne, TN 37086-7001. To order, call toll free 1-800-269-6267. Distributed outside the United States by arrangement with Eurospan, 3 Henrietta Street, London WC2E 8LU England.

Library of Congress Cataloging-in-Publication Data

Stein, Herbert, 1916–
    What I think: essays on economics, politics, and life / Herbert Stein.
        p. cm.
    Includes bibliographical references.
    ISBN 0-8447-4097-7 (cloth : alk. paper).—ISBN 0-8447-4098-5
(pbk. : alk. paper)
        1. United States—Economic conditions—1945–   2. United States—
Economic policy—1945–   3. United States—Politics and
government—20th century.   I. Title.
HC106.5.S784   1998
330.973'09—dc21   98-35375
                                                                        CIP

1   3   5   7   9   10   8   6   4   2

THE AEI PRESS
Publisher for the American Enterprise Institute
1150 17th Street, N.W., Washington, D.C. 20036

Printed in the United States of America

To

B. G.

Contents

Preface

I should explain the presence of the inclusive word *life* in the title of this book. Economics and politics are, of course, parts of life, and I could simply have called the book *Some Thoughts about Life*. But I wanted to indicate that, in addition to observations about economics and politics, which have been my stock in trade, I am including here some observations about aspects of life that are not primarily economic or political. These are mainly matters of the common experience, ranging from taste in television viewing to the relations within man-woman couples.

One can ask what are my qualifications for writing and publishing about those aspects of daily life. I do not have an academic degree in life. I was never chairman of the President's Council of Life Advisers. The explanation for my writing about such things is that I enjoy doing it. The explanation for my publishing these writings may be more difficult. But most people are amateurs of the daily business of life, and I have found that they like to share their experiences and observations with others. I hope that they will enjoy sharing these experiences with me.

PART ONE
Overview

1

What I Think

The first essay in this collection is a tribute to Henry Simons, with whom I had only one course at the University of Chicago, in 1936, but whom I regarded as a model and a mentor despite that small personal connection. When he collected his published essays in a volume, *Economic Policy for a Free Society,* he prefaced them with a new essay entitled "Credo."

I thought I would like to do something like that for this collection. But the word *credo* did not seem appropriate for me. Although *credo* literally means only "I believe," it has the sound of certitude and finality. It sounds like something one nails to the cathedral door and for which one is willing to fight and die. But I don't have such thoughts, at least about public matters. A reviewer once said that I was the master of the "Don't Know" school of economics. I don't know that I am the master of it, but I surely avow membership in it more openly than most other economists do.

So, I set down here what I think, at age eighty-two, after sixty-five years of participating in economics as a student, practitioner, teacher, and observer. (Simons lived to be only forty-six. If he had lived longer, he might have been a little restrained about nailing his theses to the cathedral door.) I don't claim that I can "prove" any of these thoughts or even that I might not be persuaded out of them by a clever, or not so clever, econometrician with a "data set."

The Success of the American Economy

I believe that the American economy serves the well-being of the American people as well as any economy could and is likely to

3

continue to do so. There are things that an economy cannot do. It cannot make everyone as rich as he would like to be. It cannot make everyone richer than his neighbor. It cannot put everyone in the top 20 percent of the income distribution. But it can create a condition in which the great majority of the population have enough wealth and income so that their happiness would not be much increased by a further increase in those magnitudes. I think the American economy does that.

How do I know that? Of course, I don't "know" it the way we know that water freezes at 32 degrees Fahrenheit. It is one of the interesting facts about economics that it is a science of how people behave to maximize something, often called their "utility," but we have no measure of anyone's utility, let alone of the relationship between income and utility. I arrive at my opinion that more income would not make most Americans much happier by considering my own experience, which is all I can know.

By the way the Internal Revenue Service measures income and the way statisticians convert dollar income into "real" income, I am much richer than I was when I was forty years old, and then I was much richer than my family was when I was ten years old. Of course, I am a different person from what I was. But when I try to abstract from that, I do not find that my degrees of happiness at those stages of my life were related to my income. Or if I try to imagine what would have made me happier at any of those stages, I don't think it was more money. And that wasn't because we always had "lots" of money. Certainly we didn't when I was a boy and my father was a blue-collar worker at the Ford Motor Company, and we probably didn't when I was forty years old. I think that what would have made me happier at all those times was better relations with myself and with other people and better appreciation of art and nature.

Sophie Tucker said, "I've been rich and I've been poor, and I can tell you, rich is better"—at least, that observation on life is attributed to her. I don't deny that sentiment. People want more income. They work, study, and save to achieve it. I would not dissuade them. I predict only that the future well-being of the American people will not depend very much on the rate at which incomes grow. Thirty years from now people will not know whether their incomes have increased by 1 percent a year or by 2 percent a year, and statisticians will be uncertain about which it was.

Per capita incomes in the United States, as well as we can make such estimates, are enormously higher today than they were anywhere, say, two hundred years ago and enormously higher than they are almost anywhere else today. It may be that the appetite for income grows on what it feeds upon and that more income will never bring us closer to the point at which having more income becomes unimportant. If so, the whole income-increasing enterprise is pointless, anyway.

I don't believe that is so. But I do believe we are in the happy state where more rapid growth of incomes—that is, more rapid than we have been experiencing recently and can reasonably expect to continue—is not very important.

Until quite recently—in fact, until early 1998—there was one big reason for thinking that the growth of incomes might not continue at the rate of the previous few decades. That reason was the prospect of enormous budget deficits beginning in about 2010. These deficits would result from the expenditures necessary to provide social security and Medicare benefits to the large bulge in the population that would begin to retire then. The deficits would exceed private saving and cause a decline in the stock of productive capital, which would slow down economic growth significantly, if it did not turn it negative. That the deficits would actually reach the levels being forecast—as much as 20 percent of the national income—was unlikely. Some corrective measures would undoubtedly have been taken in time. But the corrections might be late and incomplete, so that the threat to continued growth remained real.

This situation seems now to have changed. Thanks to unexpectedly rapid growth of revenues, coupled with limits placed on spending, we now have forecasts of substantial surpluses running as much as fifty years into the future. The uncertainty of such forecasts must be recognized, and there will surely be strong motivation for disposing of the surpluses, if they are real, by expenditure increases and tax cuts. But for now one must say that the only serious black cloud hanging over the long-run growth of the economy has lightened.

On Freedom

It is reasonable then to say that the American people enjoy an exceptionally high level of income and can expect it to grow at a rate that will make them feel that they are becoming better off economically. How did we get to this happy state? Economists studying the reasons for differences in levels or growth rates of income among different countries have identified a large number of factors, such as distance from the equator. Fourteen years ago I said that the critical condition was that 100 million people got up every morning to do the best they could for themselves and their children. Today I would say 130 million. But that was an elliptical statement. The point was that when they got up in the morning, they were free to use their resources—their time, effort, talent, and funds—in the way that was most productive for them, given the prevailing physical and technological conditions. They could apply their resources to the occupations, industries, and places that were most productive for them, which were the uses for which others would pay them the highest income, so they were the uses that were most productive for others.

Freedom is the key or, at least, a key, not only because it yielded the highest incomes but also because it was valuable in itself. People want to be free. It is almost tautological to say that people want to be free to do what they want to do. (Freedom was also key for Simons, which is why he called himself a "libertarian.")

Fifty years ago the future of freedom was in doubt. That was not only because the victory over Naziism and Fascism had been so hard-fought and because communism survived but also because of the threat perceived from socialism in Britain and the New Deal in America. Today, in my opinion, the American people have more freedom than ever before. Higher income itself increases freedom, giving people more independence of their existing employment or residence. Increased literacy and skills also add to freedom. Most striking has been the lifting of constraints on the freedom of women, blacks, and Jews to work, study, and live where they choose.

Some people make much of the distinction between "freedom to" and "freedom from." "Freedom to" is freedom from constraints imposed by nature or by poverty or by ignorance. "Freedom from" is freedom from coercion by others. I agree that coercion by others is more galling, and seems more unjust, than constraints imposed by nature, like the inability of man to fly without the aid of mechanical devices. But much of the freedom gained in the past fifty years has been freedom from coercion by others. The Jewish student who could not get into Harvard Medical School, the black householder who could not live west of Rock Creek Park in Washington, the woman who could not be employed in a major law firm—were all being coerced by others.

Today's concern is mainly about coercion by the state. We have many government regulations today, mainly related to health and the environment, that we did not have fifty years ago. We have fewer regulations about international trade, agriculture, transportation, and banking than we did then. I don't know whether there is more regulation now than there was. More important, it is essential to have some feeling about the coerciveness of government coercion. It is one thing to be prevented from producing an automobile that emits more than a specified amount of carbon dioxide by a regulation enacted pursuant to a democratic legislative process, applied objectively and subject to judicial review. It is quite a different thing to be thrown into the Lubyanka prison and shot for making a critical remark about the dictator. I agree that much of current government regulation is unnecessary and inefficient. I admire the people who diligently analyze all regulation and point out the follies that they find. They are engaged in the constant tidying up needed for a good society, but they are not carrying on a revolution.

The sticking point is taxation. Government taxation deprives people of the freedom to use their own income. I have a little trouble with the concept of "their own income." People earn income by applying their resources in this society. Few would earn the same income with the same resources on a desert island or in Central Africa. Everyone's income is a joint product of his own resources and the conditions in the society, many of which are created by government. That does not mean that the income belongs to the government. It means that the government has a legitimate interest in it and claim on it—up to a point. I don't think anyone really disagrees with this. The disagreement is about the point.

I have been "accused" of loving taxes, and in one of the articles in this collection I describe myself as a "tax-lover," but only jokingly. I don't love taxes, but I have less aversion to taxes than many other people, for several reasons:

• Although I coined the term *supply side* as descriptive of a certain approach to fiscal policy, I was always skeptical of the notion that except in strictly limited parts of the tax system tax reduction would increase the revenue. I think this skeptical view is now commonly accepted.

• Although I believe that certain kinds and rates of tax can have a negative effect on total output and its rate of growth, I believe that is true of only a limited part of the tax system, that it is not essential for the total revenue yielded, and that the effects on output and growth could be corrected without loss of revenue by revisions of the tax system. In other words, I do not complain about taxes in general.

• Given my views on the limited significance of the rate of economic growth, these complaints about the tax system do not bother me very much.

• I believe that politicians, especially Republican politicians, have exaggerated the electoral appeal of a promise to cut taxes. One reason is that it is hard to devise a tax reduction proposal that will not look to a large number of voters as favoring someone else.

But I do not love taxes. I think taxes are too high. That means, as it must, that I think some expenditures are too great. I think we spend too much in providing benefits to middle-income and upper-income people through social security and Medicare. There are also aspects of the present tax system that I do not like. I do not like to exclude from taxable income benefits that are clearly income—like medical insurance provided by employers and the rental value of owner-occupied houses—and I do not like to tax corporate profits twice. But my complaints about the level and character of taxes rest more on aesthetic than on economic grounds. I find it messy and therefore displeasing that a program designed to redistribute income from the not-needy to the needy actually takes a lot of income from the not-needy in taxes and gives it back to them in benefits. I also find it inconsistent and displeasing that a tax system described as an income tax excludes some kinds of income and taxes other kinds twice.

On Wealth and Poverty

The reference to aesthetics as a criterion of social policy reminds me of a statement by Henry Simons that has impressed me greatly. He said that "extreme inequality in the distribution of power, as of income, is unlovely." It is the word *unlovely* that strikes me. In a sense Simons's position is unassailable. If he is saying, on the one hand, that he finds this inequality unlovely, who can refute him? But, on the other hand, if someone says that he does not find this inequality unlovely, who can show that he is wrong?

I will not go into the power question. I don't think the distribution of power in the United States is well described by the word *inequality.* We have many centers of power, but they are all limited. The National Rifle Association has much power over legislation about guns, but no power outside that area. Similarly, the American Association of Retired People has much power over social security policy, but no other power. The president's power is more general but also limited in various ways—by Congress and the courts as well as by his span of attention and control even within his own administration. And almost everyone belongs to some institution that has a little bit of power.

With respect to the distribution of income, I am less fond of Simons's statement than I once was. I have found that I really don't care about the inequality, in the sense of the gap between the rich and the poor. That is because I don't care how rich the rich are. Perhaps we owe it to the gossip magazines that we know more about how the rich live. Their lives do not seem wonderful or enviable. I do mind if they have acquired their wealth in illegitimate ways or spend it with exceptional vulgarity. Otherwise I am unconcerned. I once wrote, in a little essay included here: "Apparently the chief sign of being very rich these days is the corporate jet. But, as Ethel Merman said sixty years ago: 'Riding too high with some guy in the sky is my idea of nothing to do'—especially if the destination is a stressful or boring business meeting."

I have no great desire to tax away the income of the rich. But everyone in the society may not agree with me—apparently they do not. If it satisfies the community's sense of fairness to impose a tax of 39.6 percent on incomes above a certain level, as we do now, I do not object. I do not think the adverse effects on the incomes of the rest of the population are great, and, as I have already said here several times, I don't attach much weight to those effects.

If I am not much concerned about how rich the rich are, I am concerned about how poor the poor are. That is, there are some people in America whose low income makes me unhappy, and that I would like to do something about, privately or as a taxpayer. That is, in my opinion, the most sensible definition of poverty—a condition that arouses in other people sympathy and a desire to help. I am sure that there are such people, but I don't know who they are, how many there are, and what to do to help them.

I find it difficult to believe that there are many people in poverty in America by my definition. In 1995, among households with children, 4.3 percent had adults who had been hungry during the past year because of insufficient resources; 2.2 percent of households with children had "severe physical problems with housing"; 6.6 percent experienced "crowding (more than one person per room)." Less than 2 percent did not have a color television set. Looking at such figures makes me think that the number of poor people in America is well under 10 percent—perhaps because I grew up and didn't consider myself poor without even a black-and-white television set.

We have an "official" definition of poverty in the United States according to which in 1996 13.7 percent of the population was poor. This measurement is derived from calculations of the income level below which families would be considered poor. The calculations were first made almost forty years ago. They were arbitrary even then and have been mechanically updated ever since. There are good statistical reasons to think that even if the 1960 base is accepted, the present measurement now significantly overstates the amount of poverty in America.

There are many federal government programs, such as Medicaid and food stamps, in which the official poverty line is used as a criterion for judging eligibility for benefits. The presumption is that people with incomes below that line, or below some multiple of it, are poor to a degree that elicits the society's compassion and justifies public assistance. There is no "scientific" way to locate that line. It can only reflect the community's judgment, represented by government decisions. But ideally the judgment should be based on real and current information about how people live. If the poverty line was $15,911 in 1996 for a family of four, we should know the conditions of life of typical families with such an income so that we or our representatives can see whether those conditions arouse the feelings that justify public assistance. I do not say that because I think that I know what the outcome of such a reconsideration would be or because I feel an urgent need to reduce government expenditures for assistance to the poor. I only think it would be better to know what we are doing.

No matter how poverty is defined, the problem of what to do about it will remain. Some but not all poverty is the result of poverty-creating behavior—childbearing by young unmarried women, failure to take advantage of educational opportunities, and voluntary absence from the labor force. Some poverty is inescapable; some people with the best will and effort are unable to earn an income that the society accepts as adequate for a decent life. The policy problem is how to help the inescapably poor without inducing others to engage in poverty-creating behavior.

We are now in an early stage of an experiment to try to improve the balance of antipoverty policy. The welfare policies of the past generation seem to have erred in the direction of providing too much incentive for poverty-creating behavior. Changes are now underway in the system that will make the receipt of benefits more contingent on participation in training and work. The hope is that this change will lead those who can do so to escape dependency without leaving those who can't in a state of destitution. In my opinion the experimental nature of this change in policy should be borne in mind, and we should be prepared to reconsider the policy if the hope is disappointed.

A more serious condition than that of the people who are poor in America is the plight of what is sometimes called the "underclass." These are people not only who are poor but also who live in neighborhoods with high incidence of crime, illegitimacy, school dropouts, unemployment, and absence from the labor force. How many people fall in this category is hard to say because the definition of *high incidence* is arbitrary. But some measurements that seem not unreasonable suggest that there might be 2 percent of the population, including a larger proportion of blacks, in this category.

The numbers are so small that one might be tempted to say that the existence of such a fringe is inevitable in any society and that no effort needs to be expended in trying to correct it. I do not share that view. A society as rich as ours should try to do better. The possible contribution of public policy is limited. The basic need is moral leadership and responsibility. But there are things that government could do and could well afford to do. Probably the most hopeful area is education. Many of the schools in the affected neighborhoods are miserable, even crime ridden, and do not provide an environment for learning. This condition does not exist mainly because too little money is spent on the schools but because most of the parents and children place too little value on education and because an excessively large administrative bureaucracy siphons off money that should be used for teaching. Still, more money might help. I think we learned from the example of the Department of Defense that even though the system might have been inefficient, we got better results with more money than with less. In my opinion the most attractive proposal is the school voucher plan, which would enable those parents who are motivated to do so to use public funds appropriated for education to send their children to private schools and escape the evils of their neighborhood public schools. I don't think we should be deterred by the probability that many of these private schools would be religious schools. We would be giving poor people only the opportunity that richer ones now have of sending their children to the schools of their choice.

The Stability Problem

During most of my life as an economist, the economic problem was instability. As a college student, I began to major in economics in 1933, near the bottom of the Great Depression. Concern with the possibility of serious recession and high unemployment, even if not on the scale of the Great Depression, remained uppermost in the minds of policy makers and economists for another thirty-five years. Even the advent of high inflation in the 1970s did not dispel that concern but gave it a new dimension. We then became obsessed with the possible lasting combination of high unemployment and high inflation, called "stagflation," or with the possibility of cycles in which spells of inflation led to serious recessions, as in 1975 and 1982.

There is much talk these days about whether we are in a new

economy or, as some put it, whether we have a new paradigm. This talk is stimulated by the fact that we have less unemployment combined with less inflation than we have seen in about thirty years. During 1997 unemployment averaged 4.9 percent of the labor force, and the index of consumer prices rose by 1.7 percent. But our assertion that this is the best combination in thirty years shows that this situation is not new. We are back to the balance that existed more than thirty years ago. During the 1950s and early 1960s, we experienced inflation rates and unemployment rates that were lower than we now have. We experienced those low rates fairly continuously and thought they were the normal condition, although we were always worried about possible deviations.

The interesting question now is how we departed from this benign condition, how we returned to it, and what that tells us about the likelihood of continuing in something like the present state. I don't think all this requires a new paradigm or a new model of the economy. It only requires the model of the economy that Milton Friedman and some others put forward a little more than thirty years ago: essentially, the rate of unemployment is not connected with the inflation rate but is connected with the relation between the actual inflation rate and the expected inflation rate.

Beginning in about 1965, we got an abrupt upward shift in the inflation rate from the moderate rate of about 2 percent that had persisted for the previous fifteen years. During 1979 the rate was 13 percent. This upward shift resulted from the Vietnam War and the two oil shocks and the way in which monetary policy responded to them. This shift in the actual inflation rate greatly raised the inflation rate that workers and employers expected to prevail. When monetary policy turned to fight the inflation, say, in the late 1970s, it became necessary to try to get the actual inflation rate down below the expected rate. That effort led to a period in which both the inflation rate and the unemployment rate were high. But as the disinflationary monetary policy continued, through the 1980s and the 1990s, the actual inflation rate fell, and in time that caused the expected rate also to fall, so that it no longer exceeded the actual rate. In those circumstances we could regain high employment.

Monetary policy was not the whole story. The rise in the exchange rate of the dollar reduced the cost of imports and contributed to the decline of inflation, as the spurt of productivity growth in 1996 and 1997 did. But if we want to explain the big picture of the departure from low unemployment and inflation about thirty years ago and the return to it today, in my opinion the succession of inflationary monetary policy followed by disinflationary monetary policy is the main place to look.

Many people now are surprised that we have an unemployment rate below 5 percent without an acceleration of inflation. For years economists have calculated that the unemployment rate consistent with stable and low inflation was about 6 percent. About twenty years ago I made such a calculation myself. I went out to lunch one day, when the unemployment rate was 6 percent, and observed a "help wanted" sign in a restaurant window, a sign that had been there for many months. At the end of the day, I noticed that the temporary secretary assigned to me had not typed one word of the manuscript I had left for her. I concluded that no one was looking for work and that therefore we must be at full employment, with an unemployment rate of 6 percent. Other, more quantitative economists, reached the same conclusion with more sophisticated methods.

Has the economy changed so that the rate of unemployment consistent with low inflation has dropped from 6 percent to less than 5 percent? Or were the economists who thought that rate was 6 percent simply wrong? I don't know the answer to that. My guess, however, is that the economists were wrong, simply because I think the probability of economists' being wrong is greater than the probability of the real economy's changing in any important way in the course of twenty years.

I believe our experience demonstrates that it is possible to have low unemployment and low inflation simultaneously in the United States. That does not mean that the combination of unemployment and inflation that we enjoyed in 1997 is our permanent and stable condition. No one, at least not I, can estimate that within a narrow range—say, within a range of plus or minus one percentage point. But it does mean that we have left behind the condition of high unemployment and high inflation that characterized the period 1970 to 1985.

How long we remain in the present happy state will depend on monetary policy more than on anything else. Unfortunately, we are unable to describe specifically and precisely the monetary policy that is necessary. That is, we cannot prescribe the rate of change of the money supply or the level of interest rates that will yield the desired result. This is difficult for me to say, because I was raised in the church of devotion to rules of monetary policy rather than reliance on authorities—the University of Chicago—but I do think we are consigned to depending on the good judgment of the monetary authority.[1]

The main requirement will be that the monetary authority should appreciate the danger of inflation and the difficulty of getting back to stability after inflationary expectations have been allowed to develop. We have been fortunate that for two decades we did have monetary authorities who had that appreciation. If I have one main worry about the stability of the American economy in the future, it is that after the generation of policy makers who were traumatized by the inflation of the 1970s and 1980s there will follow a new crop that has not had that experience and that will yield to the inflationary temptation again.

I recognize that the preceding judgment about monetary policy does not rest on very firm evidence. The idea that the Federal Reserve is steering this enormous economy on a stable path by gentle nudges, from time to time, of the interest rate on certain kinds of borrowing does strain credibility. The policy makers in the Fed's marble temple on Constitution Avenue in Washington may just be riding on the economy with the rest of us, with little wisdom, information, or control. The examples of the captain of the Titanic or the Wizard of Oz come to mind in a frightening way. But even though one cannot be sure, I believe that enough has

---

1. The reference to rules versus authorities in the conduct of monetary policy brings me back to Henry Simons, who wrote the article that brought attention to that subject in 1936 ("Rules versus Authorities in Monetary Policy," reprinted in Simons, *Economic Policy for a Free Society,* University of Chicago Press). Simons explained the need to have a predictable rule for the conduct of monetary policy, but he did not think that in the financial system, as it then was, a rule for the rate of growth of "money" could be effective. He believed that there were, or would be, too many "near-moneys" that the makers of monetary policy could neither predict nor control. Therefore, he proposed to rely on a rule dedicating the monetary authorities to stabilizing the price level and hoped that reform of the financial system, preventing the proliferation of assets with qualities like money, would bring about a condition in which a rule for the quantity of money could be effective and reliable. We are now even farther from the financial system Simons desired than we were in 1936.

been learned to avoid the recurrence of major recessions or inflations.

Concluding Thoughts

I return to my opening remarks. I believe that the American economy as it is and is likely to be will do as much as an economy can do to enable almost all Americans to lead a good life. That is a long way from saying that they do or will lead a good life. Whether that happens will depend on moral, psychological, and cultural factors. Although one can point to deficiencies in these respects—indicated by rates of crime, divorce, and the cultural wasteland of TV—I am optimistic about those areas also. I am certainly impressed by the great moral advance reflected in the decline of prejudice against blacks, women, and Jews. More people than ever before have access to high art, and many more than ever before are availing themselves of that access. I think we have shown the capacity for improvement in the noneconomic qualities of life. One who has lived through the century in which the quality of life in so-called civilized societies plunged to unspeakable depths cannot be confident of the outcomes in our society. But still there are reasons for hope that we will be not only richer but also better in other dimensions.

2

Reflections on an Early Libertarian

N ow that we are all conservatives, we naturally divide ourselves into various kinds of conservatives. There are traditional conservatives and neoconservatives, radical conservatives and moderate conservatives (probably no liberal conservatives), fiscal conservatives and social conservatives, isolationist, or nationalist, conservatives and internationalist conservatives. Then, of course, there are the libertarians, many of whom deny that they are conservatives. Indeed, one of their heroes, the late Friedrich Hayek, wrote a famous essay entitled "Why I Am Not a Conservative." But if you ask almost anyone whether Milton Friedman and William Buckley, probably our two most famous libertarians, are conservatives, the answer will be yes.

Libertarianism Defined

I want to speculate a little here about what being a libertarian might mean and what the policy implications of libertarianism might be. That is partly to demonstrate how hard it is, in my opinion, to get from any of the prevailing philosophies or ideologies reliable answers about the issues confronting us today. But mainly I write about libertarianism to recall the thoughts of a remarkable man, Henry Simons, who was, I believe, the first to use the word to describe a political-economic philosophy. Simons was one of my teachers at the University of Chicago in the 1930s and died, at an early age, in 1946. My essay here will consist mainly of variations on themes from Simons, not because I think he answered all the relevant questions but because he raised many of them. Although I shall pick at what seem to me some loose threads in his story, he remains for me, sixty years after I sat in his class, the most congenial of economists.

According to the *Oxford English Dictionary,* the original definition of *libertarian* is a person who believes man has free will (as opposed to a *necessitarian,* who believes he doesn't). Examples of that early usage go back to 1789. The *OED* next refers to a libertarian as one who "approves of or advocates liberty"; hence, "libertarianism" is "the principles or doctrines of libertarians." There is one example from Henry Sidgwick, an economist and philosopher who derisively referred in 1886 to an attempt "to make [Plato] talk modern Libertarianism in a quite unwarrantable way." The *OED* has no example that comes close to current usage, so I feel entitled to claim priority for Simons.

He first came to prominence in 1934 when he published a pamphlet with the title "A Positive Program for Laissez Faire: Some Proposals for a Liberal Economic Policy." This was written near the bottom of the Great Depression, at the beginning of the New Deal, and concerns itself with specifics of economic policy that I do not wish to go into here. What is most interesting is the title. Simons is arguing for laissez faire, for economic freedom. But he also recognizes, or asserts, that laissez faire would not exist, survive, or succeed without positive action by government.

In his title Simons is thus using the word *liberal* in the old-fashioned sense, which it had then and still has in Europe, as meaning the belief that individual liberty was the best route to economic prosperity and social progress. The origins of this idea in economics are usually traced to Adam Smith. When Simons in the text refers to New Dealers or other twentieth-century "planners" who claim to be "liberals," he uses quotation marks to indicate what he regards as the illegitimacy of their claim.

In early 1945 Simons wrote "A Political Credo," which he described as "an endeavor to formulate specifically the political predispositions" implicit in his work. The credo later became the introduction to a collection of his essays, published in 1948 under the title *Economic Policy for a Free Society.* By that time in America the word *liberal* had been appropriated by those who favored a massive expansion of the role of the state, and Simons felt the need for some other description of himself and the policies he favored. The description he decided upon was *libertarian* (although he also from time to time, and somewhat confusingly, reverted to *liberal*).

That he regarded his position as not only "libertarian" but "severely" so may be a little surprising to modern readers who are more likely to find it "moderate" or even "compromising." I think Simons might reply that rigorous pursuit of the libertarian goal, which by definition precludes impinging on the liberties of others, logically leads to compromise, just as the pursuit of laissez faire logically led to the need for a positive program of government. Indeed, Simons's 1945 essay quite explicitly repeats the position he took in 1934: "The libertarian policy prescription calls essentially for planning to preserve freedom."

Liberty, Equality, and Justice

The key paragraph of the 1945 essay begins on the first page:

> The distinctive feature of [the libertarian tradition] is emphasis upon liberty as both a requisite and a measure of progress. Its liberty or freedom, of course, comprises or implies justice, equality, and other aspectual qualities of the "good society." Its society, however, is a living, functioning organization or "organism"; and its good society is no static conception but is essentially social process whose goodness is progress—and progress not only in terms of prevailing criteria but also in the criteria themselves.

Libertarianism, Simons continues, "is thus largely pragmatic as regards the articulation or particularization of its values; but its ethics, if largely pragmatic, also gives special place to liberty (and nearly coordinate place to equality) as a 'relatively absolute absolute.'"

The many qualifiers Simons here imposes on "liberty" are interesting. Liberty "of course" comprises or implies justice and equality. The good society is adaptive. The application is pragmatic. Liberty is a "relatively absolute" absolute. When all this is said, being "for liberty" loses its clarity and distinctiveness as a guide to policy.

The use of the word *equality* as a value nearly coordinate with liberty rings strangely in our ears today, when someone who demands equality is likely to be accused of fomenting "class warfare." Yet Simons is very cautious about equality: "Save as the bride of liberty, equality is pale and deadly dull, if not revolting. But the ultimate liberty obviously is that of men equal in power."

Justice is the key. The word is not heard much these days, except as the name of a federal cabinet department or of a member of the Supreme Court. But Americans do pledge allegiance to a republic "with liberty and justice for all," and, however much we may value freedom, we do not really mean that people should be free to do whatever they wish. A person is free to do only what he may justly do. To the extent that he cannot do what he may justly do, he is not free. One hundred and fifty years ago, one might have said—and some probably did say—that slaves were as free as everyone else to exercise their property rights, which only happened to be negative. But it was decided that slavery was unjust and therefore a deprivation of the freedom to which the individual was entitled.

Simons distinguishes between two kinds of justice—commutative and distributive justice. Commutative justice "dictates that each shall receive according as he (or it) contributes to organized, cooperative, joint production or, in technical economic language, according to the productivity of his property, capital, or capacity (including personal capacity)." Why Simons calls this "justice" is unclear. It is presumably the result that would obtain in voluntary exchange in free, competitive markets. If A and B exchange their product, each gets the value of his product as measured by what the other is willing to pay for it.

This definition has intuitive appeal as being fair. But it implies, in the first place, that these exchange values are the true values of what each produces. That we do not always intuitively accept this is shown by our fascination with the story of Babe Ruth. When asked why he had a higher salary than the president of the United States, he replied, "Well, I had a better year." We smile and accept the logic, but we also recognize that it is a little odd, because we think that what the president does is really more valuable than hitting home runs, even if the president is Herbert Hoover.

There is also intuitive appeal in the idea that a person should get what he contributes. He seems to deserve it as a reward for his efforts. But his contribution may not be the result of his efforts, or not mainly that. The value of his contribution depends on inherited personal capacity and other wealth, family environment, education, and the nature of the society in which he lives—none of which is "his" contribution. Nowadays, players much inferior to Ruth earn incomes much larger than his partly because the society is richer but also because TV has made them more productive in the sense that far more people can watch them at the same time.

Justice and Economic Efficiency

Simons's case for commutative justice is really a case for two other things. One is the case for liberty again, because any radical alteration of distribution from the results of voluntary exchange among persons would require a degree of centralized power that would be inconsistent with liberty. This raises the question of what possibilities exist to alter the distribution of income without a dangerous concentration of power. Simons does not deny that there are such possibilities.

The other part of the case for commutative justice is a case for efficiency. Redistributing income away from the system in which each gets the value of his product impairs incentives, disorganizes production, and so reduces total output. As Simons puts it, "No large group anywhere can possibly gain enough from redistributing wealth to compensate for its probable income losses from the consequent disorganization of production." Also: "However, our primary problem is production. The common man or average family has a far greater stake in the size of our aggregate income than in any possible redistribution of income. Large and efficient production requires close approximation to the norm of commutative justice." Thus, "large and efficient production" is added to the list of values—liberty, equality, and justice—with which a libertarian must be concerned.

What is striking about these statements is that they are quantitative propositions. That is, they imply a quantitative relation between the size of the change in distribution and the size of the consequent change in the rate of growth of total output. But at the time these statements were made, we knew little about the distribution of income or about the rate of economic growth, and especially about the sources of economic growth—about which we still know little.

The nature of the quantitative relation between distribution and growth may be illustrated by some arithmetic. Suppose that the lowest 20 percent of the population receives 4 percent of the national income. Redistribution to raise that 4 percent to 5 percent will presumably slow down the growth of the national income, because it will reduce the incentive to work and save of the other 80 percent of the population, from whom income would have to be taken. In time, the 5 percent of the now more slowly growing income will be no more than the 4 percent of what the more rapidly growing income would have been. But one needs to be cautious about drawing conclusions from such calculations. Suppose that when the lowest 20 percent of the population received 4 percent of the income, the rate of growth would have been 2.5 percent per annum but that the redistribution cuts the growth rate to 2.4 percent. How long will it be before the 5 percent is less than the 4 percent would have been? The answer turns out to be 228 years.

In this example, redistribution is assumed to reduce the growth rate from 2.5 percent per annum to 2.4 percent. That may strike some as an absurdly low assumption. But it is a reduction of 4 percent in the annual growth rate, whereas the income share of the other 80 percent of the population is declining only from 96 percent to 95 percent, which is a decline of a little over 1 percent.

In any case, the numbers used in this example are of no importance. What is important is that to say that no large segment of the population can gain from redistribution implies knowing something specific about the determinants of growth that we do not know. The example does suggest, however, that the gain from redistribution could plausibly last for a long time.

Reducing Inequality

Simons's other kind of justice is "distributive justice," meaning simply equality, including equality of income. He is deeply concerned about that. He is not satisfied with the equal right of the rich and the poor to sleep under the bridges of Paris. Nor is he satisfied with the comfortable way station of equality of opportunity, although he gives much weight to it. He is concerned with progressive reduction of inequality of outcomes.

He felt no need for an extensive argument on the importance

of equality. In "A Positive Program for Laissez Faire," he discussed the question of the equitable distribution of power as well as the equitable distribution of economic goods or income. "Surely," he wrote, "there is something unlovely, to modern as against medieval minds, about marked inequality of either kind. A substantial measure of inequality may be unavoidable or essential for motivation; but it should be recognized as evil and tolerated only so far as the dictates of expediency are clear." The use of the word *unlovely* comes, in my opinion, as close as possible to saying that the issue is one about which you can agree or disagree but about which there is nothing more to say.

His warning about redistribution is really a warning against a certain way of reducing inequality. He wanted redistribution but wanted it to be achieved in a particular way. He envisaged a two-level process. At one level, production is organized in a free-market system that yields a primary distribution of income that is highly unequal. At the other level, this primary distribution is changed by transfer programs, taxation, and investment in the education of those who would otherwise be least productive. He believed that "progressive mitigation of inequality" could be achieved by policy at the second level while the free-market system could be preserved to yield both liberty and efficiency.

Fifty years later one can say that this vision has been supported by history. Societies that tried to achieve greater equality by suppressing the free-market system have failed, their economies have collapsed, and there has been poverty for everyone. Those societies that have combined a substantial welfare system for redistribution while preserving the free market have on the whole succeeded in reducing poverty while sustaining economic growth.

Distinguishing between these two levels of activity reduces the conflict between liberty cum growth on the one hand and redistribution on the other hand. But the two levels cannot be entirely isolated from each other. Simons was very interested in "neutralizing" the tax system, so that it did not distort the pattern of production that would emerge in a free market. That was one reason for his devotion of so much effort to describing a comprehensive nondistortive income tax. But the redistribution system will affect incentives to work and save and thus will affect the rate of growth. The question of whether these effects are desirable, and to what extent, will remain.

Simons placed great emphasis on education rather than transfers. His idea was to raise the incomes of the poorest people by raising their productivity. Although he was not explicit about this, one reason was probably his belief that education was cheaper, imposing fewer burdens on the rest of society, than the transferal of income. There is the homely story about teaching a man to fish, which will keep him fed for the rest of his life, rather than giving him a fish, which will leave him hungry the next day. But the story is not compelling. The costs of teaching him to fish may exceed the costs of giving him a fish a day for the rest of his life. That is, there is a cost-benefit question here, as almost everywhere else. Spending on education is a form of investment. That investment may be, for some students at least, less productive than other investments in the society. In that case, it may be cheaper to make the more productive investment and share the proceeds with underachieving students rather than trying to educate them up to a higher level of productivity.

Welfare Policy

There may be a reason to prefer education to transfer—which we now call "welfare"—as a way of dealing with inequality. That is because the society would rather see people studying, learning, and working instead of receiving welfare, even if the welfare process is cheaper. Whether a "severe" libertarian can take that position is unclear, because libertarians generally deny any right to tell other people how to live their lives.

The problem of controlling the lifestyle of others arises even more acutely in the consideration of welfare policy. The most libertarian version of welfare policy is the negative income tax, associated with Milton Friedman. The basic idea is that people should be given money in proportion as their income falls below a certain level, without any question or requirement as to their own behavior. In other words, the system was to maximize the liberty of its recipients. Eventually, two main defects in the system were perceived. First, it was expensive, because it created an incentive for people to remain poor enough to qualify for benefits. Second, and probably more important, it encouraged or permitted people to behave in ways that the society did not like—that is, not to study, not to work, and, apparently most disliked of all, for young unmarried women to have babies. Concern over this defect has led to the current interest in welfare "reform"—which means to give or withhold welfare benefits to encourage or discourage certain kinds of individual behavior. Whether a libertarian can endorse such "reform" is a question.

We also hear a great deal of talk these days about "values" and about the need to base conduct on a more elevated set of values than is believed to prevail in our society. This attitude creates a problem for libertarians. Simons says: "A moral order imposed by force or fraud, by authorities, or by threats of punishment in this world or the next is a contradiction in terms. Moral individual conduct is meaningful only within a range of responsible freedom; and social morality is, like truth, a matter of voluntary consensus. The libertarian recognizes no test of moral truth or moral wisdom save such consensus. Society is always right—provided it is the right kind of society."

But there is no answer here for dealing with the possibility that a significant number of people do not share the consensus and thus do not do what the society considers right.

I do not propose to try to parse every sentence in Simons's remarkable essay. The important point is that many problems arise when a libertarian says, as Simons does and as I believe he reasonably should, that he values not only liberty but also justice, equality, economic growth, and moral behavior. These problems are of two kinds. First, there are many relevant, factual things that we do not know. We do not know, for example, to what extent redistribution of various kinds affects economic growth, to what extent investment in education pays off in reducing inequality, or to what extent changes in welfare programs affect behavior. Second, even if we knew the size of the trade-offs—how much redistribution has how much effect on growth, for example—we have no objective way of deciding how much of one goal it is worthwhile to abandon in the name of achieving another goal.

These problems are not peculiar to libertarianism. They bedevil any general approach to policy. Simons's answer—to take recourse to process—is the only one possible. The democratic process in a free society will give better answers than any other and will give better answers as time passes. That proposition is probably one on which not only all present varieties of conservatives but also any remaining liberals can agree.

3

Brave New World *Already?*

I suppose that many people who watched the TV version of Huxley's novel *Brave New World*[1] must have asked themselves whether we are not there already. Huxley visualized a society in which the population, except for the few masters, is kept under control, not by fear of punishment but through the "reinforcement of desirable behavior by rewards" and the "non-violent manipulation of the environment and of the thoughts and feelings of individual men, women and children." In the novel everyone has free access to an unlimited supply of a drug, soma, that induces a feeling of happiness. People are constantly brainwashed with the thought that they deserve to be happy. Sex is readily available without complications. Babies are produced in vats. There is no love between individuals, no families, no devotion to anyone or anything to compete with devotion to the State.

All of this brings up thoughts of Prozac and Viagra, the "sexual revolution," the constant bombardment of product advertising, and the political imposition of "spin" on every issue. Hence the question, Are we there already?

When Huxley wrote his book, published in 1932, he placed the "brave new world" in the twenty-fifth century. But in 1958 he wrote a little book called *Brave New World Revisited,* in which he expressed the thought that we were getting there much sooner than he had earlier imagined and that, indeed, we would be far into it by the end of the twentieth century. He advised his readers

---

1. NBC, April 19, 1998.

to read that book "against a background of thoughts about the Hungarian uprising and its repression" (1956).

Population and Technology

Two forces led Huxley to advance the date at which his society would arrive: population and technology. He foresaw that the world's population would increase enormously by the end of this century. He thought that the great increase in population would cause economic misery around the world, creating the need for a dictatorship to maintain order and control future population growth. Technological change would require the concentration of production in huge institutions, controlled either by Big Business or by Big Government. Within these institutions, the technology would require that workers perform more and more as robots. But the main contribution of "advancing" technology to Huxley's world was the facility it provided for manipulating the minds of the population. Television would greatly enhance the ability of the authorities to bring their message constantly into every home. Little newspapers and magazines with dissenting opinions could not survive economically. The population would be constantly immersed in soap operas and sports on TV, effectively diverted from any thinking about the society. Mind-altering drugs would be increasingly available, cheap and without dangerous side effects.

In 1958 Huxley saw all this already happening or just around the corner. What he would say today, we cannot know. He died in 1963. But it seems to me that the main lesson, or at least one of the main lessons, from Huxley's 1958 essay is how wrong a brilliant mind can be.

He was right about the growth of population. But that growth did not produce an economic crisis, with incomes declining and government control required to maintain order. World per capita income is larger than ever and still rising. In what were the two most populous poor countries, China and India, the improvement in the economic conditions of life has been especially noticeable. This improvement of economic conditions was not brought about by an increase of centralized control. Government control of economies is diminishing everywhere. The greatest economic crisis since Huxley wrote occurred in the most controlled state, the USSR, and led to the dismantling of controls.

Moreover, technological change did not lead to a centraliza-
tion of production in a few giant institutions. The trend has been
the reverse. Improved information technology has facilitated the
efficient interaction of independent units through the market,
without central control. And technology has not changed workers
into robots. On the contrary, technology has created mechanical
robots and calls upon human beings to do what robots cannot do.

Manipulation of Human Minds

The centralized manipulation of human minds through modern
media that Huxley predicted and feared is not happening either.
He did not foresee cable TV, let alone the Internet. People have
access to more varied sources of information than ever before.
Moreover, television is turning out not to be an effective medium
for influencing human emotions. Huxley describes the rousing effect that Hitler could have on a hundred thousand Germans listening to him in person in moonlight in an amphitheater. If he had
delivered the same speeches on TV to millions of people sitting at
home in groups of two or three, eating popcorn, getting up to go
to the bathroom, and surfing the channels with their remote control, the effect would have been very small. Certainly the exposure
of our great authorities on TV has not increased respect for them
or willingness to follow their lead. And the effect of advertising,
which concerned Huxley greatly as an instrument that a dictator
might use, has turned out to be trivial. We may buy red or black
cars rather than green or brown ones because of TV, but we don't
buy cars because of TV.

The use of mind-altering drugs has probably increased as
Huxley foresaw, although probably not to the extent that he imagined. He thought that the use of these drugs would make the population indifferent and willing to accept control by political leaders.
But first there would have to be seizure of control by some group
that was not indifferent, and we do not have the atmosphere for
that sort of revolution today. Of course, we do have people who
want to be in office, but once in office they don't want to be in
control. Anyway, what causes indifference to politics today is not
drugs but politics, which seems less and less relevant to our lives.

There is a trick in Huxley's argument that makes it difficult
to refute. Unlike the people in the Gulag Archipelago, the popula-

tion in Huxley's world do not know they are not free. They have been drugged and brainwashed into thinking that they are doing exactly what they want, not what someone else, some dictator, wants them to do. So, if we say that we are free, how can we prove that we have not been programmed to say that by some master who is manipulating us? Perhaps he put soma into our drinking water.

There is, however, an answer to that. The masters in Huxley's world would not allow a movie of *Brave New World* to be shown on TV. The movie reveals what such a society could be like and what a horror it would be. The heroes of the movie are a man and woman who escape the system with their baby and are going to live like a traditional family. As long as *Brave New World* is shown on TV, we will know we are not in it.

I describe the brave new world as a horror, and Huxley thought of it as that also. He was writing a warning, not a prescription. There may be people who do not look upon it as horrible. It is a society in which people's every want is fulfilled. But, as my Professor Frank H. Knight used to say, what people want is not only to have their wants fulfilled but also to have better wants. People in *Brave New World* satisfy the wants they have but are prevented from having some good wants, like want for love and family, and deprived of the opportunity to reach for new and better wants.

4

Herb Stein's Unfamiliar Quotations

I love to browse through Bartlett's *Familiar Quotations.* It may be lazy of me, but I like to taste the plums of many authors whose full pudding I cannot digest. For example, I cannot make anything of T. S. Eliot in his entirety. But I know I am in the presence of genius when I read the following lines:

> O the moon shone bright on Mrs. Porter
> And on her daughter
> They wash their feet in soda water.

Of course, some of these nuggets are ambiguous. Thus, there is Axel Oxenstiern saying, "Behold, my son, with how little wisdom the world is governed." For a long time I thought that was a complaint that the world was not governed by more wisdom. Recently I have come to think it means that not much wisdom is required to govern the world.

As small repayment for the pleasure I have gotten from Bartlett, I am setting down here a few quotations, with explanations where necessary, that have resonated with me and that are not included in Bartlett.

- "If you meet a madman who says that he is a fish and that we are all fishes, do you take off your clothes to show him that you do not have fins?"—Milan Kundera, *Risible Amours*

I love this in part because I am proud of having translated it from the French, which was first translated from the Czech. But I love it even more because it has saved me so much trouble. In the past when I encountered some outlandish inanity—often about taxes—I would sit down at my keyboard and write an answer. I am still tempted to do that, but since I encountered that quotation, I have resisted.

You may ask, "How will I know if he is a madman?" The answer is, "Don't worry, you'll know." And if you are in doubt, assume he is mad and leave the refutation to others. There is plenty of work to be done in the world without debating with people who *may* be mad.

• "Never waste any time you can spend sleeping."—Professor Frank H. Knight, University of Chicago, in class, 1936

This seems clear enough, aside from the question of what is wasting time and what to do if you can't sleep. I have recently encountered a somewhat contradictory quotation from the poet Baudelaire, who said: "To kill that particular monster [time] is the most ordinary and legitimate occupation of each person."

It is interesting that Knight used the word *waste,* which is the gangland term for *kill.* Perhaps the reconciliation is that sleep is the best way of killing time.

• "Honesty may not be the best policy, but it is worth trying once in a while."—Richard Nixon, in a meeting, 1970

This may seem the ultimate in cynicism, but the second half of the quotation, about trying honesty once in a while, seems to be unknown to many politicians as well as to some other people.

• "Surely there is something unlovely, to modern as against medieval minds, about marked inequality of either kind [income or power]."—Henry C. Simons, *Economic Policy for a Free Society,* 1948

What fascinates me about this sentence is the word *unlovely.* It is a candid declaration that feelings on this subject are "feelings," not matters of efficiency or justice but matters of taste, of aesthetics, of emotions.

• "There is a great deal of ruin in a nation."—Adam Smith, in a letter to a friend, John Sinclair, who was lamenting the effect on Britain of the revolt of the American colonies, in 1777 after the Battle of Saratoga

This is a comfort when listening to politicians or editorialists describing the ruin that will follow if their pet policies are not adopted.

- "If something cannot go on forever, it will stop."—Stein's Law, first pronounced in the 1980s
This proposition, arising first in a discussion of the balance of payments deficit, is a response to those who think that if something cannot go on forever, steps must be taken to stop it or even to stop it at once.

- "If a plank creaks in the floor, he [Ernesto IV] snatches up his pistols and imagines that there is a liberal hiding under his bed."—Stendhal, *The Charterhouse of Parma* (1839)
I take this as a comment on many of today's pundits.

- "Three percent exceeds two percent by fifty percent, not by one percent."—Edward Denison, in conversation, about 1960
Denison made an obvious point but an important one commonly overlooked in discussion of economic growth.

- "Observe how he has made a breast of his back.
In life he wished to see too far before him,
And now he must crab backwards round this track."— Dante's *Inferno,* canto XX, circle eight—"The Fortune Tellers and Diviners"
This is Dante's vision of the fate of economic and political forecasters.

- "Where is the wisdom we have lost in knowledge?
Where is the knowledge we have lost in information?"—T. S. Eliot, *The Rock*
These Eliot lines, not in Bartlett, are an advance comment on the Information Age of which we are now so proud.

- "Don't worry, you'll do it again!"—Mother-in-law, in conversation many times
In the Jewish tradition this sardonic remark is intended to be a comfort for a person who is grieving over having made a serious mistake.

- "Thus, prediction of whether or not the capitalist order will survive is, in part, a matter of terminology."—Joseph Schumpeter, *Encyclopaedia Britannica,* 1945

"Capitalism survived its crisis and went on to great successes. But the capitalism that survived and succeeded was not the capitalism of 1929."—Herbert Stein, "The Triumph of the Adaptive Society," 1989

This joint entry is a reminder that terms like *capitalism, socialism, liberalism, conservatism, welfare state,* and *free market* have to be defined if they are to be used in intelligent discussion. The required definitions are missing most of the time.

- "We [the American colonists fighting in the War of Independence] have shed our blood in the glorious cause in which we are engaged; we are ready to shed the last drop in its defense. Nothing is above our courage, except only (with shame I speak it) except the courage to TAX ourselves."—James Madison, 1782

I was not the first person to observe this fact.

- "A person can do any amount of work as long as it is not his own."—Robert Benchley

This comes to mind frequently when I am emptying the dishwasher or similarly engaged.

PART TWO
History

5

Eighty-One Years

I am amazed these days to think of how much history has occurred in my lifetime. When I was born, in 1916, the Battle of Verdun and the First Battle of the Somme were being fought in France. In each of those battles there were a million casualties. That was the introduction to eight-one years of horror. To anyone who has lived through a significant part of those years, the horror is vividly recalled by a listing of place names—Auschwitz, Dresden, Lubyanka, Gulag (not one place but many), Shanghai, Hiroshima, Rwanda, Cambodia, Bosnia. These names conjure up plenty of testament to the evil, cruelty, and folly of man.

But that was only one side of the story. Those years also tell a story of increasing freedom, equality, and material well-being, a testament to the conscience and creativity of mankind. Some of the achievements of this period were defensive—defeating Fascism and restraining and surviving communism. There were, however, also great positive achievements. In my opinion, more progress was made in these eighty-one years than in all previous history to bring to reality the American proposition that all men—and not only all men but all men and women of all races, religions, and ethnicities—are created equal.

Then. . . .

It is necessary to recall only the most obvious facts about what the world was like eighty-one years ago.

I was born, incredible as it now seems, in the shadow of the

Civil War. The period from the end of the Civil War to the year of my birth was shorter than that from the end of World War II to the present, fifty-one years from 1865 to 1916 and fifty-two years from 1945 to 1997. I suppose this has something to do with the relativity of time, but the distance from 1865 to 1916 seems to me an extremely long time, whereas from 1945 to 1997 seems but an eye blink of history. And yet, in many ways we are now much further—not just one year further—from the end of World War II than we were from the end of the Civil War when I was born.

Although I never realized it until now, I was born in a post-war America—post–Civil War, that is. We had a president who was born before the Civil War. There was a Solid South—solid Democratic. We had Civil War veterans marching on Memorial Day, which meant the day for honoring those who fought in that war.

Most important, the emancipation of the blacks promised in the Thirteenth, Fourteenth, and Fifteenth Amendments to the Constitution had, as a matter of fact, hardly begun. Ninety percent of all blacks lived in the South. A large proportion of them lived in a state of peonage. They were effectively barred from exercising their right to vote, to receive equal education, and to enjoy the protection of the laws. In 1916 there were 54 lynchings, 50 of blacks and 4 of whites. That was down from a peak of 230, including 161 blacks, in 1892 but still a shocking number.

In the year of my birth, women did not have the right to vote in national elections. That would come four years later, with the Nineteenth Amendment to the Constitution. But the amendment could not and did not give women equal rights or opportunities in education, employment, or ownership of property.

When I was born, antisemitism was common in America and evoked no feeling of guilt among Christians. The leading person in the city of my birth, Henry Ford, was an outspoken antisemite and also one of the country's most admired figures. "Prestige" colleges and universities limited the admission of Jews. The idea that a Jew could become a member of a "white-shoe" investment bank or law firm was unthinkable.

In all the countries of Europe except France and Switzerland, and in parts of Asia, there were hereditary monarchs and aristocracies. The amount of power these people actually exercised varied, but in all cases they were generally considered to be superior to people less "well born" and so entitled to a certain respect. Even in France, a republic, there were still people who claimed and received respect as members of a hereditary aristocracy.

A large part of the world's population lived in countries that were colonies of European empires. Even small European countries, Belgium, Portugal, and the Netherlands, had colonies. Most of Africa was in colonial status and so were very populous Asian countries, including India and the Netherlands East Indies.

And Now. . . .

The world has obviously changed enormously in all these respects since 1916, and almost everywhere the changes have been in the direction of more equality, of rights, opportunities, and outcomes. Some large countries—Germany and its victim countries, the Soviet Union and its empire, and China—passed through a period of horrible oppression. But even in those places conditions have since radically improved, not only relative to the worst of times but also relative to 1916.

We can argue now about the degree of racial and gender discrimination in America today and even in some contexts about the direction of the discrimination. We can also argue about what has caused the changes that have occurred. But there can be no argument about the fact that the discrimination and inequality are much less than they were eighty-one years ago.

Stephan and Abigail Thernstrom, in their new book *America in Black and White,* have documented the great improvement in the relative and absolute condition of blacks in America since 1940. I can offer one representative figure that goes farther back. In 1916 life expectancy at birth was 52.5 years for whites and 41.3 years for "Negroes and other races." Today the figures are 77 for whites and 73 for blacks.

Diana Furchgott-Roth and her colleagues have published an excellent study, *Women's Figures,* showing the progress in the relative position of women in many respects—income, education, occupations, and others. Their statistics do not go back to 1916, but I can give some impressive comparisons in one dimension—educational attainment. In 1916 there were 32,000 bachelor's degrees granted to men and 13,000 to women. In 1995 there were 548,000 awarded to men and 630,000 to women. In 1916, 3,000 men and 1,000 women earned master's degrees; in 1995 182,000 men and 195,000 women earned those degrees. For more advanced degrees, the number granted to men is still larger than to women, but the ratio has changed greatly. In 1916 there were 7 times as many granted to men as to women. In 1995 there were 1.5 times as many to men as to women.

As far as Jews in America are concerned, the main question today is not about discrimination against them but about whether they are being integrated too much into American society and losing their distinctiveness.

There are hardly any hereditary monarchies and aristocracies left in the world, and those that remain serve only as tourist attractions, like the figures in the wax museum. America never had official aristocracies, but the respect that used to be afforded here to old and rich families has disappeared. The colonial empires are gone.

Along with this increase in equality has come a strong increase in average incomes through much of the world. Real per capita output in the United States is now four times as high as it was in 1916. The road to this outcome was not smooth. In 1933, when I was seventeen years old, at the bottom of the Great Depression, per capita output was about 16 percent lower than in the year of my birth. But the long-run story is one of remarkable economic growth. The increase was about as large in the other countries that we now consider rich; in some of these countries, Japan being the leading example, it was probably significantly greater. In many of the countries that we do not ordinarily think of as advanced—Taiwan and South Korea, for example—there has also been a large increase in per capita income. Now, as a result of recent economic growth, it is clear that average incomes are also far above 1916 levels in the world's two most populous countries—China and India. Only in sub-Saharan Africa have the past eighty-one years failed to show a marked improvement in average real incomes.

Although inequality of race, gender, ethnicity, and hereditary status has dramatically declined and average incomes have substantially increased, large inequality among individuals in family incomes persists. But even that kind of inequality has significantly declined. Although we do not have good statistics about this for the year of my birth, according to one available figure in 1916 the top 1 percent of the population received 15.6 percent of the total income in the United States. According to a presumably comparable calculation, that figure had fallen to 8.4 percent by 1948. I do not have a comparable figure for 1997, but it is surely much lower than in 1916.

Quality-of-Life Comparisons

Statistics probably cannot reveal what has happened to differences in the quality of life, however. Common observation shows a great reduction of such differences, at least for the United States.

The basic point was made by Joseph Schumpeter many years ago. He observed that the invention of nylon had greatly reduced the difference in the quality of life between the duchess, who wore silk stockings, and the shop clerk, who previously wore cotton. A much more important case is personal transportation. The gap in comfort and ease of travel a century ago between the rich man with his barouche and four horses and the ordinary man on foot was enormous. The gap between today's owner of, say, a Chevrolet and the owner of the most luxurious car there is does not amount to nearly as much. In 1916, when the population of the United States was 100 million, there were 3.4 million automobiles. Today with a population of 260 million we have 125 million cars. We have about 1.7 cars per household, and only about 9 percent of all households do not have a vehicle.

Another example is air conditioning. In 1916 the wealthy could escape the summer heat by going to Bar Harbor or Newport, while most of the population sweltered in their homes, farms, and factories. Today the typical American goes from his air-conditioned office to his air-conditioned home in an air-conditioned car. In 1993 (latest available figures), 72 percent of all households had air-conditioning, including 92 percent of all households in the South. That represents an equalization in the comfort of life that is unlikely to be caught by any statistics.

This kind of development pervades the history of the past eighty-one years. I will give only one more example. In 1916 only the very wealthy could afford to go to the symphony, opera, or ballet—or at least could afford to go often. Today almost every household has frequent access to such performances on television or videocassettes. Something else is also at work here. With the spread of education and information, the gap in taste between the classes and the masses, and therefore the gap in ability to appreciate the good things of life, has greatly diminished.

Freedom in This Century

One of the great crimes of my eighty-one-year history is that during it freedom was snuffed out for hundreds of millions of people in the Soviet Union and its empire, in Germany, in Italy, and, one should probably add, in China, although the amount of freedom the Chinese ever had is unclear. Moreover, around the middle of this period there was much concern that freedom might be extinguished even in the democratic countries by the increasing power of government. Hayek's *The Road to Serfdom* (1946) was the leading expression of that concern, but it arose earlier, in the 1930s, and still persists.

And yet the oppressed people have been liberated almost everywhere—North Korea, Iran, and Iraq being the most notable exceptions. And the fear that the democracies are on the road to serfdom now looks much less realistic than it did fifty years ago.

Some people see in the present size of the federal government a considerable abridgment of the freedom Americans enjoyed eighty-one years ago. In 1916 there were 363,000 taxable income tax returns, or about three and a half for every 1,000 people in the country. The average tax was a little over 2 percent of the taxable income shown on those returns. Today there are about 100 million taxable returns or about 400 for every 1,000 people, or about 1 per household. The average tax is about 20 percent of the taxable income, or about 14 percent of the total income on those returns. The extent of government regulation has also undoubtedly increased, although that is hard to measure.

Still, after all taxes, the average American, and almost every kind of American, has much more real income at his disposal than he did eighty-one years ago. And despite the increase of regulations, he has much more freedom than he did. The limitations of his freedom are dwarfed by the expansions of his freedom resulting from the rise of incomes and education and from the decline of the constraints that had been imposed by racial, gender, and ethnic prejudice.

People worry about the decline of our morals, and they make lists of our sins, from illegitimacy to rap music. Certainly our morals are always a suitable subject for worry. But I don't think our present sins are as great as the sins we were indulging in eighty-one years ago by repressing blacks, women, and Jews.

A Momentous Age

There have been other great and momentous ages in history, of course. When I mentioned my interest in this subject to a friend, he immediately came back with the Elizabethan Age, referring, of course, to Elizabeth I. Some might think of the Augustan Age or the Age of Pericles. I think of the years 1750 to 1830. Those were the years of Mozart, Haydn, and Beethoven. They were the years of Shelley, Keats, Jane Austen, Pushkin, and Goethe (although I could never see what was so great about Goethe). It was the time of Adam Smith, Jefferson, and Madison. And, of course, it was the time of the Declaration of Independence and of the Declaration of the Rights of Man.

That was a great eighty-one years indeed—a period of genius. We have had no Mozart, but probably more people heard Mozart's music last year than in the first 150 years after his birth. We have had no Adam Smith, but he has probably had more readers and more influence in the world in the past 50 years than in the 100 years after he published *The Wealth of Nations*. We have had no grand declarations like the American and French Declarations of Rights, but these rights have been translated into the lives of more people in the past eighty-one years than ever before.

There is probably not much point to comparing periods of history; there is no common standard of measurement. I have learned from talking to taxi drivers that everyone's life story is interesting if you know enough about it. So every period of history is probably interesting if you have lived through it. Maybe that is why I find my period so interesting. I derive a little confirmation from what was said recently by Eric Hobshawn, who is a professional historian, which I am certainly not. He said: "The past thirty or forty years have been the most revolutionary era in recorded history. Never before has the world, that is to say the lives of the men and women who live on Earth, been so profoundly, dramatically changed within such a brief period."

Hobshawn is younger than I am—by one year—and maybe

that is why he refers only to the past thirty or forty years whereas I am talking about the past eighty-one.

One has to be cautious about drawing lessons from history. Historians more learned than I have often been proved wrong within not many years after their pronouncements. Still, having nothing to lose, I will venture some judgments:

- Individual freedom has proved to be a powerful, beneficent force. We are all the beneficiaries of the freedom of scientists to pursue knowledge. We are the beneficiaries of the freedom of each individual to try to increase the prosperity of his family by working, saving, and investing in the education of his children. The world is better off because the victims of oppression and discrimination have been free to protest and to struggle.

- Human conscience and sense of justice exist and influence history. If it were not so, the liberation of blacks, women, Jews, and colonial peoples would not have proceeded so far against the power of the established forces.

- History does not go down every slippery slope. As a famous economist, Colin Clark, once said, the pig that grows up to become a hog does not go on to become an elephant. We should beware of extrapolating every movement to its ultimate possibility.

- Government is not necessarily the enemy of freedom. There are more freedoms than freedom from government. There is freedom to breathe clean air, as well as freedom to pollute it.

- Life, in the large and in the small, is full of surprises. Few people in 1916 foresaw the horrors of the past eighty-one years. Few people foresaw the advances in the conditions of life that have occurred in the same period. We cannot be blamed for failing to foresee the horrors. We can be blamed for how slowly we recognized and reacted to the horrors—Hitlerism and Stalinism—once they were apparent. We cannot be blamed for failing to foresee the blessings we have experienced. We can be blamed for failure to appreciate them after they occurred.

6

Fifty Years of the Council of Economic Advisers

M ost of the available information about the President's Council of Economic Advisers comes from people who have served as members of the council, especially from those who have served as chairman. That is, of course, an invaluable source. It is also, of course, a biased source. A person who has been named chairman of the CEA has been lifted from obscurity to national prominence, he has become a familiar in the house where Lincoln lived, he has had access to the most powerful man in the country. Naturally, he thinks that the president who selected him was a person of exceptional wisdom and that the work he did as chairman was influential and beneficial.

The essay I submit here is subject to the same qualifications. Moreover, I have not had the opportunity to do the kind of archival research that a true historian with years available might do. I have solicited information from others who have served on the CEA, and they have been generous in their response. I have also tried to learn something of the impressions of people who had worked with the CEA but were not part of it. But in the end, what is here is largely based on my own experience. I think that more than twenty years of absence from the Executive Office Building have given me some objectivity. In any case, readers of this essay have available nearby the observations of Mr. Charles Schultze and Mr. Bradford De Long.[1]

---

1. *Journal of Economic Perspectives*, vol. 10, no. 3 (Summer 1996).

Creation of the CEA

Fifty years later, the adoption of the Employment Act of 1946, which created the Council of Economic Advisers, looks like an accident that didn't have to happen. As World War II drew to a close, "everyone" knew that maintaining high employment would be a top objective of national policy after the war. President Roosevelt had declared that repeatedly, and no one was denying it.

High Employment. In 1944 the Pabst Brewing Company, celebrating its one hundredth anniversary, wanted to do something that would identify it with a goal that was universally accepted. Therefore, it sponsored a contest for essays on how to maintain high employment after the war. None of the twelve winning essays suggested any need for a legislative declaration of the intent to use government policy to maintain high employment. That intent was too obvious to require codification in law.

The proposal for legislation grew out of the desire of some people—in Congress, in the bureaucracy, in the labor movement, and in the economics profession—for something more specific than a declaration of intent. They wanted to specify the policy by which high employment or, as they preferred to say, full employment, would be maintained. The policy was simple-minded Keynesianism. That is, the government would spend enough and run a big enough deficit to keep the total of "investment"—meaning private investment plus the deficit—up to the level that, given the size of the multiplier, would yield the gross national product that would ensure full employment. In an early version of the proposed act, the required total of investment was specified—$40 billion.

Naturally, many people in Congress and in the business community were opposed to enshrining this kind of policy in law. They regarded it as a license for expansion of government spending and an invitation to government controls on the economy whose character they could not foresee. After a struggle in Congress, the offending Keynesian language was removed, *full employment* became *maximum employment, production and purchasing power,* and caveats about consistency with the free enterprise system were introduced. (Despite their success in removing the offending language from the bill, the "conservatives" of 1945 could not have imagined the expansion of government in the past fifty years.)

But when it was thus cleansed of Keynesian policy, the bill was nothing but a preamble. It required some substance, and the substance came in the form of process and institutions. That is how we got the President's Annual Economic Report, the Joint Congressional Committee on the Economic Report, and the President's Council of Economic Advisers. The original Keynesian version of the bill did not require any new institution in the executive branch. The Fiscal Division of the Bureau of the Budget was there to calculate the "gap" to be filled by government spending. Economists then in the Fiscal Division were quite willing to take on the function. But when the exclusively fiscal approach to high employment was excised from the bill, reliance on the Fiscal Division was no longer satisfactory.

The Institution. There were four main candidates for the institution to be created:

• A "czar" such as we had become accustomed to during the war, culminating in the director of the Office of War Mobilization and Reconversion. That was unacceptable as a peacetime matter, partly because it would excessively derogate the roles of the elected president and the elected Congress.

• A comprehensive public-private committee. An example is the American Economic Committee proposed by Leon Keyserling in his essay that won second prize in the Pabst competition: "To start, Congress should establish an American Economic Committee, with 3 members from the Senate and 3 members from the House of Representatives, appointed by their presiding officers, 3 members appointed by the President from his Cabinet, and 6 members appointed by the President to represent American enterprise, including two each from industry, agriculture and labor."[2] This had the attraction of seeming to get everyone into the act: it also had the defect that there would be no act.

• A presidential assistant for economics. In fact, since the reorganization of the executive office in 1937, the president had had several assistants, and one of them had been an assistant for economics (Lauchlin Currie part of the time). But many people were wary of that idea. They were afraid of some invisible, unconfirmed Rasputin whispering in the president's ear.

---

2. Leon Keyserling, "The American Economic Goal," in *The Winning Plans in the Pabst Postwar Employment Awards* (Pabst, 1944), pp. 11–15.

• A council of three economic advisers to the president. Having three was some guarantee against the president's mind being monopolized by a dangerous person. Moreover, requiring the members of the council to be confirmed by the Senate was a further guarantee.

The fourth of these is, of course, the system that was adopted. The constitution of the CEA was largely defensive. That is, it reflects fear of a dangerous presence near the president. Fundamental aspects of the CEA are, I believe, unique. I do not believe that there is any other body in the federal government consisting of three members, with only advisory functions, reporting directly to the president and requiring confirmation by the Senate.

A political scientist, Harold Gosnell, writing about the Truman period, said: "It is ironic that the presidential institution created by the Employment Act of 1946, the Council of Economic Advisers, was initiated by Congressional opposition to a full employment policy." That is probably an extreme view. But certainly many of the original proponents of the Full Employment Bill were sorely disappointed at the way the Employment Act came out, and some were tempted not to vote for it. At the same time, there was much optimism in the country when the act took effect and the first council was appointed. The new members, about whom little was commonly known, were expected to bring some great, almost magical, wisdom and dedication to the nation that promised protection against the fear of depression that obsessed the country.

When the act was passed, many key questions about the character and function of the council were not answered and not even raised. These included questions about the nature of the people to be appointed, the relations among the three members, the relations of the council to the president, to other members of the administration, to Congress and to the public, and the scope of subjects with which the council should be concerned. These questions were answered by experience, at least, for the time being, and the history of the CEA is a history of the evolution of the answers.

Who Are the Members?

The 1946 act described the qualifications of the members of the CEA as follows:

> Each of whom [Council Members] shall be a person who, as a result of his training, experience, and attain-

ments, is exceptionally qualified to analyze and interpret economic developments, to appraise programs and activities of the Government, ... and to formulate and recommend national economic policy.[3]

This did not mean that the members had to be professional economists, and especially not that they had to be economists with a primarily academic background.

The character of the first three members is somewhat difficult to define. The first chairman, Edwin Nourse, was undoubtedly a professional economist and had been on the faculty of several universities. But when appointed in 1946, he had been in Washington at the Brookings Institution for twenty-three years. One of the other members, Leon Keyserling, was a lawyer who had done some graduate work in economics but whose career had been mainly as a member of the Senate staff. The third member, John D. Clark, was a lawyer and businessman who turned to the study of economics at the graduate level at the age of forty-four. Thereafter, he pursued a mixed career in academia, law, business, and government—federal, state, and local—until appointed to the council. The successors to Nourse and Clark during the Truman administration, Roy Blough and Robert Turner, were professional economists who were at universities when appointed but who had spent most of their professional lives in the federal government.

Academics on the Council. The regime of council members with predominantly academic backgrounds began with the chairmanship of Arthur Burns, in 1953. That probably reflected Burns's own assessment at the time of the relative value of academic economists and of other economists. But it was also true that after twenty years of the New Deal, all economists with extensive experience in the government were labeled as "New Dealers," or worse, and the newly installed Republican Congress was very suspicious of such people. In that atmosphere, to be in a university, far from Washington, and with little known commitment to any specific economic policy was an advantage. Burns's first selections, Walter Stewart and Neil Jacoby, met those standards.

Starting with Burns in 1953, there have been fifty members of the CEA. All but six came from mainly academic backgrounds;

---

3. Stephen K. Bailey, *Congress Makes a Law* (New York: Columbia University Press, 1950).

two had spent most of their careers in the Federal Reserve (Lyle Gramley and Alicia Munnell). Schultze had a mixed—government, think tank, university—career. Alan Greenspan, Beryl Sprinkel, and I were exceptions. I had spent most of my working life with an organization of businessmen, the Committee for Economic Development, which was "acceptable" because it was not too businesslike. Greenspan had his own consulting firm, with many business clients, and questions were raised about this connection when his appointment was being considered. In the end, he had to divest himself of potentially conflicting interests. Sprinkel had been an economist for a Chicago bank for many years, but before being appointed chairman of the CEA, he had been "laundered" by service as under secretary of the Treasury; and when Donald Regan moved from being secretary of the Treasury to being chief of staff in the White House he, in a sense, took Sprinkel with him.

In retrospect, it seems natural that the CEA should be composed almost exclusively of academics, even though that may not have been foreseen at the outset and the economists who participated in drafting the 1946 act were not mainly academics. Academics have a more plausible appearance of objectivity than economists who come from business or labor organizations, especially to observers who are unaware of the interests and fixations that motivate professors. Academics may also find it easier or safer than other economists to take two or three years out of their careers to serve on the CEA. Possibly, academic economists are less specialized and more versatile than other economists and so may be better equipped to deal with the diversity of issues that come before the three members of the CEA.

During the discussion of the Employment Act of 1946, some believed that the new national economic policy should emanate from all sectors of the nation—meaning agriculture, business, and labor. Although that prescription did not appear in the act, the composition of the first CEA seemed to conform to it. Nourse was an agricultural economist; Clark was, or had been, a businessman; and Keyserling had been an assistant to Senator Robert Wagner on the Senate Labor Committee. This structure did not persist, although the special status of agriculture remained for a while. During the Eisenhower administration two agricultural economists, first Joseph Davis and then Karl Brandt, served on the CEA. But since then there has been only one agricultural economist on the council, Gary Seevers, and by the time he became a member, he had ceased to be primarily an agricultural economist.

Given the economic theories prevailing at the time, especially among the Democratic sponsors of the 1946 act, it is surprising that neither of the two chairmen who served under Truman was a macroeconomist. But of the fifteen chairmen since the Truman years—from Burns to Joseph Stiglitz—only Laura D'Andrea Tyson would not be classified as a macroeconomist, if that term is loosely defined. The meaning of *macroeconomics* has changed over that period, however, a subject to which I shall return later. Almost all the other members have had at least one foot in macroeconomics. The few who did not were specialists either in international economics or in "industrial organization," which in application in the CEA turns out to be the study of regulation.

The President's Role in Selection. A president's choice of an economic adviser raises the familiar question of the choice of an expert by an amateur. How does a patient choose a doctor? How does a president, who is not an economist and who has probably had little to do with economists, choose an economist? Part of the answer is that he generally doesn't. After the first (Truman) team was chosen, the chairman chose all the members, often in consultation with someone, perhaps the secretary of the Treasury, but with the unquestioning approval of the president. The only case I know in which a president took the initiative about the choice of a member was Mr. Nixon's expression, in 1972, of a desire to name a woman as a member.

Even when it comes to the selection of a chairman, the president's role has been fairly passive, because of the tendency of dynasties to emerge. Burns chose Raymond Saulnier as a member, and Saulnier became chairman after Burns left. Saulnier chose Paul McCracken as a member, and McCracken became chairman when the Republicans returned to the White House. McCracken chose me as a member, and I succeeded him as chairman. Similarly, there was the Walter Heller to Gardner Ackley to Arthur Okun succession, and Schultze can be regarded as part of that team eight years later. Tyson chose Stiglitz as a member, and he succeeded her as chairman.

When a president has already been in office for a time, he has at hand a number of people to advise him on the selection of a new CEA chairman, if he is not about to elevate one of the existing members to the chairmanship. These advisers would include the departing chairman, the secretary of the Treasury, and possibly the White House chief of staff. Thus, when Nixon chose Greenspan as chairman, he was advised by me and Treasury Secretary George Shultz. Presumably, when Reagan chose Martin Feldstein and then Sprinkel, he had similar advice from inside the administration.

So, of the fifty-five people who have served on the CEA, we are left with only about seven whose appointment by the president needs explanation. Of the first three, Keyserling was a protege of Senator Wagner, and Clark was a protege of Senator Joseph O'Mahoney. The selection of Nourse is a puzzle and apparently was to him in 1946 when he was named. There had been reports that Winfield Riefler had been chosen but then turned down for political reasons, perhaps because he was thought to be too close to the financial community. The choice of Nourse is a mystery because he had no background in the parts of economics that one would have thought most relevant to the goals of the Employment Act and because during the 1930s the Brookings Institution, where he was, had been a source of bitter opposition to the New Deal. But Nourse probably represented respectability as well as agriculture.

The other four—Burns, Heller, Weidenbaum, and Tyson— came to the chairmanship by mixed academic-political routes. Burns was recommended to Eisenhower by a committee composed of Randolph Burgess, John Williams, and Gabriel Hauge. The first two were well-established economists with connections to the financial community, but it was Hauge, the younger man, who had the contacts with the Eisenhower presidential campaign and was probably the most important in bringing Burns's name to the attention of the president-elect. Heller was well and favorably known to Kennedy's hometown economists, including Paul Samuelson and John Kenneth Galbraith, but a critical element in his appointment seems to have been the support of Senator Hubert Humphrey, from Minnesota, for whom Heller had done some work. Weidenbaum had his own political credentials, having served as an assistant secretary of the Treasury in the Nixon administration. Tyson had become known before her appointment as part of the "liberal Democratic" team of economists. But she was something of an eccentric within that group, not being a macroeconomist and having a leaning toward managed trade and industrial policy. She evidently made an impression on Clinton during early meetings with economists because of the clarity of her expression as well as the unorthodoxy of her views. He may also have liked the idea of being the first to appoint a woman as chairman of CEA. (I hope I will be forgiven for using the word *chairman* even though the Grammatik program in my word processor says I should use *chairperson* or *chair*. I am too old to change.)

Political Identity. In general, Keyserling being the most obvious exception, people appointed to the council were not at the time of their appointment political activists or most visibly identified as Republicans or Democrats. They were not the kind of people who attended conventions or participated in fund-raising. Probably at the time of their appointment, they were of the party of the president who chose them but not invariably so. And even when so, party politics were not a dominant part of their thinking. At the time of his appointment by Eisenhower in 1952, Burns was a registered Democrat. The announcement of this fact came as a surprise but was no problem. When McCracken, Hendrik Houthakker, and I were introduced to the press as Nixon's economic advisers, McCracken said that we were chosen because we were the only Republicans in the economic profession. That was, of course, a joke, because there were others, although probably only a small minority of the profession. But it was also a joke because at the time of the 1968 election, I was a registered Democrat and through most of my twenty-eight years in Maryland had been a "Dee-cline"— that is, not identified with either party.

But if they were not clearly branded as Republicans or Democrats when they came into office, members of the council soon acquired that brand and continued to wear it for a long time after leaving office. They naturally identified themselves with the president who had appointed them, and with his party, or at least with his wing of his party. And even if they did not, the outside world would so identify them. Indeed, most of the interest of the outside world in them was derived from the supposition that they were associated with some party and might speak for it. The basic fact is that a council member was not chosen because he was a Republican (or Democrat) but that he was a Republican (or Democrat) because he had been chosen.

In my own case, having been politically neutral before entering the council, I found myself a politically active Republican after leaving it. Thus, with McCracken I tried to organize an Economists-for-Ford group during the 1976 election (not a very powerful organization). I became chairman of a committee advising the Republican National Committee during the Carter administration, and in 1980 I worked with a committee raising money for the Reagan campaign. And for years when quoted in the press, I was identified as a Republican, or at least as a Nixon appointee— usually by journalists who wanted to be able to say, "Even Republican Herbert Stein believes . . ." when I seemed to be out of step with Republican orthodoxy.

I am sure that other former members have had similar experiences. As a consequence, a cadre of economists has formed who, because of their employment in one administration or another, are considered to be Republican or Democratic economists. They tend to flock together and to attract others. In turn, they are people to whom newly elected Republican or Democratic presidents look for advice on the selection of economic advisers or from whose numbers they make selections.

Relationship with President. Whoever selects the members of the CEA, whether it is the president himself or some advisers, wants them to be congenial with the president. They want economists who share the president's general point of view. But that is an exceedingly loose requirement. Presidents first entering into the position do not have very specific ideas about economic policy. The number of economists who might fit with the president is large, and among that group there would be significant differences. Moreover, a president coming into office has little conception of the problems he will face, and even less of the policy he would follow to deal with these unforeseen problems. The economist probably has a more ample medicine shelf of prescriptions for dealing with possible illnesses, but even that is not complete. It would never have occurred to a president appraising a potential CEA member in 1968 to inquire whether that person's ideas about how to deal with an energy crisis that might erupt in 1973 conformed to his.

Thus, the conformity of the new CEA member to the ideas of a new president is very general. Kennedy, when he came into office, knew that he was a liberal activist and probably that he liked fashionable economists the way his wife liked fashionable *couturiers*. But he didn't know that he was a Keynesian and didn't know what that was. In 1960 if he had chosen a CEA chairman at random from the names in the directory of the American Economic Association, the odds were very high that he would have chosen a Keynesian, and the odds were even higher if he had wanted an economist younger than he was. And even if he had decided in advance that he wanted a Keynesian, that category would have covered some variety of people, especially varied in their approach to a number of economic problems for which Keynes gives no answer.

Speaking of the selection of economic advisers, Paul Samuelson once said:

> The leaders of the world may seem to be led around through the nose by their economic advisers. But who is pulling and who is pushing? And note that he who picks his own doctor from an array of competing doctors is in a real sense his own doctor. The Prince often gets to hear what he wants to hear.[4]

That is true in a "real sense," that is, in the same sense in which a person who chooses a pig in a poke chooses the particular pig he gets. But that does not mean that the prince, or president, knowingly and in advance chooses the particular advice he gets. Instead of the picture of the adviser either pushing the president or being pulled by him, a better picture is of the two of them holding hands trying to find their way through a dark forest on a moonless night.

The Washington Adviser. Membership on the Council of Economic Advisers is the highest government position traditionally reserved for professional economists. (Some professional economists, most of them named George Shultz, have held higher positions, but they were not positions usually held by economists.) But the members of the council have not in general been the most brilliant stars of the profession. Only one member has won a

---

4. Paul A. Samuelson, "Economics and the History of Ideas," *American Economic Review,* vol. 52, no. 1 (1962):17.

Nobel Prize, although some of the younger ones may still have a chance. Of the fifty-five persons who have served on the council, only three had been presidents of the American Economic Association before joining the council. Five became president after leaving the council, but that was in most cases probably a recognition of their government service rather than of their contribution to economic science. Only four had received the award given by the American Economic Association for the outstanding economist under the age of forty. Only one had been named a Distinguished Fellow of the Association. While several identifiable innovations or revivals in economic thinking in the past fifty years have had important policy implications—monetarism, the natural rate of unemployment, rational expectations, public choice, cost-benefit analysis, supply-side economics (?)—none is associated with the name of a council member, although council members have subsequently expounded and applied some of them.

The fact that council members were not the leading scientists of the profession should be neither surprising nor disappointing. The principle of comparative advantage is not necessary to explain it. It is not only that the leading scientists had better things to do than serving on the CEA but also that most of them would probably not have been as good advisers as the people who did serve. The qualifications for an adviser are different from those for a scientist or theorist. People who invent new ideas almost invariably have a devotion to them that exceeds their demonstrated validity and usefulness. People who advise presidents should be aware of new ideas and be able to use them but should also be aware of the risks of doing so. (As Frank Knight said, "Anything very original in economics would be wrong anyway.")[5] An adviser should not be so devoted to some new idea that he is unable to give the president a true picture of the option that economics supports. (The analogy is not perfect, but although the White House doctor is not likely to win a Nobel Prize for medicine, he may be more suited to be the White House doctor than the winner of the Nobel Prize would be.)

In a piece that I wrote in 1991, I distinguished between the articles that appear in economic journals and what I called "advis-

5. Frank H. Knight, *Risk, Uncertainty and Profit,* rev. ed. (New York: Houghton, Mifflin Company, 1933).

able economics." I said that advisable economics had to have survived some period of debate and testing, had to be applicable to a particular time and place, and had to be communicable to people who are not economists. I then went on to identify the adviser's product and thus the abilities that an adviser should have:

> So the Washington economic policy adviser operates with a little stock of basic ideas that I call advisable economics, a stock that is slowly replenished and refreshed with a flow of ideas from the journal mill. But this stock of ideas is only part of the material that the adviser works with and that enters into his product. I would identify six other elements that enter into the adviser's product:
> - knowledge of the institutions in the field of his concern
> - a body of relevant statistical information
> - a set of ideas about how the government works
> - a political calculus of several kinds
> - judgment
> - communication skills.[6]

These are the qualities that have been sought for by those selecting members of the CEA and generally found in those who have accepted the position.

Relations among the Three

The authors of the Employment Act of 1946 created a council of three members, rather than a single adviser or assistant to the president, because they wanted to guard against the president's becoming the captive of a single, possibly eccentric or dangerous person, perhaps a pointy-headed intellectual. Not much thought seems to have been given to the relations among the three. Apparently, they were all to be equal. They were all to be confirmed by the Senate, and they were all to get the same pay. The president was to designate one of the members as chairman and one as vice chairman, but those designations did not have to be confirmed by the Senate. Apparently, the authors of the act did not think it very important which one would be the chairman.

---

6. Herbert Stein, "What Economic Policy Advisers Do," reprinted in *On the Other Hand . . . Essays on Economics, Economists, and Politics* (Washington, D.C.: AEI Press, 1995).

As things turned out, there was little danger that the economic advisers would have a monopoly on the president's attention. But that was not clear to the authors of the bill, who had a wrong conception, or no conception, of what the advisers would do. And the original idea of three equal advisers might have worked or evolved into a workable system over time if it had not been for the three personalities involved—Harry Truman, Edwin Nourse, and Leon Keyserling. Truman had no use for three economists. He barely had use for one. The president who said that he wished he had a one-armed economist who would not say "On the one hand, and on the other hand" could not use a six-armed council of economists. And he did not have enough interest or understanding to establish what the relationship among the three advisers should be.

Conflicts within the CEA. At the same time, Nourse and Keyserling were an extremely ill-matched couple. Nourse was the chairman, he was twenty-five years older than Keyserling, and he had a much longer and better history as an economist. He expected some deference, and he expected differences among the three to be argued out and settled privately. Keyserling was ambitious, sure of his views, and much better connected with the political powers than Nourse. He had a back channel to Truman through Clark Clifford, the president's counsel. So he was not about to submerge his differences with Nourse. Moreover, the differences were not of a kind that could be reconciled by compromise or by letting each party go his own way. The primary difference was about how public the council should be, and particularly about whether the members should testify before congressional committees. This difference could not be resolved by saying, as Truman did, that each member could testify or not as he wished. If Keyserling testified, the wish of Nourse to keep the council's advice private and to avoid having to endorse or dissent from the president's policy would be frustrated, even if Nourse did not testify.

The open, bitter controversy between Nourse and Keyserling, ending in Nourse's resignation, cast doubt on the viability of the three-man system. The Hoover Commission on Government Reorganization recommended, in 1949, that the council should be replaced by a single adviser. This probably reflected the Nourse-Keyserling experience. It probably also reflected the natural preference of professional experts on organization for arrangements in which each person gives orders to one person and receives orders from one person and their aversion to groups of people ruminating with each other. When the Republicans won the White House and both Houses of Congress in the 1952 election, the future of the council was in doubt. The new Congress provided only for a single economic assistant to the president, and Arthur Burns was appointed to that post by President Eisenhower.

A Reorganized Council. In the spring of 1953, Burns suggested, Eisenhower proposed, and Congress approved a plan for keeping but reorganizing the council. The position of vice chairman was abolished. The chairman was given control over the appointment of staff to the council, and the chairman alone was given the responsibility of reporting the council's views to the president. In retrospect, the reorganization plan seems hardly to have been necessary. The president needed only to agree that he should name council members with the concurrence of the chairman and that he would ordinarily meet in person only with the chairman alone. The formality of a reorganization plan approved by Congress, however, served as public notice that the Nourse-Keyserling situation would not be repeated.

The relationship among the members established in 1953 under Burns seems to have lasted ever since, with possible minor nuances reflecting the personalities involved. The reorganization plan gave the chairman the responsibility for reporting to the president "the Council's views," and not just his own views or the separate views of the members. That is, it is expected that there will be a council view. In fact, that has turned out to be the case. The fact that the chairman chooses the members and the three are presumably in general agreement with his philosophy has, of course, made reaching a council view easier. But it should not be assumed that the chairman dominates the council view. Although the members are chosen by the chairman, they accept the position voluntarily and would not do so if they expected to be dominated by the chairman.

Relations within the Council. A strong tradition of collegiality has developed. On some subjects a member is better informed than the chairman. His opinion would be given special weight in arriving at the council view. Reaching agreement requires no formal process. The three members work in adjoining offices, they see each other constantly, they eat lunch together, and they exchange almost all information. Agreement emerges spontaneously.

Members of the council recognize, without having to spell it out, that agreement among them is important. They testify as a group before the Joint Economic Committee, from time to time they hold press conferences together, and they all sign the Economic Report. To show disagreement on those occasions would weaken the credibility of some and probably of all.[7] Moreover, each member serves on a number of interagency committees, and his influence in those committees depends on the understanding that he speaks not only for himself but also for the council.

Typically, responsibility for each of the subjects with which the CEA is concerned and for the relevant staff is divided between the two members. The members are not, however, as is sometimes thought by outsiders and on a few occasions complained about by members, only staff assistants to the chairman with high-sounding titles. The members have been appointed by the president and confirmed by the Senate. They are part of the administration. When they speak in public, they are assumed to speak for the administration, and that gives them an obligation to speak in harmony with the administration or, at least, not in conflict with it. The extent to which members do speak in public has varied, mainly with the interest of the particular member. As far as is known, chairmen have not circumscribed the public appearances of members, although audiences and the media are naturally more interested in hearing from the chairman.

Relations within the Administration

No president would allow himself to be dependent solely on the CEA or its chairman for advice about discharging his responsibili-

---

7. I remember only one occasion of such disagreement. Paul McCracken had gone out of Washington and left me acting chairman. During his absence, the president asked the CEA for an opinion on a certain subject, to which I replied by memo, which the president approved. I learned when McCracken returned that he would have given a different opinion, but he never tried to undo what I had said.

ties under the Employment Act. A group of economists situated in the Executive Office is also unlikely to exclude itself from concern with economic issues that do not fall strictly within the scope of the Employment Act. Moreover, there are always issues of economic policy to be decided that do not have to go to the president, except possibly in a perfunctory way, but are decided at lower levels. So, contrary to idealized notions that may have existed when the act was passed, the CEA has found itself only one part of a multiparty system for advising the president and has also found itself involved in a much greater variety of questions than those entailed in the achievement of "maximum employment, production and purchasing power" and in many questions in which the president is not involved.

The others with whom the CEA advises on economic policy include most notably the secretary of the Treasury, who is the senior economic officer of the government. The list also includes the director of the budget and, varying with circumstances and personalities, the White House chief of staff, the directors of some specialized agencies, on some matters the chairman of the Federal Reserve, and others. One who should not be overlooked is the president's speechwriter. Presidents tend to judge ideas presented to them by how they sound, either when repeated to themselves or when imagined as presented to the public. So the speechwriter's skill has something to do with what the president will decide. The precise nature of the relationship of the CEA with these other actors in the economic advisory process, and with the president, has varied with the problems to be solved and with the character of the other players.

A Distinctive Role for the CEA? The group process through which advice reaches the president or some other decision point has been more formal in some administrations than in others, and whether the CEA has a distinctive role has also varied. Memoirs of chairmen tend to emphasize the one-on-one, face-to-face relationship with the president. That relationship seems to have been close only in a few cases.

Probably the most intimate and personal relationship was that between President Ford and Alan Greenspan. Some colleagues have suggested that Greenspan, having been a private consultant, was skillful in cultivating his clients, and in this case he had one client, the president. They seem to have spent a good deal of time together, watching football games on TV while discussing a variety of problems. Heller sought out his personal relation with Kennedy and is said to have haunted the halls of the West Wing of the White House to get some words with the president. Burns had regular meetings with Eisenhower; as he described them himself, they sound more like instruction sessions on elementary economics than discussions of current policy issues. Burns was proud that Eisenhower once said to him that he would have made a good army chief of staff, which is more the role of an information channel than of an adviser.

The Troika. In general, though, advising on economic policy has been a group function. It is no exaggeration to say that the life of a CEA member consists overwhelmingly of committee meetings. And since the CEA has no operating authority, its influence depends greatly on its performance in these committees with people who do have authority. The committees have been of three kinds—the formal, central; the formal, extended; and the informal. The durable and at least for a time the most important of the formal, central committees was the "Troika," consisting of the secretary of the Treasury, the director of the Office of Management and Budget, and the chairman of the CEA. This group might be augmented from time to time by the presence of the chairman of the Federal Reserve, at which point it came to be called the "Quadriad." An early version of this organization emerged in the second Eisenhower term, when Saulnier was CEA chairman. It then included the Treasury, the CEA, a representative of the Federal Reserve, and the president's special assistant for economics. In retrospect, the omission of the director of the budget seems odd. But this was a time when budget directors were usually accountants, rather than economists, and Keynesian ways of thinking had not yet taken full possession of the White House.

The centrality of the Troika in the decision-making process was natural. The budget is the focus of the administration's most important decisions about its priorities and policies. The senior officials responsible for the tax and expenditure sides of the budget—the secretary of the Treasury and the director of the budget—inevitably become chief advisers to the president. Of course, presidents prepared budgets before there was a Council of Economic Advisers, and the presence of the CEA chairman in the Troika requires some explanation.

Indeed, as already noted, the Troika did not exist until 1962. But how critical the economic assumptions were to the preparation of the budget gradually became clear, and this seemed to call for the participation of the CEA, which had the best qualifications for making the economic estimates and forecasts. Moreover, and probably more important, at least by the time of the Heller CEA, the budget came to be regarded as the chief instrument for managing the economy to achieve the goals of the Employment Act, which were the special purview of the CEA.

Arthur Okun, when chairman of the CEA, used to say of the Troika that the Treasury had the revenue, the Bureau of the Budget had the expenditures, and the CEA had the deficit. That was a joke and a redundancy since the revenues minus the expenditures equaled the deficit and if any two of the variables were determined, the third would be determined by arithmetic. But there was also a point to the remark. Okun was referring to a period when some thought that the proper size of the deficit could be determined by macroeconomic considerations—that is, one could determine how big a deficit (or surplus, but it was always a deficit) was necessary to achieve full employment—and once that had been determined, the tax and expenditure decisions had to be made to conform.

The existence of the Troika—composed of senior officials, working on a matter as critical as the budget, and having generally good relations with each other—tended to attract to its jurisdiction major economic problems beyond the budget. Thus the Troika became, for some time, an inner council on economic problems generally, and participation in the Troika was important to the stature of the council. Although the Troika did not have a chairman, the secretary of the Treasury was accepted as the leader, and meetings were generally held in his office. CEA members and staff, however, took the lead in making economic forecasts and attempting to predict the economic consequences of policy changes under consideration. As the Troika took cognizance of major aspects of economic policy beyond the budget, it also added for greater or smaller periods of time other members of the administration. Thus, for some periods officials responsible for international economic policy, for energy policy, and for price-wage controls joined in the Troika discussions. This practice, at least in the administration with which I am most familiar, reduced the occasions on which it was necessary to get a presidential decision.

Although the Troika continues to exist, its dominance in the making of economic policy seems to have diminished since about 1981. That change has been the result of a shift in the policy environment, of which I shall say more later. In sum, stabilization has ceased to be the outstanding economic problem it once was, budget policy is considered less useful for stabilization than before, and the struggle over the budget has come to be more intense and more specialized than in the past. If the key question about budget policy is a question about health care, involving a large fraction of all expenditures, for example, the Troika can no longer play the key role it once did, and that affects the role of the CEA.

Interagency Relations. Since early in the Eisenhower-Burns administration, there has almost always been an interagency committee on economic policy more inclusive than the Troika. Since much was said during the consideration of the Employment Act about the need to "coordinate" economic policy, it is surprising that such machinery did not emerge earlier. Nourse, in his early reports, refers frequently to the cooperation he requested and received from other agencies, but those comments seem to have meant mainly the exchange of information, not consultation about policy. Perhaps it was too early for the CEA to have found its way into the policy-making machinery. But there were probably other reasons as well. The Truman administration was divided into its liberal and conservative wings, and the CEA did not fit comfortably in either—or, rather, Keyserling fit in one and Nourse in the other. Some interagency committees appear to have been reluctant to invite the CEA because they would have had to include all three members, who could be counted on to disagree with each other. Some people found Keyserling difficult to work with. After Nourse left and Keyserling became chairman, Roy Blough joined the CEA as a member. The Treasury and the Federal Reserve discussed matters with Blough, but they did not feel comfortable dealing with Keyserling. Frank Pace is said to have left his position as director of the budget and moved to the Pentagon because he did not like to work with Keyserling. Meanwhile, Keyserling had his own interagency committee, which was, however, outside the government manual. He was a member of the liberal wing of the administration called the "Ewing Group," because they met regularly in the Wardman Park Hotel apartment of Oscar Ewing, the secretary of the interior. The leading figure in this group was Clark Clifford, the president's counsel and confidant. Through Clifford the ideas of the group, among whom Keyserling was the only economist, came to the attention of the president.

When Burns and Eisenhower came into office, Burns suggested and Eisenhower approved the establishment of the Advisory Board on Economic Growth and Stability (ABEGS). This apparently served the president's idea of an orderly organization. It also served to put Burns in a leading position: he was to be chairman of ABEGS, and the other members were under secretaries (of Treasury, commerce, labor, agriculture, and health, education and welfare), the vice chairman of the Federal Reserve, the deputy director of the Bureau of the Budget, the president of the Export-Import Bank, and the special assistant to the president for economic affairs.

What ABEGS did is not clear. Burns has said that, unlike some of his successors, he did not want to deal with every economic issue that arose in the government but wanted to confine himself to the macro matters affecting aggregate production, employment, and inflation. Similarly, ABEGS addressed macro matters. But there is no evidence of any contribution of ABEGS to Burns's thinking or to the president's policy on macro matters. Perhaps we should regard ABEGS as an early abortive effort from which the Troika and the Quadriad later emerged. It also served as a channel for information from the agencies to Burns, who had an enormous appetite for information.

Some years after he left office, Burns said that he had been mistaken to constitute ABEGS with under secretaries but should have made it a committee of cabinet secretaries. But in that case, of course, the chairman of the CEA would not have been the chairman of ABEGS.

In January 1960 President Eisenhower established a Cabinet Committee on Price Stability for Economic Growth. This was a committee of cabinet members, and although the chairman of the CEA was a member of it, the chairman of the committee was Vice President Nixon. Eisenhower's creation of this committee was apparently intended to underline his determination to fight inflation, then running at about 2 percent a year. The committee had a small staff of its own, headed by W. Allen Wallis, and produced a commendable statement on the general principles of fiscal policy,[8] but it had no visible effect on policy at the time.

Following the usual practice of a new administration of showing that it knows a new and better way of doing things, the Kennedy-Heller team abolished ABEGS and the Cabinet Committee on Price Stability, formalizing the Troika instead. It probably conformed more to the Kennedy style of government, which tended to emphasize the distinction between the inner circle of White House people and personal friends, on the one hand, and the outer circle that included most cabinet secretaries and the vice president, on the other. At this time, a committee on international finance was also established, headed by the under secretary of the Treasury and generally known by his name, as the Roosa Group or the Volcker Group, and so on. The chairman of the CEA or a member served on that committee.

The termination of agencywide committees like ABEGS and the Cabinet Committee on Price Stability for Economic Growth did not mean that the Heller-Ackley-Okun Council withdrew from participation in discussion of economic issues outside the strict purview of the Employment Act. On the contrary, this council greatly expanded the area in which it operated and set the standard for all future councils in that respect. Its method of operation was to establish confidence with the White House chief of staff— Theodore Sorenson and later Joseph Califano. When an issue of interagency concern arose, it was the responsibility of those people to set up a mechanism for dealing with it. The usual mechanism was an ad hoc interagency committee on which the CEA was represented. This was, in fact, standard procedure thereafter, even when a cabinet-level committee under some title formally existed.

Before the end of his term in 1968, President Johnson established a new Committee on Price Stability. Johnson created that committee partly to symbolize a commitment to price stability, as Eisenhower had done eight years earlier. But also by that time the administration had become heavily involved in trying to influence particular prices, and although the CEA had played an active role

---

8. At least, I commended it in my book, *The Fiscal Revolution in America,* 2d ed. (Washington, D.C.: AEI Press, 1996).

in that effort, the effort was beginning to exceed the capacity and the essentially advisory role of the council. Since the Johnson administration was near its end, however, the committee did not accomplish much, except to leave behind the idea of a more active government role in price control, an idea that probably had some effect in 1971.

The Nixon administration began with a Cabinet Committee on Economic Policy, on an even grander scale than Eisenhower's ABEGS. This committee included all the agencies with even a marginal claim to interest in economics, each represented by its secretaries except for the State Department, which was represented by an under secretary. The president served as chairman. All three members of the CEA participated in meetings of the body, labeled CabComEcoPol by William Safire. Whether the members of the CEA other than the chairman were members of CabComEcoPol was not clear, but that did not matter since membership entailed no powers or responsibilities. (Members attended meetings of the committee and participated in its discussions.)

The chairman of the CEA, McCracken in this case, briefed the president in advance of the committee's meetings. Usually the meetings were devoted to discussions of briefing papers, most of which had been prepared by one of the members of the CEA. These discussions covered a variety of subjects, including such things as the lumber situation or copper affairs. But the committee focused much attention on the aggregate economic situation, budget policy, and monetary policy.[9] These sessions did not usually arrive at conclusions; the president seemed not to like to reach or state conclusions in the course of meetings with a large number of people. But they helped to direct the president's thinking and also to give the others present a sense of the president's leanings that they could use in their subsequent actions.

The president also established at the outset of his term a Domestic Policy Council, of which he was also the chairman and Daniel Patrick Moynihan was director. The division between the Domestic Policy Council and the Cabinet Committee on Economic

---

9. I have reported in some detail on these discussions and on subsequent discussions of fiscal policy in other venues in a 1995 essay, "The Fiscal Revolution in America, 1964–1994," included in *The Fiscal Revolution in America*.

Policy was not clearly established. At one point the Domestic Policy Council Staff disagreed with the CEA about whether unemployment was a domestic policy problem or an economic problem. This vagueness did not matter, however. CEA members did much staff work for the Domestic Policy Council. For example, when the president's welfare program, the Family Assistance Program, was being developed and there was much contention over the facts and the estimates, the president turned to McCracken to generate an accurate picture. In 1969 I headed a task force on the post-Vietnam dividend as a project for the Domestic Policy Council that could just as logically have been a project of CabComEcoPol.

These formal organizations did not remain important in economic policy for very long. President Nixon decided before 1969 was over that meeting with a dozen officials to discuss a subject on which most had little competence was not a good use of his time. He turned the chairmanship over to the vice president, after which CabComEcoPol soon faded away. The Domestic Policy Council became concerned mostly with monitoring the agencies and shepherding legislation through Congress.

Except for two cases that I will note, I shall not trace the succession of National Economic Councils, Economic Policy Councils, and other such cabinet-level interagency committees since 1970. There has always been such a council. The secretary of the Treasury has usually chaired it, with a few exceptions, and the chairman of the CEA has always been a member of it. These councils have rarely been the means by which work got done and decisions made. That has almost always been the province of ad hoc groups including the relevant and competent parties, and these groups would reach policy decisions by themselves or, if necessary, refer them to the president. The National Economic Council established by President Clinton, with the usual assertions of novelty, seems organizationally like many of its predecessors. Whether it has turned out to be different in function and effect from the earlier councils is too early to say.

In its January 1973 report, the CEA noted that the chairman or members worked with the Cost of Living Council, the Council on International Economic Policy, the Domestic Council, the National Commission on Productivity, the Regulation and Purchasing Review Board, the Property Review Board, the Oil Policy Committee, the Joint Board on Fuel Supply and Transport, and the Defense Programs Review Committee. In addition the council and its professional staff served as members of approximately *thirty* other interagency working groups.

In this maze of committees, the CEA established two roles for itself. First, it was a preferred research organization that could be counted on to assemble, analyze, and present the information relevant to a subject under consideration. The CEA staff was highly regarded for its competence. It was able to obtain from agencies information that they might have been reluctant to share with each other. The CEA maintained a reputation for being willing to present all the "respectable" points of view, including those with which it disagreed. In addition, the CEA placed great weight on the ability to produce a clear, brief paper quickly.

Second, the chairman or member of the CEA participated in all these committees as an equal, even though he had no appropriations to dispense or regulations to issue. That much was accepted by virtue of presidential appointment and tradition accumulated over time. But within the committee the influence of the CEA member depended on the cogency and persuasiveness of his argument. Usually in such cases opinion is divided, and people line up on one side or another. The council member adds some weight to the side with which he lines up, partly because of his argument and partly because he counts for one. It is sometimes said that the council chairman achieves influence because he can go to the president. That is unrealistic, in my opinion. If the CEA chairman cannot convince some other member of the group—the secretary of the Treasury or the director of the budget or the secretary of commerce—he is exceedingly unlikely to convince the president. Basically, the influence of the CEA chairman depends on the alliances he can form with other members of the team.

I will refer briefly to two groups because they were important and because they illustrate how different interagency committees can be. After President Nixon declared his new economic policy, on August 15, 1971, he established a Cost of Living Council to govern that policy, especially its wage and price control aspects. The secretary of the Treasury was chairman, the chairman of the CEA was vice chairman, and about ten cabinet secretaries and presidential assistants were members. The council met almost every day. All the members were present (perhaps in part because there was such national interest in the subject that television filmed the openings of the meetings). There was real work to be done—reviewing the general rules of the price and wage bodies, deciding on decontrol of rents or small businesses, recommending the provisions of phase two of the control system—subject in that case to the approval of the president. Discussion was lively, not much influenced by departmental interests, and decisions were reached under the leadership of a strong chairman (John Connally), who was more insistent on reaching decisions than on their particular content. This condition did not last, of course. After the big decisions had been made, interest faded. But for a while it was a model of intense application of a group to a real problem. The CEA played a significant role, partly because I was the only person present who had studied, or participated in, price control in World War I, World War II, and the Korean War.

A quite different setup was the meeting held each morning, at 8:00 A.M. in the White House office of George Shultz after he became both secretary of the Treasury and special assistant to the president for economics. Those in attendance were from the "inner circle"—CEA, OMB, NSC, Committee on International Economic Policy, Energy Office, and Cost of Living Council. Issues were discussed, but these meetings served mainly to set an agenda. They decided what had to be worked on and who would do what, so that important issues were not neglected and relevant players were not omitted. The meetings also served to establish a cooperative atmosphere that might not otherwise have existed.

The CEA and the Treasury. The relation of the CEA chairman to the secretary of the Treasury is extremely important, probably more important than the relation of the chairman to the president. The secretary is the senior economic officer of the government, and he is likely to have been chosen directly by the president rather than by an intermediary, as is usually the case with the CEA chairman. He may be the president's friend, they speak the same language, and he may have a political constituency of his own. Moreover, he has direct day-to-day control over three powerful instruments—taxation, debt management, and international finance.

The chairman is unlikely to induce the president to adopt any policy to which the secretary is opposed, but the president is likely to be influenced by an agreement between the secretary and the chairman. There is much opportunity for rivalry here but also for cooperation.

Several cases of disagreement are well known. John Connally saw no reason for the existence of the CEA. When, in the spring of 1971, Paul McCracken suggested, both publicly and privately, an expansive policy that Connally rejected, the president reminded the council forcefully that Connally was his spokesman. No doubt the president was reflecting Connally in this, and no doubt it contributed to McCracken's resignation, although not before McCracken's policy had been adopted.[10] Donald Regan resented Martin Feldstein's repeated suggestion of the need for a tax increase in 1984 and publicly suggested that the council's Annual Economic Report should be thrown away. George Humphrey, Eisenhower's Treasury secretary, seemed to have an amused and tolerant attitude toward what he called Burns's "kit of tools" for dealing with the 1954 recession. But when a little later Burns expressed disagreement with Humphrey about taxation, Humphrey told Burns to stay off his turf.[11] Burns resisted, and the two agreed to go to Eisenhower, who announced, even before hearing their arguments, that he took the same position as Burns—which made the argument unnecessary.

But there have been important cases of productive cooperation between the CEA chairman and the Treasury secretary. That seems to have been the case in the relationship between Heller and Douglas Dillon, after Heller's arguments, in addition to concern about the state of the economy, persuaded Dillon to support the large tax cut proposed by the CEA. Dillon's support was critical to getting Kennedy's approval. My own relation with George Shultz was critical for me. We came from a somewhat similar ideological background and usually, but not always, agreed. As leader

---

10. H. R. Haldeman reports that in 1972 Connally complained that a number of people in the administration, including me, were conspiring against him; see Robert Haldeman, *The Haldeman Diaries* (New York: G. P. Putnam's Sons, 1994). When the relative power positions of Connally and Stein are considered, one can see to what lengths paranoia can go.

11. The Treasury is particularly jealous of its role in tax policy. In 1969, when I became a member of the CEA and had spent twenty-two years writing about taxation for the Committee for Economic Development, I phoned the assistant secretary of the Treasury for taxation—a lawyer—to tell him that I was on the job and ready to cooperate. He replied, "If any economics comes up, we'll call you." Of course, it did come up within a few months.

of a group of economic officials, Shultz typically did not reveal his own decision until there had been considerable discussion and a consensus had been neared. I felt that my own arguments helped Shultz bring the group to agreement on the position he had probably favored from the outset. In addition, when, as chairman of a task force, I had developed the plan for phase two of the price and wage control system, I thought that Mr. Nixon had more confidence in signing on to it because Shultz also supported it.

These stories could be multiplied. The basic point is a simple one that should have been obvious from the outset, but many outside observers probably still do not appreciate it. The CEA is a cog in a large decision-making machine, and like other cogs it has its special functions and capabilities. But the outcomes depend on the relations among all the cogs—the most important of which for the CEA is the relation to the Treasury.

What the CEA Believed

Several generalizations may introduce a description of the "economic philosophy" of the successive CEAs:

• Each CEA coming in with a new administration produces a statement of its philosophy indicating how it is different from, and superior to, its predecessors.

• Each philosophy is "moderate" and "practical." No one is for a controlled economy. No one is for laissez faire. Everyone believes that government has a role to play but not a dominant one.

• These initial statements of philosophy are not invariable guides to what the CEA will say when faced with particular circumstances.

• On the unavoidable subject of Keynes, the best guide is the birthdate of the council members. Those born before 1915 were not Keynesians. Those born between 1915 and 1940 were Keynesians or had a strong leaning in that direction. For those born after 1940, Keynesianism was a minor and unreliable tool, to be used on some occasions but not relevant to the major problems.

• All CEAs were free traders, at least within the range of options being seriously considered by the administration. When Ms. Tyson was appointed, some questioned whether she fit this pattern, but she turned out to do so.

- Again, within the range of practical options, the CEA has been a strong advocate of deregulation, and where deregulation was not possible, it has been a strong advocate of prices as the preferred means of achieving the object of regulation, as in the environmental case. I shall not try to tell that story here. Charles Schultze is one of the heroes of this story and knows it much better than I do, so I refer the reader to his essay for insights on that matter. I would, however, point to the distinction between *regulation* and *promotion,* both of which are interferences with the market. CEAs have not been nearly so clear in opposition to promotion—for preschool education, for worker training, or even for some of the activities that go under the name of "industrial policy."

Policies through the Years. I will now briefly call the roll of some of the policies avowed by successive CEAs.

Although, as noted at the outset, the Employment Act of 1946 had its origin in a kind of simple-minded Keynesianism, the first council did not subscribe to that philosophy. In its first report to the president, the council explicitly disavowed what it called the "Spartan" view and the "Roman" view. The Spartan view was thoroughgoing laissez faire. The Roman view, associated with the idea of bread and circuses, was that everything could be made all right by the correct dosage of fiscal and monetary measures. The private economy was said to be much too independent and complex to be managed by such simple instruments.

What emerges, more or less explicitly, from the reports of the first CEA—in which Nourse and Keyserling seem to have agreed—is something like this: merely to prevent recessions is not sufficient. The goal is maximum and continuously growing production. That required attention to what was later called the "supply side." The government had to look after the supply of natural resources—which involved an early environmentalism—and the training of the labor force. But the critical element was the amount of private investment.

Because private investment would depend on the expectations of business about the growth of the market, one of the main functions of the CEA was to educate businessmen about how big the future market was going to be. But this big and growing future market depended on big and growing consumer demand, and that could come only from consumers who were not rich, since the rich consumers were already consuming all they were likely to consume. That made the distribution of income between the rich and the not-rich critical. But the CEA had no way of knowing what that optimum distribution was, or any way of bringing it about if it had known. So the whole idea was left without any practical application, even if it had been correct.

There seems to have been some connection between this line of thinking and the Department of Agriculture's annual "outlook" conferences, in which Nourse had been a participant for many years. The department assembled a very large number of representatives of farmers and talked to them about the forecast market for corn, or cattle, or other farm products, in the hope of keeping the farmers from overproducing or underproducing. The CEA seemed to think that it could talk to business and labor in the same way and bring about a balanced distribution of income.

The Arthur Burns team came into office with a different outlook. Burns had devoted much of his working life to the study of business cycles, seeking regularities in the behavior of economic magnitudes that would enable him to explain and predict cyclical fluctuations. He regarded his main function in the White House as keeping his eye out for cyclical downturns—*recessions,* although that word was taboo—and suggesting methods for preventing or reversing those downturns. The preferred method went back to pre-Keynesian economics and had a long history at the National Bureau of Economic Research, where Burns had done most of his work. The method was the timely increase in expenditures for "public works," which might, however, be broadly defined to include ships under construction for the government. Burns's main institutional contribution during his term as chairman, aside from the 1953 revision of the role of the chairman in the CEA, was to establish within the CEA the position of public works coordinator, under the direction of a general from the Corps of Engineers.

The attitude of the Saulnier Council was not significantly different from that of the Burns Council. Probably because of his own background, Saulnier had more interest than Burns did in credit policies affecting sectors of the economy, such as small business and housing. There may also have been some small infiltration of Keynesianism through the influence of the younger members of the staff.

be achieved consistently with any expected rate of inflation, including zero. One implication was that "incomes policy" would be both ineffective and unnecessary.

The new approach suggested by the McCracken-Houthakker-Stein team emerged from this combination of experience and analysis. Fiscal fine-tuning was out, except in extreme and rare circumstances. The basic fiscal position would be kept stable, although the automatic variations in the size of the surplus or deficit that came with economic fluctuations would be accepted and, indeed, welcomed. This was essentially the policy of balancing the budget at high employment, although in the effort to spell that out some refinements were developed that need not concern us here.[13]

The position of fiscal restraint—balanced budget—that had finally been achieved by the Johnson administration would be continued. Together with restrictive monetary policy that would raise the unemployment rate—3.3 percent when the Nixon team entered office—to a little more than 4 percent. Four percent was considered "the natural rate of unemployment," so when the actual rate exceeded that, even by a little, the inflation rate would come down and would do so fairly promptly. There would be no incomes policy. Neither would there be any balance of payments concerns. The balance of payments policy would be "benign neglect," meaning that the United States would not apply policy fixes to reduce the balance of payments deficit but would expect the countries accumulating dollars to take corrective measures if they felt the accumulation was excessive.[14]

Obviously the CEA could not continue to live by this theory, and it adapted in various ways as events developed. The basic problem was that if there was a natural rate of unemployment, it was not 4 percent. Unemployment rose toward 6 percent—which seemed extremely high in 1971—and there was little sign of an abatement in the inflation rate. The council tried to devise mea-

---

13. I have written about this in my essay, "The Fiscal Revolution in America, 1964–1994," published in the second revised edition of *The Fiscal Revolution in America*.

14. This policy was recommended by a task force headed by Gottfried Haberler in 1968, one of several charged with preparing for a possible Nixon administration. The term *benign neglect* as applied to international finance was first used in a pamphlet written by Haberler and Thomas Willett for the American Enterprise Institute.

sures to meet the rising demand to do something—which meant "incomes policy"—with a minimum violation of its devotion, and the president's devotion, to free markets. The CEA also found itself trying, without success, to explain that its stabilizing budget policy—balance at high employment—was an effective response to the unemployment problem. For the conservatives, that meant too much deficit, and for the liberals it meant too little. The council looked to the Federal Reserve for assistance in getting the unemployment down but found little help in that quarter.

It was in these circumstances, in the spring of 1971, that the CEA became a supporter of expansionist policies, including a possible tax cut, which caused the rift with Connally to which I have already referred. The CEA also helped to bring about an effort, of only moderate effectiveness, to give the economy a dose of fiscal stimulus in the first half of 1972. But by that time we were living in a new world of price and wage controls and a devalued dollar.

The years 1969 to 1974 were a hard school of economics, and the CEA learned some hard lessons. It learned that however useful the idea of the natural rate of unemployment was, it did not know what the natural rate was. It learned that it could not fine-tune fiscal policy and could not sell the idea of not fine-tuning it. It learned that although it believed monetary policy was terribly important, it did not know what the optimum monetary policy was and had little chance of getting it adopted if it did know. But it did cling to some of its earlier ideas. Consigned to a world of price and wage controls, it worked to define the rules of that system in a way that would be least harmful to production, and it was a constant advocate of decontrol wherever possible. When it had come into office in 1969, the CEA had been more worried about inflation than most others in the government, including the president. By 1973 it had seen inflation rise to rates previously inconceivable for the United States and had become even more concentrated on fighting inflation. It resisted supporting the exchange rate of the dollar and was among those most in favor of the floating system reached in early 1973. It became more impressed than ever with the prospect of rapidly rising federal expenditures and the attendant budget deficits. It remained a supporter of trade liberalization and deregulation.

During the later Nixon years, the Ford years, and the Carter years, the CEA struggled with problems for which it and the economics profession were unprepared. High unemployment and high inflation existed simultaneously, and the relative position of the two evils changed unpredictably. Fiscal policy was dominated by concern with rising expenditures and deficits and could not be diverted by efforts to deal with the imperfectly foreseen oscillations of the economy. The growth rate of potential output seemed to be slowing down, for reasons that were not understood. "Incomes policy" in all its variants was discredited. The energy problem, with potentially large but not well-understood effects on both the supply side and the demand side of the economy, rolled around the deck like a loose cannon.

For this period it is impossible to draw a coherent picture of what the CEA believed. Alan Greenspan described the attitude with which he came into office in 1974 in these words:

> I believed that we should stop trying to engage in short-term fiscal fine-tuning, which, at best, we are poor at and, at worst, is counterproductive. We should try instead to focus on solving longer-term problems and in that process engage in as little policy as was both economically and politically possible. My view was that we had to slow down the pace of governmental policy actions, if we were to restore a level of risk in the system consistent with long-term non-inflationary growth.[15]

But within a few weeks of entering office, he was supporting a war against inflation that included, among other things, a tax increase, and a few months later he was supporting a temporary tax cut to counter the recession. Although this was to be the deepest recession of the postwar period up to then, he correctly foresaw that it would be brief and resisted stronger measures to deal with it. Thereafter, his main concern seems to have been trying to keep expenditures and the deficit under control. The Carter-Schultze era looked for a while like a replay of Kennedy-Heller, but the world was different and had become resistant to the old prescriptions. As Schultze later said, they were chasing after a moving economy always six months too late.

The CEA that emerged from the turbulence of the 1980s would have been a great surprise to the original proponents of the

---

15. Edwin C. Hargrove and Samuel A. Morley, *The President and the Council of Economic Advisers* (Boulder, Colo.: Westview Press, 1984), p. 418.

Employment Act of 1946. They had operated on the belief that the great national problem was unemployment, that the cure was in the budget, and that a body of economic experts would from time to time calculate the size of the budget deficit needed to achieve full employment and that thereafter the president and Congress would adapt expenditures and taxes to conform to the required deficit. By 1981 that whole line of thinking was gone, or almost so. A faint reflection of it appeared in some suggestions by the CEA for limited fiscal measures to promote recovery from the 1990–1992 recession. In 1993 and 1994, the CEA was claiming that the deficit-reduction package enacted at the president's urging had contributed strongly to the recovery then underway, and in 1995 it was warning that more rapid deficit reduction would retard economic growth. But these seemed to have been afterthoughts and not very important in the decisions being made.

Basically, the problem of stabilizing the growth of demand and so avoiding rapid inflation or serious inflation was left to the Federal Reserve. Although some in the administration, especially in the early Reagan years, were inclined to try to push the Fed in one direction or another, that was not the attitude of the CEA. Notably, when the disinflationary process entailed a rather serious recession in 1982, neither the CEA nor the president put pressure on the Fed to pump the economy up.

Although fine-tuning the deficit was no longer a central concern of the CEA, the budget was. By now the concern was primarily with the long-run and supply-side effects of the budget. On this subject, the Reagan-Bush team had three central propositions. Expenditures, at least at the level then prevailing or proposed, were bad, because they were a wasteful use of the nation's resources. Murray Weidenbaum, Reagan's first CEA chairman, was even willing to assert this of defense expenditures, a subject later chairmen were loath to enter. Taxes, at least at the level then prevailing, were bad because they weakened incentives to work and save. Deficits were bad, primarily because they absorbed private saving that would otherwise go into private investment. At least, that was the reason most commonly cited by the CEA.

For some people this formulation might have seemed to create an arithmetical problem. If deficits are bad and taxes are bad, is a tax increase that reduces the deficit good or bad? To some in the administration, this was not a real question, because they thought that a reduction of tax rates would increase the revenue. The CEA, however, although willing to give considerable weight to the possibility that some of the revenue lost through reduction of tax rates would be recouped through the resulting increase in the tax base, did not believe that there would be a net revenue gain, except for limited, special cases, which might include a cut of capital-gains taxes.

There were others, in the administration and out, for whom the taxes-versus-deficit trade-off did not exist because they believed that an increase of taxes would cause an equal increase in expenditures, leaving the deficit unchanged. Essentially, they believed that the size of the deficit was a constant. The CEA did not agree with this, and the behavior of the deficit in the 1980s gave them no reason to think so.

Thus, the CEA, like many others in the administration, was repeatedly faced with the question of whether it should support a tax increase to reduce the deficit. The view of Feldstein on this is clear. He thought that the administration should recommend a tax increase or at least be willing to recommend a tax increase if reasonable estimates did not show the deficit to be declining significantly. That was part of the reason for his disagreement with the secretary of the Treasury, Donald Regan, to which I have already referred. The position of the other chairmen of the CEA during the Reagan and Bush administrations is less clear. Their usual formulation was that they were for "deficit reduction by expenditure restraint," which relieved them of the need to take a public position about taxes. We do know, however, that the debate over raising taxes went on almost continuously during the Reagan and Bush years and that, in fact, taxes were raised in many of those years. Probably the CEA was not among those in the administration most averse to raising taxes of some kinds and in some amounts.

Although the CEA always believed that the deficit was a serious problem, it did not, at least as far as the public record shows, make a calculation of an optimum path of the deficit. Its answer to the question of the proper size of the deficit was always "less," just as the Pentagon's estimate of the proper size of the defense budget was always "more." The administration's budgets were the outcome of pushing and pulling among parties with conflicting interests, among which the CEA was one whose interest was a smaller deficit. Of course, it had some allies. But the size of the deficit does not seem to have been an initially agreed upon constraint to which the other decisions had to conform, except that there was sometimes a desire to show on paper that the deficit would get to zero in five years.

During most of the Reagan-Bush years, people were much concerned with "the twin deficits," meaning the budget deficit and the balance of payments deficit. The CEA seemed to share the concern about the balance of payments deficit—mainly because other people were concerned about it and would do undesirable things to try to eliminate it if it persisted. But in general the CEA did not support intervention in the exchange markets as a way of reducing the balance of payments deficit and had little confidence in the idea, then fashionable, of international coordination of economic policy.

Beyond this, the councils of the Reagan-Bush period look very much like their predecessors. They were supporters of trade liberalization and opponents of restrictionism. They were for tax reform—meaning reducing discrimination in the treatment of different kinds of economic activity, especially different kinds of investment, and assisted in bringing about the Tax Reform Act of 1986. Perhaps even more than their predecessors, they were eager to eliminate government regulation where they could and rationalize it where they could not.

The advent of President Clinton and Chairman Tyson in 1993 looked as if it might bring a change in the general philosophy of the council. Ms. Tyson seemed more favorably disposed toward managed trade and incomes policy than her predecessors. That belief, in fact, caused some alarm in the economics profession. The participants have not yet written their memoirs or confessions, so it is too early to say what went on within the suites in the Old Executive Office Building. But a preliminary view is that the new council soon found its old niche as a supporter of free markets, economy in government, prudence in fiscal policy, and willingness to allow the Federal Reserve to bear the responsibility for management of aggregate demand.

Achievements and Failures

Even if there had never been a Council of Economic Advisers, there would have been economics, economics would have had some effect on policy, there would have been economists in the government, and there would probably have been some economists in the Executive Office. Moreover, as Alec Cairncross, long-time adviser to the British government, said:

> When the issue is in dispute, who except the Minister (or even including the Minister) knows what clinched the matter? It is very rarely that one can say with confidence that the decision would have been different if x had not been there. The people who think they know and say so may, in fact, be ill-qualified to judge.[16]

So, the history of the Council of Economic Advisers in the past fifty years is not the same as the history of American economic policy in that period, and an evaluation of that history is not the same as an evaluation of the CEA. To separate what the CEA did from what everyone else did is, at least for the time being, impossible, and to judge the merit or demerit of what was done is a highly subjective matter. Taking advantage of the fact that I have observed this history and to some degree participated in it for longer than almost anyone else, however, I will offer some impressions.

I will not give a chronological history but will attempt to identify certain classes of conditions that recurred during the period. Moreover, with apologies I will pass over almost all the "micro" aspects of the story. That is not because they are unimportant. On the contrary, almost all economic observers agree that they have been very important and have become increasingly so. But their story is less interesting just because it has been, in the eyes of economists, at least, less controversial and more successful. My own interests have also made me less capable of telling that story, however much I appreciate it.

CEA Advice Rejected. In three important cases, policy went against the strongly held opinion and advice of the CEA. In 1951, against the advice of Chairman Keyserling and also contrary to the wishes of President Truman, the Federal Reserve and the Treasury entered into an "accord" that ended the Federal Re-

---

16. Alec Cairncross, *Essays in Economic Management* (Albany: State University of New York Press, 1972).

serve's support of the prices of government bonds. I suppose there is little question now that Keyserling and Truman were wrong.

In 1965 the CEA urged President Johnson to raise taxes to help pay the costs of the Vietnam War, and the president rejected that advice. From an economic point of view, the council was probably correct. But presidents have to think about more than economics. The president had to think about how congressional support for the Vietnam War would have been affected by a request for a tax increase at that time, so a judgment about the president's decision involves hard questions beyond the scope of economics.

In 1971 President Nixon imposed comprehensive, mandatory price and wage controls against the advice of the CEA, advice that had been given to him with clarity and persistence for almost three years. The CEA may bear some responsibility for not visualizing how long and difficult the process of extraction from the control system would be, but still, that deficiency was not the primary cause of the decision, which was economically unwise and probably politically unnecessary—although people more expert than I in politics thought otherwise. On a related matter, the CEA, in the Nixon administration and later, sought with limited effect to decontrol the price of oil, which would have been an advantage.

Successful Policies. But, of course, it is comforting for economists to say that we knew what to do and the politicians kept it from being done. The more interesting cases, the ones requiring more self-examination by economists, are the ones in which the CEA, always with some allies, of course, did get its way. Some of these cases are, at least in my opinion, success stories. Probably the Oscar on the shelf of the CEA is the Kennedy-Johnson tax cut. More than any other major economic policy decision of the past fifty years, this was originated and promoted by the Council of Economic Advisers. Taken by itself, the tax cut was an economic and political success. But it was part of a package that generated serious problems. First, it was visualized as fitting into a context of rapid economic growth—4 percent per annum or more—in which growing budget surpluses would be a drag on the growth of the economy unless constantly offset by the distribution of fiscal dividends. That helped to set the stage for commitments to programs whose growing, largely underestimated costs would weigh on the economy for years to come. Second, the package included "incomes policy" to restrain the inflationary tendencies of a full-employment economy. This idea did not originate with the Heller team. Traces of it can be found in the economic reports of the Eisenhower administration and elsewhere. But the Heller team gave it a prominence that lasted and created the impression that the government had an instrument by which it could reconcile high employment and price stability without pain if only it was not hampered by a "theological" devotion to free markets. That created a difficult atmosphere for the Nixon administration and helped to lead that administration into the mandatory controls system.

The Nixon team, of course with allies, notably George Shultz, influenced policy in some ways that I consider successful. As already noted, having gotten into the price-wage control system we were an instrument for managing it, and getting out of it, in the least harmful way possible, with the unfortunate exception of an inability to do much about the ceiling on the price of oil. Moreover, we ranged ourselves on the side of first devaluing and then floating the dollar, which I think was a great step forward, although there are those who disagree.

Policy Errors. The most serious error of the Nixon CEA came, in my opinion, at the outset of the administration. Fascinated by the idea of "the natural rate of unemployment," we thought it necessary only to get the unemployment rate slightly above that to bring the inflation down, after which we could all live happily with the natural rate of unemployment and reasonably low inflation. We also thought that 4 percent was the natural rate. So we thought, and, worst of all, allowed the president and the country to think, that we only had to go through a rather painless transition to reach the goal. When that turned out not to be the case, when unemployment had risen to 6 percent and there was still no sure sign that inflation was abating, confidence in the policy of "gradualism" evaporated, and the stage was set for the radical move to price and wage controls. Perhaps that could have been avoided if the president and the country had been warned in advance of the likely difficulties.

Mixed Success. Some of the cases in the history of the CEA in relation to economic policy are more mixed. Suppose, for example, that Saulnier had been more vigorous and effective in promoting an expansive fiscal and monetary policy in the second Eisenhower term. Richard Nixon might have won the 1960 election, which was extremely close anyway, and the world would have been different in many respects. Suppose that in early 1974, during the first energy crisis, the CEA had been less rigid in clinging to restrictive fiscal policy—along with the other economic officials of the time. Might the recession of 1974–1975 have been averted, and if it had been, would the subsequent inflation have been even worse?

One cannot help being troubled about the possible connection of the past operation of the CEA with what seem to be the big problems of our times—the poverty problem and the long-run deficit problem. The Heller council was certainly involved in launching the War on Poverty. Whether the members initially contemplated as ambitious a program as President Johnson started is unclear, but still they participated. Moreover, the Nixon CEA was also sympathetic to it, although hoping to reform it in some ways. But none of us foresaw the size to which these programs would grow. Probably more worrisome, none of us foresaw the behavioral consequences that might follow and, some say, have followed, from these programs. Even if these were only possibilities, they were possibilities of which the decision makers should have been warned, and I think they were not.

From about the middle of 1972, in my experience, CEAs have been increasingly worried about the rising trends of expenditures built into existing programs and about the deficits likely to accompany those trends. But I think they have not been sufficiently alarmed and have not sufficiently alerted their principals or the public, because they did not look far enough ahead. (This is an error of which I was also guilty.) If they had started earlier to consider how the budget was going to look in the year 2030, we might now be on a more reliable path to avoiding possible catastrophe.

Closing Thoughts

I will close with a few general observations. I believe that the CEA has given the government and the public as good economic advice as the economics profession has to offer. There are always, every year, some economists who could have given better advice, just as every year there are some mutual fund managers who do better than the average. But they are not the same people every year, and no one knows how to choose the best pickers in advance. The government is going to get advice, and the presence of the CEA makes the quality of that advice better than if it all came from under secretaries of various departments and the presidential assistants who come up through the political process. Compared with other sources of advice, the CEA has more, or different, objectivity; it has more allegiance to professional standards; and it has by now a tradition that allows it to attract extremely able and hard-working staff.

I believe that the history of the CEA suggests two kinds of deficiencies that might be corrected. One is that it does not look far enough ahead but becomes too engrossed in immediate problems. That cannot be entirely avoided, but it might be useful to segregate a portion of the staff, under the guidance of one of the members, to think of what the economy and its problems might look like in, say, twenty-five years.

Second, the CEA, like the government as a whole, is deficient in contingency planning. It is not sufficient to say that we think that the economy will grow by 4 percent a year. It is necessary to consider also what should be done if it grows by 3 percent or 5 percent. It is not sufficient to launch a War on Poverty. It is necessary to consider also what should be done if that war yields a large crop of illegitimate babies born to teenaged mothers. Examples could be multiplied. I think the council has been good about giving the president a fair picture of his options. It has been less good about preparing him for the possibility that the option he selects turns out not to have the expected consequences.

A few years ago, reflecting on fifty years of experience as a Washington economist, I summed up my lessons as follows: (1) economists do not know very much and (2) other people, including politicians who make economic policy, know even less about economics than economists do.[17] I have not changed my mind about that.

---

17. Herbert Stein, *Washington Bedtime Stories* (New York: Free Press, 1986), p. xi.

7

Washington before the War

Perhaps I should explain for the younger readers that when I refer to "the war" I mean World War II. When "before-the-war" ended in Washington is somewhat arbitrary. It could mean September 1, 1939, when the war began in Europe. It could mean December 7, 1941, Pearl Harbor Day. For my purposes, I take January 20, 1941—the day of Franklin Roosevelt's third inauguration.

Newcomers

When my wife, Mildred, and I arrived in Washington on the overnight train from Chicago, in April 1938, we did not know what to expect. I had never been in Washington before. Mildred had been here briefly, as a sightseer with her high school senior class, and remembered little about it. We knew only that Washington was one of the few places at that time where a person with some graduate study in economics might find a job. We were twenty-two years old, had been married less than a year, and were about to make our first flight out of the school-college-university nest.

Looking out from the exit of Union Station, seeing the Capitol dome before us, we thought we were in the center of town. So we checked into a hotel in Union Plaza. That was in the days when you could check into a hotel without a reservation.

I soon learned that the area around the Capitol was not the center of town for me then and would not be for any part of the many years since. Shortly after entering the hotel, I called my friend Taylor Ostrander, and he informed me that I was in the wrong place to start out looking for a job. Ostrander had been in the class three years before me at Williams College, had returned as an instructor in economics when I was a senior, and had later been my supervisor on a Works Progress Administration project in Chicago. He was to be my first guide to Washington.

Ostrander not only told me that I was in the wrong place but also insisted that Mildred and I should leave the hotel and move into their apartment, which we did. They lived on the second floor of a three-story building at 1734 Eye Street (as I learned to write it). Their small apartment was furnished in the style then fashionable among young people—Swedish modern, meaning blond, unadorned wood and rustic, rough upholstery and drapes. In many cases there would be couches made of flush doors to which iron legs were affixed and bookcases made of boards stacked on bricks. At Ostrander's we slept on a convertible sofa in the living room.

This style was a trivial symptom of something more important about Washington in the years of which I write. It was a city of youth. I mean not merely that we were young or even that almost all the people we knew were young. I mean that an unusually large proportion of the people in the city were young. And if they weren't young, they were fairly new to the city, working at jobs they had never done before in agencies that had not existed five years earlier. The impression of Washington was not of the majesty of its history or the boredom of having seen it all before, but of its newness and prospects.

But back to my story. . . . When we arrived in April 1938, it was cherry blossom time, and the Ostranders took us for a drive around the Tidal Basin in their little Nash coupe. The traffic was heavy, and, perhaps because I had more serious things on my mind, I was not much exhilarated by the spectacle. In fact, I have not been much impressed by the cherry blossoms around the Tidal Basin at any time since. I find the display of azaleas around private homes on upper Sixteenth Street and in Silver Spring and Takoma Park much more amazing, not only for their beauty but because they are the product of hundreds of individual householders seeking to express themselves, not of the hired hands of the National Park Service.

My attitude toward the cherry blossoms at the Tidal Basin

probably had another significance. From the beginning, I never liked the idea of being a tourist in Washington. It was not that I objected to being a tourist in general. I have done all the tourist things in London and Paris and Rome and Tokyo and Beijing. But being a tourist in the town where I lived and worked seemed, in a word then much in use, *corny,* or unsophisticated. I never went to the White House or the Capitol or the Library of Congress until I had business there, or to the Arlington Cemetery until, alas, I had a friend to be buried there. I have still not been to the Supreme Court or the National Archives or the Jefferson Memorial. I took pleasure and pride in seeing these places as I went about my daily life. I liked to think that I was part of their neighborhood, but I didn't want to be a tourist in my own neighborhood.

I came here in 1938 as a job seeker, not as a tourist. Ostrander worked in the Division of Monetary Research of the Treasury, the director of which was Harry D. White, who would achieve subsequent fame and notoriety. He took me to meet White, but no job offer came of that. I then went to see two other of my former Williams College teachers who were working in Washington, one at the WPA and one at the Department of Agriculture. After leaving the Agriculture building, on Independence Avenue, I walked across the Mall to the National Press Building for my next interview. I was wearing my Chicago overcoat and Washington was very warm in April that year. I always remember how hot I was and how thin I was.

My interview at the National Press Building was at the Federal Deposit Insurance Corporation, where I went to see Homer Jones, a former University of Chicago student to whom I had been recommended by one of my Chicago professors. It was this interview that resulted in a job offer, which I accepted.

Residence in Washington

After a return to Chicago for me to finish my studies and Mildred to finish her job, we came back in June and moved into our first Washington apartment. It was sublet, furnished, for the summer. A large brownstone house in Georgetown, which had originally been the home of a single family, had been divided into four apartments, and we had one of them. The house still stands, at the corner of Thirtieth Street and Dumbarton, and looks just as it did then. Its distinguishing architectural feature was a wide, curved, external staircase, of stone with iron railings, leading up to the main entrance. Our apartment was off the hall immediately inside the front door.

The apartment was small, but no smaller than we had been used to in Chicago. The impressive thing about living in Washington was the heat. Chicago had been hot in the summer but not day after day and night after day, and with such humidity. This was, of course, before air conditioning was common. In fact, this memoir could just as well have been entitled "Washington before Air Conditioning" as "Washington before the War." Air conditioning made about as much difference to life in Washington as the war did. We all fought the heat with electric fans, but it was a losing battle.

It was in this apartment that I performed the most dextrous and courageous feat of my life. Early in our stay, we discovered that we shared the apartment with a family of mice. Somehow, I managed to scoop them up with a broom into a wastebasket and then dump them down a sewer on Dumbarton Street, where their descendants probably still live.

Structurally, Georgetown has changed little over the years, except for the building of Georgetown Plaza on the 3100 block of M Street. The residential streets were occupied by narrow, old, two- or three-story houses, mainly frame, with little or no space between them and tiny gardens behind. The commercial streets, M Street and Wisconsin Avenue, were lined by a ragtag of stores with one or two floors of offices above them. But socially Georgetown was different then. The residential streets had not yet been established as an elite area—the bedroom of Camelot, as it would become in the Kennedy years. Some well-known New Dealers lived there. I think that was where Corcoran and Cohen lived, but that did not give Georgetown a distinctive aura—or, if it did, we were not aware of it. At the same time, the commercial streets had not yet become the hangout of tourists and students. Perhaps people who lived in the rest of Washington occasionally came to one or another of Georgetown's specialty shops or restaurants, but basically the local stores were patronized by the local neighbors. We bought groceries at the Sanitary (later known as the Safeway) and occasionally at Magruder's, a fancy store down the street from us on Wisconsin Avenue. We went to the movies at the Georgetown Theater, which was only a few steps away. That was the era of the screwball comedies, and we saw them all there. *Bringing Up Baby,* with Katherine Hepburn and Cary Grant, was a big hit. Coming across it recently on TV, I found it sickeningly silly, which I suppose is the difference between being twenty-two and being eighty.

I went to work from Georgetown to the National Press Building, at Fourteenth and F Streets, on the streetcar that ran down Wisconsin Avenue, east on M Street and then down Pennsylvania Avenue. In 1935 the District had begun a transition from the old-fashioned, boxlike street cars with a motorman and a conductor to the modern, streamlined cars in which there was only one attendant, who both drove and took fares. When we came in 1938, the transition was not complete, and both kinds of cars were running. In fact, the war interrupted the transition, and it was not completed until a few years after the war, just about in time for the advent of the buses. My trip to work was not long—about a mile—but even then I was not a great walker, especially in the Washington heat.

When our summer sublet expired, we moved to an apartment on Seventeenth Street, between L and M Streets, now the site of a thirteen-story office building. Even for me that was within walking distance of my office—a short stroll through Lafayette Square and I was there. By this time, in the fall of 1938, Mildred was also working, at the Railroad Retirement Board, at Twelfth and G Streets. Her walk was a little longer than mine but quite manageable.

Our new apartment was on the third floor of a three-story building, the first floor of which was occupied by a greasy-spoon restaurant and an exterminator's establishment. We had what I believe is called a railroad apartment. There was a living room in front, looking out over Seventeenth Street, a narrow hall off which there were a bathroom and a bedroom, and a kitchen at the back, looking out over the backyard that was paved with cinders.

This was our first occasion to furnish an apartment for ourselves. Mildred made several trips to New York—up and back by train in the same day—to visit Macy's and Altman's and some other places. In this way we acquired, among other things, a blond mahogany desk, which our son now has and which I think of as representative of the style of the times. Even a rather ordinary record player had to be bought in New York. (We had learned not to say "Victrola.") A record player was obligatory for young "cultivated" households. Records we bought in Washington. This was before LPs and before vinyl. A symphony might consist of twelve heavy, glass records. Listening to music was quite a chore. There were automatic record changers, but they were expensive and had a tendency to chew up the records from time to time.

Going to New York to buy furniture was symptomatic of a more general attitude. Even though we were living in a pretty big town, we—especially Mildred—were still sufficiently New Yorkers to think that Manhattan was the place to shop. We regularly bought the Sunday *New York Times.* And the *New Yorker* magazine was our arbiter of culture. (These were the days of James Thurber, E. B. and Katherine White, Robert Benchley, Wolcott Gibbs, and S. J. Perelman—names that still hold a charm for me.) The attachment to being New Yorkers was reinforced by the Civil Service regulations of the time. Civil Service employment was supposed to be apportioned by state, so there was an advantage to claiming to be from almost anywhere but Washington, D.C., Virginia, or Maryland. Everyone clung to identification with some other state. We maintained the fiction of being New Yorkers for some time and voted in New York in the 1940 presidential election.

This location on Seventeenth Street gave us more the feeling of being in the nation's capital than we had in Georgetown. Connecticut Avenue was the stylish commercial street, analogous to Fifth Avenue in New York. On Easter Sunday women and girls in their best dresses would parade up and down Connecticut Avenue. When it was not Easter Sunday, one could see women in Washington's most fashionable street wearing what even to me looked like cotton housedresses. More than almost anything else those symbolized that Washington was, as northerners then called it, a "sleepy Southern town."

When we lived on Seventeenth Street, we could walk out on Connecticut Avenue in the evening and see important-looking people strolling or hurrying around. One of our big thrills was seeing Senator Vandenberg, unmistakable with his bow tie and cane, walking up the avenue. But our biggest thrill was looking out of our front window at the rear entrance of the Mayflower Hotel, across the street, and seeing President Roosevelt in his wheel chair being lifted into the hotel where he was to give a speech.

Housekeeping on Seventeenth Street provided our introduc-

tion to one of the distinguishing features of prewar Washington—
the availability of cheap household help. We could have a mature,
responsible, capable woman as a dayworker who would come to
the apartment in the afternoon, clean up, and prepare dinner for
us—for twenty-five cents an hour. Of course, almost all 1938 prices
seem absurdly low today. As a rough rule, one can multiply them
by ten to put them into 1996 dollars. Anyone in Washington can
see that $2.50 an hour is still very low. A better way to understand
the situation is to recognize that Mildred, a junior economist in
the government, was making about one dollar an hour, so the
dayworker was making one-fourth of Mildred's pay per hour. I
would think that the cost of a comparable dayworker today would
be at least three-fourths of the hourly pay of a junior economist.
The dayworker "of course" was black or, as we said then, *colored.*
This "of course" opens up an important subject to which I shall
return.

After about a year, the attraction of living on Seventeenth
Street began to fade. We had acquired a car—a second-hand
Chevrolet—and that reduced the need to live downtown and
raised the possibility that we could get more room and cooler air
if we moved farther out. The car itself was a source of trouble. We
parked it in the yard behind the apartment building, a parking
place that was also used by the taxi drivers who hung out in the
restaurant on the ground floor. They resented our presence, and
often we would find that they had taken out their resentment by
lifting the hood of our car and disposing of chicken bones around
the engine. Finally, we decided to move when the owner of the
apartment refused to replace the old refrigerator that had broken
down.

Looking for an apartment was an introduction to another facet
of prewar life in Washington. We discovered that a large proportion of the classified ads for rental apartments in the newspaper
carried the words *near churches.* That was not a tribute to the piety
of apartment seekers in Washington. It was code for "No Jews!"

We looked at one apartment, in Glover Park, for which the ad
had not contained that warning. The agent told us, however, that
the owner did not want to rent to "Orientals," which included us.
This attitude survived in Washington for many years. Some time
later, shortly after the war, we were prepared to make an offer to
buy a house in Rollingwood, a middle-class section in nearby

Chevy Chase. On our second visit the owner told us that he could not sell to us because it would be "unfair to the neighbors."

As I look back at it now, I don't think that I was angered by such incidents. I thought that they were wrong and stupid. But I did not feel that I was being deprived of particularly attractive neighborhoods or neighbors. I remember telling the story about the "Orientals" as an amusing example of how bizarre some Gentiles were. "Restrictions" in housing gradually wore off or became less blatant. But it is revealing that from 1943 to 1974, when we lived in houses we owned, we always lived in neighborhoods with a large majority of Jewish families. I should point out that from the time of our arrival in 1938, I never felt any attitude of antisemitism in my work or in any other connections except for housing.

Late in 1939, we settled in an apartment in a bungalow in Takoma Park that had been divided into two parts. We lived on the ground floor and the owners, an elderly couple, lived in the basement. Why they did not object to Jewish tenants I don't know. Perhaps being in a community dominated by Seventh Day Adventists had accustomed them to infidels, although we learned later that toleration of Jews did not extend to selling a house to them.

The bungalow had a large, level back yard with huge trees and azalea bushes. There was a front porch where we could sit out and a screened back porch where we would sometimes eat. Still without air conditioning, we made a definite gain in coolness when we moved to Takoma Park.

From Takoma Park we drove in to work together. Parking lots were conveniently scattered around empty spaces in downtown Washington, and traffic, on Fifteenth Street or Thirteenth Street, was not terrible. From our apartment we could walk two blocks to the Takoma Park shopping district, where the shopkeepers were friendly and there was a small town atmosphere. We also had a convenient drive to Georgia Avenue, which was a center of Jewish-style food stores. Hofberg's Delicatessen, at Georgia and Alaska, and Posin's, at Georgia and Missouri, were attractive. Farther down Georgia Avenue was the New Yorker Bakery, with the best bread we have yet encountered in Washington. The Takoma Park bungalow would be our home when our first child was born, and it was in the living room of this apartment that I heard the radio report of the bombing of Pearl Harbor.

Work in Washington

When I reported for work at the Federal Deposit Insurance Corporation in June 1938, its offices were in the National Press Building, at the corner of Fourteenth and F. That corner was then the center of downtown Washington. The FDIC was the only government agency in the building. Aside from it, and the Press Club on the top floor—which I never visited until years later—the building was filled with little offices of the Washington bureaus of newspapers from all over the country and the world. Walking those corridors, one had the feeling of being in a Raymond Chandler movie—Sam Spade might come out of one of those doors with their ground-glass windows at any time. The most numerous occupants of the National Press Building were cockroaches. In 1939 the FDIC moved to the Washington Building, at Fifteenth Street and New York Avenue. That was a newer and cleaner building. It also had the S&W cafeteria on the ground floor, where I received my introduction to Southern cooking and, I believe, my first meeting with black-eyed peas.

By 1938 the hectic days of the banking crisis were over. Roosevelt had closed all the banks in March 1933. After that, all the banks deemed fit to reopen were allowed to do so, many with an infusion of capital from the government. The creation of the FDIC had calmed the worries of depositors. The work of the FDIC at that point became routine, to examine the banks within its jurisdiction and take remedial action if any seemed necessary, which was rare. Some of the people who had been involved in examining the closed banks to decide which were fit to reopen now worked in the Examination Division of the FDIC.

The chairman of the FDIC was Leo T. Crowley, from Wisconsin. He might have been an Irish pol from central casting. He was a big man with a broad face and a lot of white hair. He kept a cuspidor alongside his desk and used it from time to time. He had no visible background qualifying him to be chairman of the FDIC, but neither was there any visible deficiency in his performance. I had little to do with him, but he once had my boss, Homer Jones, and me to dinner in his suite at the Mayflower to discuss something and I was pleased by that.

Although I had little direct contact with Crowley, most of my work at the FDIC was derived from him personally. Crowley was a great rival of Marriner Eccles, who was chairman of the Federal Reserve. This rivalry was connected to animus between Crowley and A. P. Giannini, a power in Democratic politics and a friend, perhaps the sponsor, of Eccles. Giannini was head of the Trans-america Corporation, which controlled the Bank of America, the largest bank in California, as well as banks in other Western states, insurance companies, land companies, and other financial institu-tions. So, a lot of my work, under the direction of Homer Jones, was anti-Eccles and anti-Giannini.

With respect to Eccles, the contest took the form of a turf war. There were then three main federal agencies supervising banks. The Comptroller of the Currency supervised national banks, the Federal Reserve supervised state banks that were members of the Federal Reserve System, and the FDIC super-vised insured banks that were not members of the Federal Re-serve System. The Federal Reserve was engaged in showing that this was a source of "duplication and confusion" and that it should be given control of all the banks, or at least of the ones that the FDIC supervised. The FDIC, including me, was engaged in refut-ing these claims. Of course, the memos that I and others wrote on the subject made no difference. The state bank supervisors and the associations of state banks were too powerful to allow the Fed to have its way, so the FDIC was safe.

The other part of the conflict—contra-Giannini—took more time. Jones and I were trying to show (a) that there was a big problem of monopolization in the banking industry, with the Gian-nini empire as the leading example, and (b) that there was a big problem of self-dealing between banks and their nonbank affili-ates, again with the Giannini empire as the leading example. In connection with the first of these issues, I spent many weeks with a Monroe desk calculator doing computations that a modern com-puter would do in seconds. In the end nothing came of this either. The powers in the banking business were too strong for the anti-monopoly and divestiture policy we were looking for, and anyway the whole subject would soon be swept away by the war.

And I have learned since that a good deal of time and effort is devoted everywhere to intramural conflict. I found that not only in various government connections but also in a university and in other private institutions. My work was probably useless, and I could well have been described as a "faceless bureaucrat." But nevertheless, I found it a challenge to intelligence and ingenuity. I was satisfied with what I was doing, and it never occurred to me to be bored or frustrated.

It was my additional good fortune that my boss, Homer Jones, had interests beyond this competition with the Federal Reserve. He was interested in all the economic issues that floated around Washington in those days. He liked to write little memos about those issues and encouraged me to do the same. He would then circulate the memos to his friends in other agencies. That was a source of satisfaction to me, and it was in this connection that I discovered that writing little memos was the area of my comparative advantage. This discovery also had something to do with my staying in Washington for almost all the rest of my life. That is, I found that I was better suited to the kind of economics that goes on in Washington than to the kind that goes on in universities.

In June 1940, I left the FDIC, not knowing at the time whether I was leaving permanently. By then, the economic implications of the European war for the United States were becoming important. British purchases here were rising. Our own defense expenditures, although low, were going up. And someone, at some level, may have contemplated the possibility that we would become active participants and wanted to prepare for the economic consequences of that. So the president activated the National Defense Advisory Commission, for which provision had been made after World War I for such circumstances. I thought that I had some special competence in that field because I had written an essay, while a senior at Williams College, entitled "Government Price Policy in the United States during the World War." (I didn't foresee that there would be a second world war.) So I offered my services, and they were accepted.

I found myself then a member of the staff of the Price Stabilization Division of the NDAC. The division was headed by a veteran Democratic political economist—with emphasis on the word *political*—Leon Henderson. The research staff had codirectors, my old friend Taylor Ostrander and Raymond Goldsmith, who came with Henderson from the Securities and Exchange Commission and who was known at the time as one of Washington's leading economists.

The research staff included in its small number two who would later win a Nobel Prize in economics, George Stigler, and

William Vickery. In general, we were looking for ways to avoid the inflationary consequences of the defense buildup without price and wage controls and without interfering with defense production. This position did not go without challenge for very long. After the November presidential election, Leon Henderson acquired a second research staff. It consisted of people, led by Richard Gilbert, who had served as economic advisers to Roosevelt's campaign and for whom a place had to be found when the campaign was over. This new group was all-out for price controls. So a competition went on within the Price Stabilization Division between the pro- and anti-price controllers. Of course, my side was to lose this struggle in 1941, as my side lost a similar struggle thirty years later.

Entertainment and Recreation

The movies were our first line of entertainment. That was not only because the movie theaters were an air-conditioned refuge from the Washington heat but also because we were of the movies generation, probably the most addicted to movies of all generations. Of course, we had no television. As children, say, up to the age of twelve, if we had radio at all it was only a crackling noise in a headset. But the Saturday afternoon movie had been a feature of our lives from earliest days.

We knew the movies. Mildred and I would have disdained to read a movie magazine. But we had seen enough movies to know who all the people were. When the picture started, no preliminaries were necessary to establish the character and the personality of the performers. Greta Garbo was the glamorous beauty, Katherine Hepburn was the pert ingénue, Spencer Tracy stood for strong integrity, Clark Gable for strong flippancy, Ginger Rogers and Fred Astaire for grace and elegance, and so on. We recognized and welcomed our old friends, like children wanting to be told the same fairy tale over and over.

The fairy tales were comforting, not frightening. Among the pictures we saw in those years were Disney's first full-length feature, *Snow White and the Seven Dwarfs,* Judy Garland in *The Wizard of Oz,* Katherine Hepburn in *The Philadelphia Story,* and, the biggest hit of all, *Gone with the Wind,* with Vivien Leigh and Clark Gable. One exception to the fairy tales was *The Grapes of Wrath,* but even that seemed the story of a misery that we were in the process of correcting. There were lots of gangster movies, but they never seemed to show ordinary, law-abiding citizens in danger. Of course, most of the movies then were quite forgettable, and I have forgotten them. Scanning the old newspapers reminds me of how terrible much of them were, but we had more tolerance for even terrible movies than we do now.

There were three big downtown movie theaters, two of which also played vaudeville. But we didn't go to them very much. In general, the vaudeville was poor, and it was cheaper as well as more convenient to go to the smaller neighborhood theaters, especially after we moved to Takoma Park.

All the movie theaters showed newsreels, and there was one, the Translux on Fourteenth Street, that showed nothing but newsreels and documentaries. In those pre-TV days the newsreels gave us the most vivid picture we had of what was going on in the world. It was through them that we saw the awesome march of the Nazis through Austria, Czechoslovakia, Poland, and Western Europe. But that was not, as in today's TV, in real time. There was always a delay of at least a few days between the event and its appearance on the screen, and that diluted the impression of being there.

Washington had at the time one "legitimate" theater, the National. (I use the word *legitimate* to mean live performances but to exclude the Gayety, which was a burlesque house on Ninth Street.) Washington was in part a tryout stop for shows aiming at Broadway. Generally, the shows did not stay in Washington for long, which meant that even though there was only one theater, the number of different shows seen in the course of a year was large. We went with fair frequency. We were young enough to climb to the cheap seats in the balcony, and we could park for a low fee in a large vacant lot on Fourteenth Street across from the Department of Commerce.

By far the highlight of our prewar theater going was a performance of *Knickerbocker Holiday,* with Walter Huston in the lead role of Peter Stuyvesant. That play is still remembered for the "September Song," which is even more poignant to me at age eighty than it was at age twenty-three. But the reason it remains enshrined in our minds is that on the night when we were there, Huston had the whole cast bow toward the box in which Franklin

D. Roosevelt was seated. The drama of that was heightened by FDR's New York Dutch connection. I have the feeling that Huston stopped the play in the middle to make this gesture, but I may be wrong about that and it may have come at the end of the show.

According to connoisseurs, the Washington Symphony at that time was not much good. That did not bother us, because we were not connoisseurs and, besides, never went to hear them at their regular concerts, which were performed in Constitution Hall. But in the summer they performed for no charge at the Water Gate. That was two words then and didn't mean an office-hotel-apartment complex but had its dictionary meaning of a "gateway leading to the edge of a body of water." Just west of the Lincoln Memorial there was, and still is, a series of concrete steps leading down to the Potomac River, and these steps formed the seats of an outdoor theater. The symphony performed on a barge moored in the river. In addition to the audience seated on the steps, there were hardy or romantic souls who rented canoes at the boathouse in Georgetown and came downstream to listen. The music would be drowned out by airplanes preparing to land at the airport down the river, at Gravelly Point, but that wasn't much of a problem because there weren't many planes.

As I have said, radio was largely static when we had been children, fifteen years earlier, but by the years I am writing about—1938 to 1940—it had entered its golden age. There were the great comedians—Jack Benny, Burns and Allen, Fred Allen. The most famous broadcast from a studio—radio or television—there has ever been came on October 30, 1938, when Orson Welles scared half of America out of its wits with a news report of the landing of Martians in New Jersey. Mildred and I were either too smart or too unimaginative to be taken in by that. In a major bow to high culture, CBS engaged Toscanini to organize and conduct symphony broadcasts. We were devoted to what I still think of as the best of all broadcast discussion programs, the *University of Chicago Round Table,* on Sunday morning. The *Round Table* was frequently led by a Chicago professor, T. V. Smith, who gave himself the admirable identification of "an honest man and a philosopher." We were entering the period of the personality newscaster—H. V. Kaltenborn, Raymond Gram Swing, Elmer Davis, Lowell Thomas, and others. Toward the end of this period, we began to get the on-the-scene broadcasts of the war from Edward Murrow and his associates.

We listened to much of this, but radio never dominated so much of our time as television would later do. One could do many other things while listening to the radio—wash your car or your dishes, mow the lawn, even read. And radio was not as hypnotizing as TV. It was easier to turn off. And there was lots of trash to turn off, even in the golden days of radio.

Washington produced two radio stars during the 1930s. One, of course, was FDR. The other was Arthur Godfrey, who ran a wake-up show that occupied the city between 7:00 and 9:00 AM. He told jokes, played the banjo, and reported the news and weather. He had one running gag that now sounds silly but that we all enjoyed at the time. A furrier named Zlotnick had a huge, white stuffed bear standing on its hind legs, and Godfrey had some joke about it every morning. Later, Godfrey parlayed minimal talent into a spot on national radio. But finally he ran into trouble because he owned a "restricted," that is, no Jews, hotel in Florida beyond the time when that was acceptable.

We were not great readers of books. For a time we succumbed to the lure of the Book-of-the-Month Club but after a while found that to be a bore and a burden. For about fifty years thereafter we moved from home to home a book, *Young Man of Caracas* by T. R. Ybarra, that was a relic of the Book-of-the-Month Club. We read *The Grapes of Wrath* and *For Whom the Bell Tolls,* but even mentioning these novels shows that our main interest was in current events rather than in literature. After war broke out in Europe, I became an amateur of military affairs and an avid reader of Col. A. B. Liddell-Hart and Maj. George Fielding Eliot. (I was recently surprised to learn of Churchill's disdain for Liddell-Hart, who seemed to me in 1940 to be a great expert.)

If we were not great book readers, we were great newspaper readers. Radio did not sate our interest in news as TV now does, and we probably were not as sated with the news as we later became. There was certainly a lot of news, with the outbreak of war, and there were many newspapers. In Washington there were four papers of general circulation, plus two "Negro" newspapers. The *Times-Herald* was the paper of Col. McCormick and Cissie Patterson. No self-respecting intellectual read it. The *Daily News* was a Scripps-Howard tabloid that seemed to specialize in horse-racing news and civil service news. Although the government in Washington was much bigger than it had been ten years earlier, it was still not too big to have a shop newspaper, in which the reader could learn about people and agencies with which he had some personal contact. The *Daily Newspaper* was that shop paper.

The main papers were the *Washington Post* and the *Evening Star*. We had the *Post* delivered in the morning and bought the *Star* on the way home from work in the evening. The *Post* was the paper with the better features—better comics, including " 'Lil Abner"; the best advice giver, Mary Haworth, who was much superior to all her later imitators; and the best columnists, including Walter Lippman, who was regarded at the time as one of the country's deepest thinkers. But the *Star* was always considered a more reliable and comprehensive news source, perhaps just because it seemed less interesting. As I have said, we looked on the Sunday *New York Times* as a kind of bible but did not read it on weekdays. The *New York Times* and the *Wall Street Journal* did not have nearly the presence in Washington that they later attained.

Mildred and I had both spent many years in upstate New York—in Mildred's case, her whole precollege life. We were used to having access to pleasant lakes in the summertime, and we missed that when we came to Washington. The nearest swimming place, aside from a few not very pleasant public pools, was the Chesapeake Bay. A few visits to beaches on the bay showed that to be unsatisfactory. The beaches were narrow and gritty, and the water was full of sea nettles. And even some of these miserable beaches were "restricted"—open to sea nettles but not to Jews.

The place to go was Rehoboth Beach, on the ocean. Unlike Ocean City, Rehoboth had a certain "class." When Washington closed down for the summer and Congress went home, the diplomats went to Rehoboth. At least, so it was said. We never saw them and wouldn't have recognized them. Getting to Rehoboth was a drive of many hours—probably five or six. There was no bridge across the bay; crossing was by ferry. (That was also true of driving to New York, which we did several times; there was no bridge across the Delaware River, and one crossed by ferry.) The ferry ride itself was delightful, but of course it added to the time needed to get to the ocean. And on a busy weekend, there could be a long wait to get on the ferry. But the drive across the Eastern Shore was lovely, and the beach was great. We spent some single weeks and some weekends there during the years I am writing about. We did not stay at the big hotel, the Henlopen, although we ate some meals there. We stayed in rented rooms in private houses a few blocks back from the beach. And one of the treats in Rehoboth was a snackbar called George's, on the main street leading to the beach, which we remembered for years thereafter as having wonderful French fries.

Another thing we—and especially Mildred—missed from upstate New York was ice skating on a frozen pond. We did find a substitute for that at an indoor rink on Wisconsin Avenue near Van Ness. We skated there under the auspices of the Treasury Department's employees recreational society. Across the street from the rink was a root beer parlor, one of a few that had been established in Washington by J. Willard Marriott and his wife in the previous ten years. From those little acorns the Marriott empire grew.

Those were the days when going for a ride was still a form of entertainment. We had not yet spent miserable years in traffic, having a car of one's own was fairly new to us, and driving could stir up a breeze against the heat (cars were not air-conditioned). In a few minutes one could get away from the city, onto a country road between fields where cattle grazed and corn grew in rows. When we lived in Takoma Park, the preferred drives were out Colesville Road or out Wisconsin Avenue. Along either road one could buy from the farmer melons, tomatoes, and corn. If one continued to Frederick, one could get a half-bushel of delicious peaches at a wonderfully low price.

Those were the simple pleasures of the young in a simpler day.

The Policy Environment

When we arrived in Washington, in 1938, the New Deal had passed its most active phase. All the legislation that we now associate with the New Deal had been enacted. The Roosevelt administration had no big new plans for the economy, and even if it did, Congress was in no mood to listen. There was one more domestic economic policy show before the war shut that all down. The recession of 1937, coming before we had fully recovered from the Great Depression, the uncertainty about policy for getting out of the recession, and the still-controversial rise of Keynesian economics combined to raise the question about what our long-run strategy for sustaining prosperity was going to be. Congress set up a joint committee to study that subject and held endless hearings. If there was any outcome of this study, it was washed away by the war, but it had special significance for a young economist in two respects. First, it produced enough free reports, certainly more than fifty volumes, to constitute an economist's library, and I dragged them around with me for several years. Second, it was the first time that I had observed economists testifying before a congressional committee. That seemed to me, in my naiveté, about the greatest height that an economist could reach.

The people with whom I worked, my friends from Chicago, and I considered ourselves "conservatives" in economics. We were not Keynesians, we were not planners, we were not controllers or regulators. And yet we were all for Roosevelt. In fact, I think I knew only three people who were against Roosevelt. They were old men at the Brookings Institution who were, at least so I thought, embittered because the New Dealers had not called upon them for advice. Why were we conservatives for Roosevelt, who has since become the epitome of liberalism? I think it was because the Roosevelt regime was open to the talents. It had room for economists and lawyers and other intellectuals. Roosevelt himself had no fixed ideology, and if it was the liberal wing of his intellectual court that got most of his attention, there was also an opportunity for others. So we conservatives who thought of ourselves as intellectuals felt that we belonged with the Roosevelt team. Roosevelt had possessed a brain trust. There was no Republican brain trust.

In 1938 the political crisis in Europe was pushing domestic economic policy out of the spotlight of national attention. Shortly after we got settled in Washington, we were all watching the negotiations in Munich that ended up giving Hitler a green light to occupy Czechoslovakia. In the newsreels we saw Chamberlain coming home to London with his piece of paper. On the radio we heard Hitler's triumphant speeches—with a voice-over in English. The trial run for World War II was going on in Spain.

We were all wrapped up in this. And yet, I, and people like me, who read several newspapers, who listened to the commentators on the radio, and who read serious books, had no comprehension of the horror that was going on or of the greater horrors that were to come. As Jews, we might have been expected to be particularly sensitive to what was happening to the Jews in Germany, but we were far from realizing the gravity of the situation.

We were all supporters of the Loyalists in Spain. At the solicitation of people in the office where she worked, Mildred subscribed money to "adopt," that is, support, an orphaned child of Loyalists. The fact that the Loyalist government was Communist, and was supported by the Soviet Union, did not disturb us. I was enough of an economist to know that the Soviet planned economy could not work. But neither I nor my friends knew how Stalin oppressed his own people or how he might later oppress others. At least, he was not Hitler. This was an atmosphere in which, as was later alleged, Soviet agents could swim without detection in Washington. Colleagues of Taylor Ostrander at the Treasury and of Mildred at the Railroad Retirement Board were later said to have played that role. But there was no reason for suspicion at the time, and I still don't know the validity of the charges.

After June 1940, I was working in an agency that had as one of its functions preparing for war. In the fall of 1940, Congress passed the Selective Service Act. On October 16 of that year, I registered for the draft, and on October 29 a lottery was held at which the order of call-up for draftees was determined. One might think that even a blind man could see that the nation might soon be at war and what that might mean for him personally. I suppose I did realize that with part of my brain. But I was not obsessed with it, and I did not feel it with the same emotional chill that I feel when I think about it now, many years later. (For the record it never did happen to me. In 1944, at age twenty-eight, I became an ensign in the navy working on economic plans for the navy's occupation of various Pacific islands held by the Japanese. There was always the possibility that I might be put ashore on one of these islands—Formosa was my specialty—to impose the Stein tax plan on the natives. That was a worrisome thought but also too bizarre to be taken terribly seriously. It never did happen.)

The Black Condition

I was brought up in a city with many blacks—Detroit—and just before coming to Washington, I had spent three years in a city with many more—Chicago. In both places, the blacks were mainly poor and were segregated from the white population primarily by their poverty and also by cultural attributes brought with them from the South. But Washington was my first encounter with official and semiofficial segregation.

I have already referred to the low wage a responsible black woman earned as a dayworker in 1938. The blacks were poor and were a disproportionately large share of the welfare population. Thousands of blacks lived in "alley dwellings," shacks in the alleys between some "white" residential streets—shacks that had been built shortly after the end of the Civil War. (In those days we didn't say *black* but said *Negro* or *colored*.) Schools were segregated. Even the public golf courses were segregated. There were forty-five holes in public golf courses, of which nine holes were open to black golfers. Theaters were segregated. In 1933 *Green Pastures* played at the National Theater with an all-black cast, but blacks were not admitted to the audience. The District of Columbia could not have home rule but was governed by a Board of Commissioners appointed by the president, because Southern congressmen did not want to live in a city that might be governed by blacks. Whenever the newspapers referred to a black person, they always named him as such—saying "John Smith, colored" or "Mary Jones, colored"—as if that was an essential and probably sufficient identification. Sample headlines were "Colored Man, 25, to Face Special Jury in Assault" and "800 in Colored Classes Move to Upper Grades."

I was a white intellectual, as a Jew familiar with racial discrimination and considering himself to be free of prejudice. Why was I not outraged by this outrageous situation? Part of the answer may be that I was in my early twenties, engaged in starting a new family and a new career in a new town in a world that was in crisis. I had many things other than the condition of the blacks to absorb me.

But that is not the whole story. Mildred and I and our friends did pay attention to the black condition. What impressed us was less that things were terrible than that things were getting better. Many of the blacks in Washington had recently come up from the South, where, especially in the depression, conditions had been much worse for them. Many lived in alley dwellings, but the number of those was declining, and there was a public authority devoted to improving their living conditions. It was called, candidly enough, the Alley-Dwelling Authority. Many worked for the federal government, and although they usually had menial jobs, the federal government was a more color-blind employer than most in the country. Some were on welfare, but at least there was welfare. They went to segregated schools, but some of those schools were very good. (At the college I attended, Williams College in Massachusetts, there were usually one or two brilliant black students from one of the good Washington, D.C., high schools.)

The defining episode in the black condition in Washington in those years was the Marian Anderson affair. The Daughters of the American Revolution owned Constitution Hall, then the only decent concert hall in town. The DAR refused permission for Marian Anderson, a world-celebrated contralto, to sing there, because she was black. There was a furor, in Washington and in the country. Eleanor Roosevelt got Harold Ickes, secretary of the interior, to arrange for Anderson to sing on the steps of the Lincoln Memorial, which she did, triumphantly, before a crowd of 75,000 people, black and white. One could look at this as a story of how sick America was that the DAR would refuse Anderson the use of Constitution Hall. But one could also look at the sequel as a story of our getting better.

Although we viewed the condition of the blacks with optimism, there was one matter, probably trivial in itself, that always offended us when we saw it or thought of it. Woodward and Lothrop, one of the city's leading department stores, had a restaurant on the top floor where all the waitresses were of exactly the same shade of brown. That seemed to us to be carrying color consciousness too far.

The End of Before-the-War

On January 20, 1941, I took Mildred's mother downtown to see the Inauguration Day parade. (Why Mildred didn't come I don't remember. Perhaps we had only two tickets.) We sat on wooden bleachers on Pennsylvania Avenue across the street from the Willard Hotel. The day was cold but sunny. Before the parade the president gave the first ever, and probably last ever, third inaugural address. His remarks were very general, almost platitudinous, but on close reading they noted the end of the New Deal and the preparation for war.

Then the parade came up from the Capitol. And there was

General George Marshall, chief of staff of the army, riding up the avenue on his horse, perfectly erect, holding an unsheathed sword upright against his shoulder. It was a thrilling sight. He could have been Robert E. Lee or even George Washington. And behind him came a small company of light, clanking tanks, the most the U.S. Army could muster. Marshall on his horse signified for me the end of an era, and the pitiful tanks signified the beginning of another. We were not yet at war, but we were through with before-the-war.

8

Inside Washington's Old Executive Office Building

N othing illustrates the difference between being "in" in Washington and being "out," to me at least, as much as what is now called the Old Executive Office Building.

When my wife and I came to Washington in 1938, the building was known as State, War, and Navy, because it housed those three departments. It was also generally considered ugly, a monstrosity, an opinion that Mildred and I shared. It was, and is, an enormous pile, west of the White House and separated from it by a closed street, West Executive Avenue. It is three blocks long, one block wide, and five stories high. Built in the 1870s, it was, in a way, a balance to the equally large Treasury Building on the east side of the White House, which was, however, older and of a different architectural style. The Treasury was classical, whereas State, War, and Navy was Second French Empire.

Its curlicues, pillars supporting nothing, and other superfluous ornamentation did not fit with our ideal of architectural beauty. Moreover, its gray stone always looked dirty. During World War II, the State, War, and Navy Departments outgrew it, and the building was taken over by various offices attached to the president, the largest of which was the Bureau of the Budget. State, War, and Navy was renamed the Executive Office Building (EOB). When the Council of Economic Advisers was established in 1946, it was also installed there. I had occasions in those years to visit either the BOB or the CEA, and seeing the building from the inside did not improve my impression of it. There were end-less hallways floored with black and white tile that might have been better suited to a railway station or a public toilet. The curv-ing stairways were a strain for me to climb even when I was in my thirties. The rooms always seemed dark, being too big for their windows. Sometime during the Eisenhower administration I went to call on a moderately high official in his office there. The office was enormous, probably half a block long, lined with bookshelves in which there was only one book—the Bible. In the summertime, before air conditioning was general, the offices had louvered doors opening into the corridors to permit circulation of air. All in all, it seemed a musty and inefficient place in which to do business.

A Changed Impression

When in 1969 I moved into the EOB to stay, as a member of the President's Council of Economic Advisers and not as a visitor, my impression of it changed radically. What had seemed merely heaviness now seemed an indication of the gravity and durability of what was to be done there. What had seemed old-fashioned now seemed an indication of stability and continuity in doing the country's serious business. One had the feeling of being part of a chain of public servants who had worked there through a century of great development and many problems. I was delighted to dis-cover, at one point, that my office was immediately above one that had been occupied by Dean Acheson and was just like it. I didn't feel that I was a successor to Dean Acheson or Elihu Root or John Hay or the young Franklin Delano Roosevelt, who had worked there as assistant secretary of the navy during World War I. But I could think of myself as a successor to generations of lesser offi-cials who had made some anonymous contribution.

This impression of continuity and gravity was fortified by the presence in the building of hundreds of civil servants, most of whom had been there before us and would be there after us. At the opening of business on a cold morning, one could see them hurrying or sauntering to their offices from the cafeteria carrying steaming cups of coffee. For some reason that always made me think of a scene from a nineteenth-century Russian novel, set in St. Petersburg. I discovered that in general these people were highly competent and devoted. I think, perhaps this is romanticizing, that the atmosphere of the building contributed to their feeling of pride, seriousness, and obligation toward what they were doing there.

This atmosphere of the EOB may be compared with the atmosphere of the White House, which was even more exciting but in some ways less nourishing. I did not have an office in the White House, but I went there freely and frequently—to meetings, to lunch in the Mess, even to get my hair cut. The White House did not convey the feeling of age as the EOB did. Almost all my dealings with the White House were in the West Wing, where the Cabinet Room, the Roosevelt Room, the Oval Office, the Mess, and the offices of various presidential assistants were. The West Wing was much younger than the EOB, having been built in the time of Theodore Roosevelt. Moreover, the West Wing was always spick-and-span, and the decor much brighter than in the EOB, so that it gave the impression of being even newer than it was.

Even the main building of the White House, the residential part, which was, of course, much older than the EOB, did not give the impression of age, since it had been redone so frequently. In fact, the State Rooms were more suggestive of Jackie Kennedy than of Abraham Lincoln or Andrew Jackson.

Whereas the EOB was mainly peopled by civil servants who had been there and would be there for a long time, almost everyone in the West Wing was new. They had come with Nixon and would go when he went. There was a feeling of impermanence about being there. In the EOB you were part of a continuing government. In the White House you were part of a passing administration. That was exciting, but it was also somewhat unreal.

I don't mean to suggest that the feeling of unreality was at the front of my mind whenever I was in the White House. I had real and absorbing work to do there, and that was usually the focus of my attention. But I often had the sense of watching myself with wonderment. One day toward the end, probably in late 1973, I attended a meeting of an interagency committee chaired by George Shultz. Afterward, when we were alone, I said to him that I felt as if we were a bunch of high school seniors who had been allowed to sit in the offices of City Hall and pretend to be the City Council for a day. I didn't feel that at the EOB—that was a place where real people worked.

So the combination of being in the EOB most of the time

and in the White House frequently was the best of both worlds. I experienced the gravity and seriousness of the EOB and the glitz and excitement of the White House.

"At Home" in the EOB

During my term there, from 1969 to 1974, the EOB housed not only the Office of Management and Budget and the Council of Economic Advisers but also staffs of the National Security Council, the Council on International Economic Policy, the press secretary, and various presidential liaisons. The speech-writing staff was there, and when my son worked on that staff in 1973 and 1974, that added to the feeling that EOB was home to me.

Up on the fourth floor was a large room, with a tiled floor and cast-iron decorations, called the Indian Treaty Room, a name dating back to dealings with Indian nations a century earlier. The room was usually empty but would be furnished with tables and chairs as the occasion required. In January 1970 the Council of Economic Advisers held a press conference there, talking about the first-ever trillion-dollar GNP in the room where bearded presidents and feathered Indian chiefs had signed papers to pacify the frontier. In retrospect this seems bizarre, but at the time it seemed perfectly natural. We were bit players in the same historical drama as the presidents and Indian chiefs, on the same stage, the EOB.

The White House doctors, except the chief of them who was on duty in the White House itself, had a clinic on the second floor of the EOB. The Californians, Bob Haldeman and John Erlichman, had arranged for a little exercise room to be installed on the first floor. I was not one to use the exercise equipment, but on those few occasions when I had to dress for dinner, the gym was a convenient place to take a shower and change my clothes. There was said to be a bowling alley in the basement. I once tried to take some visitors to see it, but we couldn't find it.

The vice president had an office on the third floor, and the president had his hideaway office on the second floor. Perhaps Mr. Nixon (alas) also welcomed the sense of permanence that came with the EOB, as distinguished from the West Wing of the White House.

In the EOB the Council of Economic Advisers had a suite of offices on the third floor, along the western and southern side of the building. From the beginning of the CEA in 1946 until 1961, the chairman had occupied the corner office, with windows facing west toward the Corcoran Gallery and south over the Mall and into Virginia. When Walter Heller became chairman, he decided to move out of that office to the one to the east of it, which was larger and gave him access to a large room for his secretaries and administrative assistant. After my appointment, my friend Otto Eckstein, who was a CEA member in the Johnson administration, advised me to get to the building as soon as possible and occupy the corner office, which I did. Later, when I became chairman, I continued to use the corner office, and subsequent chairmen for twenty-four years have done the same.

The office had an area of 567 square feet, divided about 28 feet by 20 feet. The ceiling was exceptionally high, higher than one ever encounters in a modern building, about 18 feet. With high windows on the south and west, it was usually bright during most of the year. One of my first perks was the right to choose my own draperies, which I did with Mildred's advice, selecting a Swedish-modern pattern. The office came equipped with a fireplace, which had been blocked up. For furnishing there was a large wooden desk, with a high-backed desk chair, two leather sofas, a conference table that would seat eight, and assorted chairs. I also asked for and received a typewriter table with an IBM Selectric typewriter, this not yet being the era of the word processor. I was to do a lot of writing. A little later I received a television set that was hooked up to the Signal Corps receivers on the roof. I could see not only the current broadcasts but also a large selection of previous broadcasts, including all the news and talk shows, that the corps had taped. In January 1973, when we were working on the council's Economic Report, a large part of the staff joined in my office on a Sunday afternoon to watch the Redskins in the Super Bowl. In 1971 I acquired another electronic gadget. I was regularly chairing a committee that included two cigar smokers, Charls Walker, under secretary of the Treasury, and James Lynn, under secretary of commerce, and I obtained a device for removing smoke from the air.

From my windows on the west side, the Seventeenth Street side, I could look down at the Winder Building, where Abraham Lincoln used to go to read the telegrams reporting on the progress of Civil War battles. Looking out the south windows, I could see the airplanes rising and descending at National Airport, across the Potomac, in the old Confederacy. Down the hall from my office, on the south side, was the EOB library. It was a scarcely used room, with an antique and haphazard collection of books. But it was a place where a visitor could sit in quiet. The librarian was an elderly lady whose hobby was collecting miniature ceramic cats, which were lavishly distributed among the tables and shelves. The room had a gallery, reached by a narrow, winding iron staircase and protected by cast-iron railings. French doors led out from the library to a portico that was one of the best places in Washington from which to see the fireworks on the Fourth of July.

One of our perks was an endless supply of photographs that could be framed at the government's expense. The White House photographer, Ollie Atkins, and his assistants took great photographs of almost every visible thing that happened and would provide any number of copies. I soon had several of them framed on my wall, led by the picture of President Nixon, along with the copy of my certificate of appointment. This was, of course, standard for all presidential appointees. Some lived surrounded by such pictures of their former glory for the rest of their lives. I never had a place, after I left the government, where that seemed appropriate. Even at the EOB it seemed to me a little tacky. I took advantage of the government's willingness to frame anything to put up on the wall some cheap prints that I brought back from Paris, instead of more and more photographs with the single theme of our lives with the White House. I didn't need the photographs to remind me of that. I was there.

I rarely get inside the EOB any more. (It is now called the Old EOB, having acquired the name during our stay there, when a New EOB was opened on the other side of Pennsylvania Avenue.) But I sometimes drive by in the evening and look up to see the windows lit up on the southwest corner on the third floor. I think that someone is up there seriously and happily working at a continuing and worthy cause. And I also think of how little people who haven't been there know about what goes on in the halls of government.

9

Reading the Inaugurals

President Clinton's inaugural address of January 1997 is the fifty-third in the series that began in 1789. They are all worth reading—all of them—not just the highlights such as Washington, Lincoln, and FDR. They will give you a feeling of being there, not as an omniscient historian of the present looking back at 1837 or 1897 but as an ordinary citizen sharing, and limited by, the information, the concerns, and the values of those times. (Thanks to Columbia University, all the addresses can be found at http://www.columbia.edu/acis/bartleby/inaugural/index.html.)

Among all the past presidents and their speechwriters, there was only one literary genius—Abraham Lincoln. After 132 years, his second inaugural still brings tears to your eyes and chills to your blood. None of the others are in that league. But by and large, they are good speeches. Those now-forgotten men (they were all men), Pierce, Garfield, Hayes, and others, rated as "average presidents" by historians, were not average men. They would not have been elected president if they had been. They were articulate men, in touch with their times, and aware that their inauguration was the most solemn occasion of their life. They gave, within the context of their circumstances, dignified and intelligent speeches.

Three Phases

The stance and style of the inaugurals seemed to go through three phases. The first phase, lasting until Lincoln, was one of the modest, classic public servant. The second, lasting through Taft, was of the prosaic government executive. The third, the current one, is the phase of the assertive, theatrical, leader-preacher. This classification is not waterproof. Theodore Roosevelt may belong in the third phase and Harding-Coolidge-Hoover in the second. But the trend is clear.

On picking up Washington's first inaugural, one is immediately struck by the modesty. He had just been elected unanimously by the electoral college. He was more respected at that moment than any subsequent president has been at the time of *his* inauguration. And what does he say?

> The magnitude and difficulty of the trust to which the voice of my country called me, being sufficient to awaken in the wisest and most experienced of her citizens a distrustful scrutiny into his qualifications, could not but overwhelm with despondence one who (inheriting inferior endowments from nature and unpracticed in the duties of civil administration) ought to be peculiarly conscious of his own deficiencies.

No later president has made the point as forcefully as that. But some echoes of that are to be found in almost every president for the next sixty-eight years. (John Adams was an exception. He was apparently so envious of Washington that he spent a large part of his address spelling out his excellent qualifications for the job.) That era ended with Lincoln. Subsequent inaugurals routinely contain protestations of humility, but they are perfunctory and do not sound sincere.

The antebellum modesty may in part have been a reflection of the conventional etiquette of the time. There is, however, a more political side to the later decline of modesty in inaugural addresses. In the early days, starting with Washington, some people feared that the republic might be transformed into a monarchy and the president into a king. The presidents' assertion of modesty, not only about themselves but also about the powers of the presidency, may have helped to alleviate that concern. A little later, perhaps after 1820, a new worry arose. Would the power of the federal government be used to interfere with the "peculiar domestic institution" of the Southern states? The presidents' assurance of the limitation of their own powers, personally and as prescribed by the Constitution, may have been intended to give comfort to those states.

Lincoln faced a different situation. Like his predecessors, he had taken an oath to "preserve, protect and defend the Constitution," but whereas they might have thought they could do that by giving assurance of the limitation of the federal executive power, Lincoln, with the South already seceding, could preserve the Constitution only by asserting the power of the federal government and his own power as chief executive of that government. It was no time for modesty. Lincoln's successors inherited a federal government with much more authority and more need to use it than before the war and less motivation to belittle themselves and their powers.

In the third phase the inaugural address metamorphosed from describing the government's policy to inspiring the public's behavior. Presidents recognized—or, at least, believed—that the country had problems they ought to deal with but could not manage by using the instruments of government alone. Thus, in his first inaugural, Woodrow Wilson said:

> At last a vision has been vouchsafed us of our life as a whole. We see the bad with the good, the debased and decadent with the sound and the vital. With this vision we approach new affairs.

If the country is debased and decadent, the cure has to come from uplifting the people, not from acts of government. Similar diagnoses and prescriptions appear in later inaugurals.

Presidents derived their license to serve as leader-preacher from the remark of Theodore Roosevelt that the presidency is "a bully pulpit," a remark that did not appear in his inaugural address. The metaphor of the pulpit suggests not reading but oral and visual contact between the preacher and his flock. Radio and, even more, television made this possible on a national scale.

A tell-tale sign of the leader-preacher inaugural is the use of the phrase *Let us,* meaning, "You do as I say." This expression appears occasionally throughout the history of inaugurals, but it hit its stride in recent years. Kennedy's inaugural contains it sixteen times, and Nixon's second has it twenty-two times.

The change in literary style from classical to colloquial can be demonstrated by one statistic. In all the inaugurals from Washington through Buchanan, the average number of words per sentence was forty-four. From Lincoln to Wilson, it was thirty-four; and since Wilson it has been twenty-five. I do not consider this a deterioration (this article has seventeen words per sentence), but it does reflect the change in the size and character of the audience to which the inaugurals were addressed and in the means of communication. William Henry Harrison could talk about the governments of Athens, Rome, and the Helvetic Confederacy and expect his audience to know what he was talking about. That wouldn't be true today. But Harrison's audience would not have known what the Internet was.

Presidents and their speechwriters have mined their predecessors for memorable words and repeated them without attribution. Kennedy's trumpet call, "Ask not what your country can do for you: Ask what you can do for your country," has an ironic history. In his inaugural, Warren G. Harding, surely no model for Kennedy, had said, "Our most dangerous tendency is to expect too little of government, and at the same time do for it too little." And even earlier, in a speech in 1916, Harding had said, "In the great fulfillment we must have a citizenship less concerned about what the government can do for it and more anxious about what it can do for the nation."

Issues in the Inaugural Speeches

Many an issue frets its hour on the inaugural stage and then is heard no more. That includes the Indians, the coastal fortifications, territorial expansion, the Isthmus Canal, civil service reform, polygamy, and Prohibition. Some subjects that you expect to appear don't. Hoover's inaugural, March 4, 1929, gives no hint of economic vulnerability. In January 1937, Roosevelt's second inaugural contains no reference to Hitler or to Germany. But what is most amazing, at least to a reader now, is the silence of the inaugurals on the subject of women. The word *women* does not appear at all until Wilson's first inaugural, and it always appears as part of a phrase *men and women,* never as referring to any special concerns of women.

One subject that does get ample treatment is taxes. *Taxes* or some equivalent word appears in forty-three of the fifty-two inaugurals spoken to date. Coolidge in 1925 said: "The time is arriving when we can have further tax reduction. . . . I am opposed to extremely high rates, because they produce little or no revenue, because they are bad for the country, and, finally, because they are wrong." Federal taxes were then about 3 percent of the gross domestic product. Ronald Reagan said essentially the same thing in 1981, when they were 20 percent.

The most disturbing aspect of the whole series of inaugurals is what is said and unsaid on the subject of race relations, which Arthur Schlesinger, Jr., calls "the supreme American problem." The words *black, blacks, Negro,* or *race* (as applied to blacks) do not appear at all until Hayes in 1877. James Monroe, in 1817, asked, "On whom has oppression fallen in any quarter of our Union? Who has been deprived of any right of person or property?" These were rhetorical questions, intended to get the answer No one! as if there were not millions of slaves in America.

Before the Civil War the word *slavery* appears only in Van Buren, 1837, and Buchanan, 1857, and then only as something that, to adhere to the Constitution and preserve the Union, should not be interfered with. But although generally unmentionable, the subject was boiling and would boil over in 1861. After the Civil War, in the inaugurals of Hayes, Garfield, and Benjamin Harrison we find the most explicit and positive discussion of the need to convert into reality the rights and freedom granted to the "freedmen" on paper by the Thirteenth, Fourteenth, and Fifteenth Amendments. Garfield's was the strongest among these. (He had been a student at Williams College in the 1850s, eighty years before me, when the college had been a station on the underground railway.) But the subject then began to fade. McKinley said: "Lynchings must not be tolerated in a great and civilized country like the United States," but he said it without horror. Taft raised the subject of race relations only to express satisfaction at the progress that had been made. And then the subject disappeared. FDR never mentioned it in any of his four inaugurals.

After World War II, the subject comes back to inaugural addresses, but in a weak and abstract form. That is true even of the presidents we think of as being most concerned with race relations in America—like Truman, Lyndon Johnson, and Clinton. Perhaps each thought he had made a sufficient statement by having a black woman—Marian Anderson, Leontyne Price, or Maya Angelou—perform at his ceremony. In Clinton's first inaugural the only allusion to the race problem is in this sentence: "From our revolution, the Civil War, to the Great Depression to the civil rights movement, our people have always mustered the determination to construct from these crises the pillars of our history." I recall this not to suggest that their concern was not deep and sincere but only to indicate what is acceptable to say in a speech intended to appeal to the values shared by Americans.

There is much to ponder in these speeches—much more than I have suggested here. There is much to be proud of, in what we have endured and achieved, in the peaceful transference of power, and in the reasonableness and moderation of the presidents we have elected. There are no Caligulas, no George IIIs, no Lenins, and no Hitlers among them. But there is also much humility to be learned from reading these speeches. We look back with amazement at the ignorance and moral obtuseness revealed by what our past leaders have said and our past citizens believed. We should recognize that fifty or a hundred years from now readers will shake their heads at what we are saying and believing today.

10

Looking Back to
August 15, 1971

On August 15, 1971, President Nixon came down from
Camp David and announced his new economic policy to
the nation on all networks. The plan included freezing all
prices and wage rates for ninety days, stopping gold payments,
imposing a 10 percent surcharge on imports, and cutting various
taxes and expenditures. I don't propose to retell the story of that
announcement, which seemed so dramatic at the time but is memorable now only to the few who were direct participants. Instead, I
would like to make some observations about the policy-making
process that are suggested by recalling that experience but have,
I believe, more general applicability. These observations mainly
fall in the category of "looking ahead."

Big Decisions

Even now, I am amazed to think of how little we looked ahead
during that exciting weekend at Camp David when we (the president, really) made those big decisions. We were going to freeze
wages and prices for ninety days. What would happen after the
ninety days? I don't remember any discussion of that. We all assumed that the comprehensive freeze would not last beyond the
ninety days. Some people, at least, assumed that we would then
fall back to what used to be called "some kind of incomes policy,"

meaning moral suasion addressed to the largest unions and businesses. But that idea was not explicitly raised.

As it turned out, we were in the price-and-wage-control business, although with diminishing coverage and rigidity, not for ninety days but for nearly a thousand. We were in the business of controlling energy prices for much longer. Would the Nixon team have embarked on the controls in August 1971 if we had foreseen that? I don't know, but it is surely a real question. Was it foreseeable? Perhaps it was not a certain outcome, but it was surely a possible outcome. Probably the whole idea of the controls was so alien to us that we could not imagine that we would be living with them for very long. About two months later, when George Shultz and I gave Mr. Nixon the suggested plan for phase two of the controls, to follow the ninety-day freeze, the president said, "If this baby gets too strong we can strangle it in its cradle." But we could not strangle it in its cradle.

We had created a system upon which tens of millions of people depended, and we could get out of it only gradually. Some time in the fall of 1971, when I was working on the plans for what would follow the freeze, a Canadian economist concerned with price controls in his country sent me these lines from *Macbeth:* "I am in blood stept in so far that, should I wade no more, returning were as tedious as go o'er." The lines were all too apt.

Some people at Camp David had a theory of what we were doing with the ninety-day freeze. The theory was that the inflation then under way (about 4 percent a year as measured by the consumer price index) was propelled by expectations of inflation and not by underlying demand and supply conditions. The ninety-day freeze would knock those expectations in the head by demonstrating that prices and wages would not rise rapidly forever and the economy would then subside into price stability. It was a rather flaky theory, and we were not prepared for the strong possibility that it was wrong.

The story of closing the gold window was only a little different. What was decided at Camp David was that we wanted to get the exchange value of the dollar down. Closing the gold window and imposing the surcharge were ways to do that. But how much did we want to get the dollar down? Having gotten it down, did we want to keep it at its new level indefinitely, or did we want to provide for its subsequent adjustment? If we wanted an adjustable-rate system, what would be the rules of that system? Or did we want exchange rates to float, without any limiting rules? Some of the participants at Camp David had in mind answers to these questions. But they were different ideas, and they were never discussed.

In the year and a half after Camp David, we went through the process of answering those questions. It took until the end of 1971 to determine a new set of exchange rates. During 1972 an effort was made to establish the rules of a system for adjustment of rates. And in early 1973 we moved to floating. The difference from the price control case was that once we had made the decision to freeze wages and prices, there was no way out except slowly and uncomfortably to get back to where we had been before. In the exchange rate case, though, there was a way forward to what some people, at least, thought was a better system—floating. But in neither case had there been any looking ahead.

Failure to Look Ahead

I describe the incidents of that weekend in August 1971 because they are a dramatic example of not looking ahead, but they are by no means unique. *Looking ahead* means something more than sketching out the most comfortable, or even the most probable, future scenario. It means recognizing that even the most probable forecast is uncertain and preparing for the eventuality that the forecast turns out to be incorrect. Defined in this way, failure to look ahead is extremely common in government policy making. (I refer to government in this connection only because I have had more experience with it, not because I know that things are any better in the private sector.)

The Bay of Pigs venture and various injections of troops into Vietnam are probably good examples of failure to look ahead. The decision to launch Medicare is another important case. When the Johnson administration made that decision, it had estimates of its future cost. But these estimates were highly uncertain. There was no preparation in the public mind or in policy for action to be taken if the costs grossly exceeded the estimates, as they did. Thirty years later, we are still struggling with that problem. Ronald Reagan's decision in 1980 to make a big tax cut the centerpiece of his election campaign is another example. There were in his camp several theories about what would happen after the tax cut was enacted, but there was no agreed theory and no plan for what to do if none of the theories turned out to be correct, as was the case.

Looking back at these failures to look forward raises questions about what is going on today. When we sent ground troops to Bosnia, there was, I suppose, a theory about what would happen and how our troops would get out. Is there a theory about what to do if the first theory proves to be incorrect? We are about to end "welfare as we know it." Implicit in the new policy are some estimates of how many fewer unmarried teenage women will have babies, how many will find self-supporting employment, and how much money states will provide for employment and child care and other paths to self-reliance. Possibly someone has explicit estimates of such things, although I have never heard of them. But does anyone have any plan for what we should do if the assumptions underlying "welfare as we are going to know it" turn out to be wrong? Now we have Republican proposals for big tax cuts, and also Democratic proposals for tax cuts, although smaller ones. Have the proponents of these tax cuts looked head, with due awareness of the uncertainties, to the consequences for the year 2002, 2020, or even 2030?

Perhaps there are good answers to these questions. I hope so.

11

The Nixon I Knew

D etermined scholars and journalists have fished through the Nixon tapes and recovered enough material to fill books and articles showing that Nixon was obscene and unscrupulous. I do not deny that there was *a* Nixon like that. But that was not the only Nixon or the most usual and important one. Richard Nixon performed the daily, difficult duties of being president responsibly and respectably. I was not a confidant or crony of Mr. Nixon. But I saw him frequently during his whole tenure of office, when I was a member and then chairman of his Council of Economic Advisers. On all these occasions, he impressed me as a civil, serious, dedicated, judicious, and highly intelligent man. I believe that others who worked with him in a professional way had the same impression.

An Informed President

I first met Mr. Nixon on December 18, 1968, after his first election, when he was about to name me a member of the CEA. If I was a Republican at all, I was not a Nixon Republican. He was about to assume the most powerful office in the world. I was a little-known economics essayist. But I felt comfortable with him. He did not try either to glad-hand me or to impress me with his importance. He showed genuine interest in what I had to say about the matters on which I was assumed to be well informed, and he was unreserved about expressing his own opinion.

I was also struck by my observation of him at the first meeting of the Cabinet Committee on Economic Policy, shortly after the inauguration. I and my colleague, Hendrik Houthakker, as members of the CEA, were the lowest-ranking people in the room. But the president wanted to hear what we had to say. He also made it clear that he did not expect his economic advisers to engage in political activity, although we might make speeches on economic policy to groups of economists and others interested in a professional way. I thought he showed courtesy, consideration, and desire to learn. (Later, after the 1972 campaign, some of my Democratic friends thought that my speeches had been too political. If so, it was because I enjoyed being in the political game, not because Mr. Nixon urged me on.)

In the next six years, I went through many meetings in which three or four people—Treasury, budget, Federal Reserve, CEA—would discuss economic policy with the president. He usually listened to the interchange quietly. When the discussion was over, he would summarize the discussion in a systematic way—distilling what order could be obtained from the discussion and indicating what he thought the main considerations and options were. These were scenes light-years remote from the locker-room conversations with Haldeman, Erlichman, and others that have become the subject of much recent interest.

The president appreciated both the value and the limitations of economics. He understood that it had something to contribute and should be heard, but he also understood that economics is a limited and uncertain science. There were no complaints or recriminations when the economic forecasts turned out to be wrong. At the beginning of 1972, the CEA had forecast that unemployment would be down from about 6 percent to 4 percent by the end of the year. In December I had to report to him that unemployment was still about 5 percent, and I said that was "in the neighborhood" of 4 percent. All he replied was that it was a streetcar ride across the neighborhood. That realistic attitude was a great comfort to an economic adviser.

I don't recall his ever using an obscenity, unless you want to count the time he said that he would rather have Mr. X inside the tent and p. . .ing out than outside the tent p. . .ing in. (I believe this was borrowed from LBJ, and probably from generations of earlier politicians.) I remember Mr. Nixon's once saying, "Honesty may not be the best policy, but it is worth trying once in a while." But that was an occasion when he was arguing for honesty.

Judge Not

I think it important in view of the grossness of some of the language selectively extracted from the tapes that Mr. Nixon showed an appreciation of, and capacity for, good writing and wit. He probably had the best staff of writers any president ever had since the time Alexander Hamilton wrote speeches for George Washington. The exchange with him that I best remember came in early 1973 when he was considering the reimposition of a wage and price freeze, which had been so popular when first done in August 1971. In a smart-alecky kind of way I said, quoting Heraclitus, "You can't step in the same river twice." He immediately responded, "Yes, you can, if it's frozen."

In my opinion the imposition of price and wage controls was President Nixon's one serious mistake of economic policy. But that decision was within the range of options urged upon him by respected economists, mainly Democrats. The control system gave the administration extraordinary power over individual businesses. I do not believe there was any case in which this power was improperly used.

Mr. Nixon recognized and used talent, whatever its political connection. The leading example was George Shultz. He saw in this professor, whom he had never met before he invited him to be secretary of labor, a man of extraordinary intelligence, management ability, and integrity. He quickly elevated him from the secondary position of secretary of labor. There must have been few administrations that had as much talent in the two senior cabinet positions—state and Treasury—as Kissinger and Shultz.

I do not put down these few recollections to excuse Richard Nixon. I knew him and liked and respected him. I am not inclined to judge him. I do not feel I have the wisdom and moral elevation to do that. Anyway, what would be the point? He is now beyond our—or, at least, my—power to add or detract. I want to suggest only that those who feel the need and ability to judge him should try to look beyond the revelation-of-the-day.

PART THREE

The State of the Economy

12

A Rich Country with Problems

The American people are bathed in information about the
economy, as they are about many other subjects. Their economic information comes to them in snippets in newspapers or on television and refers to some current event or currently
released bit of news. The bits of information are not seen in the
contexts—national, international, and, especially, historic—that
would give them meaning.

To pretend to give a comprehensive, objective picture of the
American economy would be presumptuous. The subject is too
big and complicated. Some facts one would like to have are not
available, and some are not even conceptually obtainable. People
disagree about what constitutes facts and about which facts are
significant. Nevertheless, it may be a service to put down what
seem to be the basic facts and the story they tell.

America's Wealth

America is very rich. This does not mean that America has no
economic problems. But for the most part, they are problems relative to the expectations of a rich society. Many conditions that
appear as problems here would not seem problems if they occurred in a society that was not so rich and that did not seem to
have so much capacity to overcome the problems.

By the best measure we have, output per person is now about
eight times as high as it was 125 years ago. Many qualifications
must be acknowledged about such a calculation, but there can be

little doubt that output per person here is much higher than it was even within the memory of people now living. Output per person in the United States is now probably about 25 percent higher than in Japan or Germany, the other large countries with the largest output per person.

The relative richness of the United States is not a new phenomenon. Already at the beginning of this century, output per person in the United States was higher than in other industrial countries, many of which have grown faster than the United States has since 1900. In economic terms, the Americans of this generation are the beneficiaries of the efforts and achievements of much earlier generations.

About 60 percent of the world's population lives in countries where the average output is less than 20 percent of that in the United States. Today, however, some of the poorest countries, such as China and India, have higher growth rates of output per person than we do.

Facets of the U.S. Economy

Role of Government. Almost all of America's huge flow of goods and services is produced in private businesses—85 percent in 1997, almost exactly the same percentage as in 1929. The role of government in the economy has increased greatly since 1929, but it has not increased in its capacity as a producer, which is still small. Rather, it has increased as a purchaser from the private sector, buying all kinds of things, such as computers and gasoline, which it uses in providing services to the public. Most of all, government has grown as a transferrer of income from taxpayers to various recipients of cash benefits, like social security.

The Business Sector and Unions. At various times earlier in this century, some have been concerned that the private business sector that supplies almost all our output was, or was becoming, monopolized by large businesses, with bad economic and political consequences. This worry was unfounded and has faded. Although there are many large firms in the United States, more than half of all American workers are employed in firms with fewer than 500 employees. There is no evidence that concentration within the American economy has increased, and there has been a great increase in competition from firms in the rest of the world.

The fear that the American economy would be dominated by large labor unions has also passed. Union membership has declined as a share of nonfarm employment since its high point in the 1950s and now stands at around 18 percent. It is fair to say that on the production side the American economy is not only private but also competitive.

A Service Economy. The American economy has been a service economy for a long time, in the sense that at least since before World War II more than half the output purchased has been services and more than half the output has been produced in service industries. The share of services has been rising. In 1996, over 60 percent of all private output was produced in service industries.

There is a common tendency to think of the service industries as typically low-productivity, low-wage industries, symbolized by fast-food restaurants. But the service industries include finance, advertising, entertainment, and transportation as well as retail trade. In 1996, the average compensation of all service workers was about 94 percent of the average compensation of all private workers.

Personal Consumption. The output of the American economy is basically devoted to personal consumption. In the 1990s about two-thirds of total output went to personal consumption directly. But in a fundamental sense the share of consumption is much greater. The part of output that is invested goes to increase consumption in the future, and most of the output used by government provides services for consumers—such as education or health care—or services used in the provision of consumer goods, such as highways.

From 1959 to 1997, real direct consumption expenditures per person increased at an average rate of 2.2 percent a year. The character of these expenditures has changed greatly. The share spent for food has fallen sharply, and the share going to medical care has risen sharply, so that by 1997 personal expenditures for medical care were higher than for food.

America's Problems

Although America's is the world's most productive economy, it has nonetheless been beset with real problems, as well as with unjustified complaints. The great trauma of the American economy was the depression of the 1930s. Unemployment rose to 25 percent of the labor force. Total output fell by 28 percent from 1929 to 1933 and did not regain its 1929 level until 1939. The causes of this great depression are still being debated among economists. Undoubtedly, the steep decline in the supply of money was a contributing factor, but there were probably others, at home and abroad.

For many years after the depression was over, fear of a recurrence haunted America. But the fear that anything of a similar scale will happen again has abated. We now see that the depression of the 1930s was unlike anything that had happened before, and we have now had more than half a century in which nothing like it has happened again. In our worst postwar recessions, unemployment reached 8.5 percent in 1975 and 9.7 percent in 1982 and then receded fairly quickly. Confidence that America will avoid another major depression is strengthened by the belief that monetary policy will not repeat the mistakes of the early 1930s. Moreover, stability is increased by the fact that government expenditures are much larger, relative to the size of the economy, than they were in 1929, and the government expenditures tend to increase, rather than decrease in a recession, which helps to support private incomes and avert what might otherwise be a cumulative decline.

Unemployment. Even in the best of times, we have some unemployment. The rate of normal unemployment seems to have risen, although no one knows with certitude what it is. In the 1950s, it was thought to be about 4 percent; in the early 1980s many economists thought it was around 6 percent; and more recently, it has looked like 5 percent. In 1997, half the unemployed had been out of work for less than eight weeks.

Inflation. During most of our history before World War II, there was no long-run trend toward a higher average level of prices. The price level surged during the Civil War and again, although not so much, during World War I. After each of these surges, however, the price level stabilized or even declined, so that between 1860 and 1940 the average annual rate of increase of the price level was only about one-half of 1 percent. After the inflation of World War II, however, the price level did not decline or even stabilize. The level of prices rises every year, by greater or smaller amounts.

In the 1970s, the American economy experienced two big spasms of inflation. Consumer prices rose 12 percent in 1974 and, after slowing down, by 13 percent in 1979. Each of these surges was connected with a big increase in oil prices, but it is probably also true that fiscal and monetary policy were not very resistant to the translation of the oil price increase into the rest of the price level. The rate of consumer price inflation is now about 3 percent a year. (All the foregoing figures refer to the official measurement, which may overstate the actual increase by around 1 percent a year. Improvement of the calculations is, however, unlikely to change the story that the inflation rate was much higher from about 1970 to about 1990 than it was earlier or has been since.) The rate of inflation will undoubtedly fluctuate somewhat. Responsibility for avoiding serious inflation lies with the monetary policy of the Federal Reserve. The instruments and strategy of monetary policy are not sufficiently precise to keep the rate of inflation constant at any specified number, whether zero or 3 percent or some other. How to deal with a major shock like the oil price increase, if one should occur, is uncertain. But still it seems to be within the capacity of the Federal Reserve to keep the long-run average rate of inflation moderate.

Government Programs. Total government expenditures—federal, state, and local—now equal about one-third of the gross domestic product, compared with about 15 percent in 1929. Most of the increase in the government share had come by 1949, as a result of new federal programs adopted during the depression and even more as a consequence of World War II and the heightened costs of defense connected with the cold war. In the postwar period, expenditures have fluctuated within a range of 30 to 35 percent of GDP. There has, however, been a major shift in the character of expenditures. Defense as a share of GDP has been on a declining trend, punctuated by increases for the Korean War, the Vietnam War, and the 1980s buildup. This declining trend has been offset by a rising trend of nondefense spending.

Between 1959 and 1997, government nondefense expenditures rose from 17 percent of GDP to 30 percent. About three-fourths of this increase was for three functions—health, education, and payments to individuals, the largest of which was for social security. By 1997, federal payments to individuals amounted to about 10 percent of GDP. About one-fourth of these expenditures were "means-tested"—that is, given to people who were eligible only because they were poor.

Since 1960, federal tax revenues have fluctuated between 18 to 20 percent of GDP, and in 1997 they were 20 percent. The composition of the total has changed radically. Revenue from payroll taxes has risen from 1.6 percent of GDP in 1950 to 6.8 percent in 1997. These taxes are dedicated to specific purposes—programs for retirement, disability, medical care, and unemployment. As a percentage of GDP, the revenues available for all other purposes have declined, because of the decline in revenue from corporate profits taxes and excises. The percentage of GDP going to personal income taxes has risen irregularly, fluctuating somewhat with the business cycle. It was 7.9 percent in 1960 and 9.3 percent in 1997.

Since 1985, the federal income tax burden on families in a wide range of income classes has declined. In 1985, for example, a family of four with an income of $75,000 in 1995 dollars would have paid about 18 percent of its income in income tax. In 1996, that percentage was 15 percent. In 1985, a family with an income of $20,000 in 1995 dollars would have paid a tax of about 5 percent; in 1996 they would have received an earned-income tax refund equal to about 4 percent of their income. Extending the comparison back to 1970 would still show declines or, at least, stability in the income tax burdens of families with comparable incomes.

Except for wars and recessions, federal expenditures and revenues have moved closely together, keeping budget deficits small until the 1980s. In that decade, a combination of tax reduction and increased spending for defense raised the deficit to around 5 percent of GDP. But by 1998, the budget had come into balance again and surpluses were expected for at least the next five years, if tax and spending programs were not changed.

Family Income. The American economy now suffers from two main problems. The first is that real average incomes have been rising much less rapidly than they did earlier in the postwar period. The second is that the incomes of the workers and families with the lowest incomes have been rising especially slowly and may have actually declined in the past twenty years.

Median family income, adjusted for inflation according to conventional measurements, increased by only about 3 percent between 1978 and 1996, but that figure is sensitive to the measurement of inflation, which is now believed to be highly uncertain. If, as some experts believe, the conventional measurement overstates inflation by about 1 percent a year, the increase of real median income over that period has been 24 percent. (Half of all families have income below the median, and half have incomes above.) Figures are commonly cited to show that family incomes have declined, but such figures do not adjust for the declining size of the average family and do not use the best available price index for calculating real incomes. Nonetheless, the increase in the past twenty years is almost certainly below our earlier experience.

Most family income is derived from the compensation of labor, and the slowdown in the growth of family incomes is a reflection of a slowdown in the rise of real compensation per hour of work. Here again some calculations would show an actual decline in earnings since 1973, but these calculations do not take account of the rise of compensation in the form of fringe benefits, which have increased substantially relative to cash wages. They also use an inferior price index. By the best available measures, average compensation has continued to rise but much less rapidly than before 1973.

The slow growth of incomes and labor compensation is a reflection of the slow growth of productivity, most simply defined as real output per hour of work. Over time, labor compensation and labor productivity have moved closely together, which is inevitable since it is the value of the worker's product that determines what an employer can and will pay. From 1948 to 1973, real output per hour rose by 3.4 percent a year; from 1973 to 1992, it rose by only 1.2 percent a year. Again, overstatement of inflation in the official price may cause understatement of the rate of productivity growth, but that there has been a significant decline in that rate seems highly likely. The causes of this decline in productivity growth, which occurred in all the advanced countries, are still a mystery. Economists can measure some of the factors that contribute to the growth of productivity. These include the increased education of the labor force, the increased stock of capital per worker, the investment in research and development, and the movement of workers from low-productivity to high-productivity industries. But with what is known about all the measurable factors accounted for, most of the decline in the rate of growth of productivity still remains unexplained.

While average incomes were rising slowly, the incomes of the lowest-income families were apparently rising even more slowly and may have been declining. One has to say "apparently" because the statistics we have relate to income in a single year; these statistics may be distorted by the inclusion in the lowest-income group of families those that have higher total incomes over a period of years but fall into the lowest-income group in a single year. In the past two decades, the incomes of less-educated workers have declined relative to those who are better educated. That trend would contribute to relatively slow growth in the incomes of low-income families. The rising gap between the incomes of less-educated and more-educated workers is probably due to technological change that reduces the demand for less-skilled workers. Change in family composition also probably contributes to the lag in the incomes of the poorest families. Whereas increasingly the average family tends to have two earners, the lowest-income families more typically have only one earner, and increasingly that one earner is a young woman.

Although the gap between the lowest-income families and the rest of the population seems to have widened, there has been a reduction of inequality in some other dimensions. Over the postwar period taken as a whole, the earnings of blacks have risen relative to the earnings of whites with the same number of years of schooling, although a gap remains. Similarly, the earnings of women have risen relative to those of men, and there the remaining gap seems small. Incomes in what were formerly the poorest regions of the country have also come much closer to the national average than they formerly were.

What Is Poverty?

The statistics on poverty shed light on what has been happening to low-income families. We have no objective way to identify the income level that draws the line between poverty and nonpoverty. By some plausible definitions, the number of people in poverty is three times as high as by other plausible definitions. No great weight should thus be placed on the "official" definition of poverty that shows about 14 percent of the American population in poverty. But the available evidence does support some conclusions:

• After a rapid decline in the proportion of the population in poverty in the decades before 1973, the proportion has been fairly stable since then, or, again recognizing uncertainty about the inflation rate, has been declining less rapidly.

• The proportion of blacks in poverty is perhaps three times as high as that of whites.

• Poverty in America has increasingly become a problem of persons in households headed by females, not because the proportion of female-headed families who are poor has increased but because their poverty rate has always been higher than that for the rest of the population and because the proportion of the population in female-headed families has increased.

• The proportion of children in poverty is much higher than for adults and has been increasing.

The meaning of *poverty* in America is unclear. The word commonly suggests living in areas in which a large fraction of the population is poor and may experience other disabilities, such as high rates of illegitimacy, school dropout, persistent unemployment, and welfare dependency. By different definitions, the proportion of the population living in such areas in 1990 was between about 1 percent and 4 percent, whereas the official estimate of the total number in poverty in that year was about 14 percent.

Conclusion

A point made at the outset needs to be repeated. America's problems are the problems of a rich country and are problems relative to the expectations of a rich country. We are getting richer more slowly than we used to, but we are getting richer at a rate that is still faster than has been experienced through much of human history. The incomes of the poorest Americans have been growing especially slowly, but they are far above the average incomes of countries where most of the world's population lives. Our problems are not cause for alarm, but they deserve attention. One advantage of being rich is that we have the capacity to deal with our problems, if we are aware of them.

13

The American Dream

"The American dream" is one of today's buzzwords that baffles me. In what sense is it a dream? It is not one of those things that floats through your unconscious while you are asleep. I am not a student of Dr. Freud, but I never heard that he had isolated a kind of dream called "American." Among the many definitions of the word *dream,* probably the one that comes closest to what people have in mind when they refer to "the American dream" is *aspiration.* What makes aspiration so dreamlike is that it suggests a reach for something lofty, worth striving for, probably not fully attainable but somewhat approachable. It is different from intention or expectation. I could say that I intend and expect to go to the grocery store. I would never say that I aspire to go to the grocery store or that I dream of going to the grocery store.

There was a time, and not so long ago, when the American dream referred to that kind of aspiration. In his invaluable *New Political Dictionary,* William Safire gives these examples of the use of the term:

> In 1893 Katherine Lee Bates wrote in "America the Beautiful" of a "patriot dream that sees beyond the years."
> In 1960 the poet Archibald MacLeish, debating national purpose, said: "There are those, I know, who will reply that the liberation of humanity, the freedom of man and mind, is nothing but a dream. They are right. It is. It is the American dream."

The Dream Degraded

But the American dream has been degraded from the status of a noble aspiration to a commonplace expectation. It used to be an aspiration for the perfection of society; it has become the expectation of individual enrichment. We measure the achievement of the dream in increasing dollars of per capita national income. We expect that increase to be substantial, and when it is not, we are disappointed, complaining that the dream has not been fulfilled.

President Clinton describes the dream as the belief that "if you work hard and play by the rules," then something good will happen to you. That good thing is measured in income. One possible implication is that if you work hard and play by the rules, you will make more money than if you don't. There is nothing here about virtue being its own reward or about the reward coming in the hereafter. The reward is to be here and now, cash on the barrel head. It is probably true in America that if you work hard and play by the rules, you will make more money than if you don't. The question is, What are the rules? Are they the rules of Moses, of William Bennett, of P. T. Barnum, or of Willie Sutton? The proposition is tautological: if you work hard by the rules for making money, you will make money.

But I don't think that when people refer to the American dream as something now in danger of evaporating after two centuries of realization, they are talking about just getting richer if you work hard and play by the rules than if you don't. I think they are saying that if you work hard and play by the rules, you will be richer than your parents were. We all take that as a rather obvious expectation, but it is not really obvious. After all, our parents worked hard—much harder than most of us—and played by the rules at least as well as we do. So why should we expect to be richer than they were?

The Efforts of Others

In fact, of course, each generation in America has been richer than the preceding one, and that is true of the present generation as well. How has that happened, for the great majority of us who are not smarter than our parents and don't work harder and play more correctly by the rules? I think of my own case. I have a higher income because someone—my parents, taxpayers, philanthropists who endowed two colleges—supported my education. In addition, various people over the past two centuries developed a body of knowledge that I was able to absorb and sell. Some people in one way or another enriched themselves enough so that they could afford to buy my product—which is, after all, a luxury. Others over the years have invented and invested in capital equipment that has enriched me as producer and consumer. And that is true of almost everyone.

Of course, some people, maybe most people, have acted in ways that enriched others. But that is not what the "dream" is about. It is not about giving; it is about getting. It is not about obligation; it is about entitlement. The American dream is the expectation of being enriched largely by the efforts of others.

That is a peculiar dream for a country that regards itself as the land of individualism and independence. We have an image of how people "get ahead." It is the image of the sturdy farmer who goes out into the prairie, clears the land, builds a cabin, and raises a crop. But he goes into land purchased by the government, explored by the government, and protected by the government. His crop is valuable because someone else has invented and invested in railroads and steamships to send the crop to Europe. And his descendants become really rich when the automobile, the paved highway, and the growth of population enable him to sell the farm as a site for a shopping mall.

Is this "just" semantics? Would it make any difference if instead of "American dream," we said "feeling of entitlement to being enriched by the efforts of others"? I don't know. It would certainly change campaign oratory. But it might have other effects as well. It might soften the notion that the world is divided between good, upstanding people who have made it on their own and others who claim entitlement to share in the incomes they have earned. More important, it might raise the question whether getting richer is a good enough dream for America.

14

The Debate over Income Inequality

Inequality in the distribution of income is one of today's hottest
topics. Almost every day a new statistic demonstrates great
and increasing inequality and a new sermon deplores it. As
one who has always regarded himself as sensitive to the problem
of inequality, I find myself only more and more confused by the
current discussion. I explain my confusion here in the hope—
admittedly not very great—of showing other people that they are
also confused or of inducing someone to come forward and clarify
the subject.

I have two problems. First, I don't know what inequality
means, and, second, I am not sure what I would think about it if I
knew what it meant.

What Is Inequality?

My first problem can be illustrated by looking at some examples.
In 1973 the median income of households headed by a person
fifteen to twenty-four years old was only a little over half that of
households headed by a person forty-five to fifty-four years old.
Surely that is inequality, in arithmetic. But in economics and in
conscience it is not inequality. It is not a fact that occasions surprise or dismay. We *expect* fifteen- to twenty-four-year-olds to earn
less than forty-five- to fifty-four-year-olds, and it doesn't bother us.
This may not be a very interesting case, but it shows that what we

are interested in is not inequality as such but inequality that violates our notions of a proper relationship among different people or different kinds of people.

But we don't have clear notions about what are proper relationships, and so attention has tended to focus not on the level of inequality but on its change. We don't know what to say about the degree of inequality among specified classes of people at a given point of time, but we feel more confident in saying something about an increase of inequality over time. Some kinds of inequality may have decreased if we look back, say, fifty years, but today's talk usually refers to the past twenty or twenty-five years.

To return to my previous example, between 1973 and 1992 the median income of households headed by fifteen- to twenty-four-year-olds fell from a little over half that of forty-five- to fifty-four-year-olds to a little over 30 percent. Is that not surely a significant increase of inequality? Well, we can't be sure. There were not the same people, or even the same kind of people, in each category in 1992 as in 1973. By 1992 the fifteen- to twenty-four-year-old category included younger household heads and more female household heads than in 1973. By 1992 the forty-five- to fifty-four-year-old category also included more households with two adult workers than in 1973. So we don't know, at least from these figures, that the gap between the same kinds of households increased between 1973 and 1992.

Let us now move to a larger screen. According to the 1996 Annual Report of the Council of Economic Advisers, the real average income of the poorest fifth of families declined by 15 percent between 1979 and 1993. The average real family income of the richest fifth of families rose by 18 percent in the same period. That does not mean that the income *of any person or of any kind of person* who was in the bottom fifth declined. (I leave aside the problems of adjusting nominal incomes for inflation, adjusting for family size, taking account of the value of transfer benefits in cash and in kind, and taking account of the difference between annual incomes and lifetime incomes.)

Suppose that in 1979 the bottom fifth consisted half of female-headed families with average incomes of $10,000 and half of male-headed families with average incomes of $20,000, so that the average for the whole group was $15,000. Then, suppose that between 1979 and 1993 the real income of each type of family rises by 10 percent but that now instead of 50 percent being headed by females, it is 84 percent. Then the average income of the group will be $12,760, a decline of, roughly, 15 percent.

I don't need to go through the same arithmetic for the top fifth of the income distribution to show, for example, that if the average incomes of male and female doctors remain constant, the average income of the top fifth of all families will rise significantly if the doctors marry each other. Thus, the "gap" between the lowest fifth and the highest could widen without the gap between any two individuals widening.

Another common observation is that the difference in earnings between people with little education and people with much is large (which is no news) and is widening (which is news). At the same time, the average educational attainment of the work force is rising. In 1973 about 30 percent of the civilian labor force aged sixteen to sixty-five had not finished high school; in 1993 that proportion was down to about 10 percent. One possible inference would be that on the average those who did not finish high school in 1993 were different in some way relevant to their incomes from those who did not finish high school in 1973. Another possible inference is that the dispersion of educational attainment in the work force has diminished, so that the dispersion of earnings among all workers could have diminished. The probability at birth that a person will have a relatively low lifetime income if he does not finish high school has increased, but the probability of his not finishing high school has diminished.

Clarifying the Changes

I am not denying that the distribution of income in the United States has become more unequal. I am saying only that I don't know what that means, without further specification. The discussion would be clarified if we distinguished among at least four kinds of changes:

• changes in the degree of inequality among persons of similar relevant characteristics, such as fifteen-year-old unmarried mothers who are high school dropouts

• changes in the degree of inequality between persons of different relevant characteristics, such as between the fifteen-year-old

dropout unmarried mothers and the forty-year-old male lawyers who were on the *Harvard Law Review*
- changes in the degree of inequality between groups containing an assortment of people that changes through time, such as the group of people in the poorest fifth of the population or in the richest fifth
- changes in the proportion of different kinds of people in the whole population

How we put the question and which classes of people we choose to compare will profoundly affect the degree of inequality we find, the direction and degree of change, and the implications for policy and for sentiment. It is worth pointing out, in some qualification of the trend of current discussion, that if we classify people in certain ways, we will find that inequality has decreased. At least by some measures, inequality of incomes between blacks and whites, between men and women, and between residents of low-income states and residents of high-income states have decreased.

Evaluating the Gap

My second problem is that even if we abstract from questions of classification and focus attention on the fact that some people are very rich and some are very poor, and even that the gap between them is increasing, I am not sure what I think. If I consult my feelings, I find that I don't care how rich the very rich are. I care if they became rich in an unethical way or if they use their riches in a particularly vulgar or revolting way. I don't attach much weight to the idea that they deserve their riches, and I wouldn't mind if they lost some or had some taxed away. But I don't mind if they keep their money either. I don't even find the lifestyle of the very rich particularly enviable. Apparently, the chief sign of being very rich these days is the corporate jet. But, as Ethel Merman said sixty years ago, "Riding too high with some guy in the sky is my idea of nothing to do!"—especially if the destination is a boring or stressful business meeting.

For years I have gone around with Henry Simons's dictum in my head that extreme inequality in the distribution of income is "unlovely." I now think that he had it backward. I would say that a distribution of income that I find unlovely is extreme. But, of course, as the word *unlovely* suggests, such judgments are highly personal. I don't find the richness of the very rich unlovely, and so I don't find it extreme.

But I do find the poverty of the very poor unlovely, and so I find it extreme. Poverty is a relative concept. The poor in America are not poor by the standards of Bangladesh. They are poor by American standards. But their poverty is not measured by the contrast between their incomes and the income of Bill Gates. That comparison is irrelevant. We do not consider a person handicapped if he cannot run as fast as Carl Lewis. We consider him handicapped if he cannot walk nearly as easily as the average person. Similarly, we consider a person poor by comparison with average Americans, not with Bill Gates.

What makes poverty in America unlovely to me is not only a low level of income but the association of that condition with a high probability of being a victim or a criminal, of attending an unsafe and disorderly school, of living in an atmosphere of drug and alcohol abuse, and, most of all, of not having a supportive spouse or two caring parents. All people with low incomes do not have these problems, and some with higher incomes do have them. But the association of these problems with lowness of income is close enough to describe the condition of poverty that I find unlovely. That condition deserves, in my opinion, our most intensive care. I believe that the present focus on inequality of income diverts national attention from it.

But I recognize that this is a personal view and that others, perhaps better informed or less sentimental, may evaluate the situation differently.

15

Am I Better Off?

R emember the 1996 presidential campaign? Remember the
question Bill Clinton asked repeatedly, Are you better off
than you were four years ago? That was, of course, the
same question Ronald Reagan asked in 1980.

Personal Experience

Note that this was not a question about what statisticians reported
on the basis of surveys as the experience of some hypothetical
average American. No, this was an appeal to the personal experience of individual Americans about their own lives, of which they
were presumed to be better witnesses than the statisticians. And
everyone seemed to know the answer—everyone but me. I not
only don't know the answer but don't even understand the question.

One thing I do know is that I am four years older than I was
four years ago. That is one of the most important things about my
life of the past four years. I don't know whether Mr. Clinton was
asking whether I was better off than four years ago *adjusted for
age*. Am I supposed to answer whether I would be better off in
1996 if I were still seventy-six years old than I was in 1992 when I
actually was seventy-six? To answer that would be a tremendous,
I would say impossible, feat of imagination. Is the question one
about the facts or about the feeling—whether I feel better than I
felt four years ago or whether I really am better off? And what
does "really being better off" mean if it is something other than

149

feeling? In any case the answer requires a great feat of reconstructing the facts and feelings of four years ago.

One might say that of course I was better off in 1992 when I was only seventy-six and had a longer life expectancy. But I'm not sure that even on that simple test I was better off if "expectancy" really means what I could have expected. Four years ago I had a number of ailments that could have made my life miserable and carried me off. Today my doctor and I are surprised that, for reasons not entirely clear, I am still here in fairly good shape. So I don't know that in terms of expected years I am worse off than I was. I don't want to pursue that lugubrious subject. A more important point is that all years are not alike. I believe that I have learned some things that enable me to appreciate my years more, and not simply because there may be fewer of them. That is a major aspect of how well off one is—how capable one is of appreciating what life has to offer.

I use the story of an old man only as an example. I could use the example of a young married couple that four years ago had no children and now has one or two. Or I could use the example of a middle-aged couple that four years ago was enjoying family life with two teenaged children who now have gone away to college and left them alone. I am trying to make three points:

• Changes in the conditions of a person's life make it difficult even for that person to be sure whether he is better or worse off than he was in a previous time.

• Certainly statisticians have no way of adding up these changes for the country as a whole and concluding whether the representative person is better or worse off.

• These important changes have almost no connection with anything President Clinton or any other president did.

Everyone's Asset

Everyone has a certain asset, which is the present value of his expected future life. The value of this expectation depends not only on the number of years expected but also on income, health, personal relations, capacity to appreciate life, and undoubtedly other factors. If a person's life follows exactly the expected path and the expectations do not change, the value of this asset will decline with the passage of time, because of declining life expectancy—although the value will remain positive. But surprises can occur. A young man may meet and marry the most wonderful girl in the world—something he never expected. Or, less romantically, he may discover Mozart. In that case the value of his asset will rise, even though he is aging. He may, however, incur an unexpected illness, which will reduce the value of his asset.

I suppose that one could adjust the value of this asset for age. Then, we could say that a change in the age-adjusted value of this asset would indicate whether a person has become better off or worse off. But, of course, no one thinks like that, and if anyone did, he would be unable to measure the value of that asset or its change between two points of time. Our knowledge of how well-off we are would be, as Lord Kelvin said of the knowledge of other unmeasured things, of a meager and unsatisfactory kind.

If President Clinton were asked what he meant by his question, Are you better off than you were four years ago? he would surely answer that he didn't mean anything so deep and complicated. He would probably say that he was referring to something simple and measurable, like a person's income. That is, he was referring to an element in a person's well-offness that is important but not the whole of it and often not the dominant part of it.

But measuring the change in one's income from four years ago turns out not to be so simple, either. It is easier, for me at least, to find out what the national gross domestic product was in 1992 than to find out my own income in that year. After some search, I retrieve my income tax return for that year. What the IRS calls "adjusted gross income" on my tax return, however, is not my income. I am mainly retired, and most of what the IRS calls my income is distributions from retirement accounts, which were not income in 1992 but returns of capital. The adjusted gross income does not include the value of unrealized capital gains that, *pace* IRS and Jack Kemp, are income. It does not include the value of living in the apartment I own or driving the car I own.

If I could, by some research, figure out my income for 1992 and 1996 to compare them, I would have to remove the inflation factor by converting both figures to the same price level. I could use the consumer price index for that purpose. We already know, however, that the CPI is not an accurate measure of inflation, although we don't know by how much it is in error. Anyway, the

CPI is not my price index. I don't buy things in the proportion in which they are represented in the CPI. I surely do not spend as much on movie admissions, gasoline, or foreign travel as is included in the marketbasket the Bureau of Labor Statistics prices to calculate the CPI. I surely spend more on pills and restaurant meals, and probably more on computer hardware and software. But I cannot compute my own price index. I have not saved all those little pieces of paper showing how much I paid for everything. And even if I had that information, I would still have the problems the BLS has in taking account of quality changes, introduction of new products, and changes in the composition of the marketbasket.

So I can't figure out whether my real income was higher in 1992 than in 1996. I don't want to exaggerate the problem. If I won a $1,000,000 lottery in either of these years, I would know in which year my income was higher. But in the ordinary course of events, the calculation would take a lot of work. And what would be the point of doing it? Suppose I discovered that my income had been higher in 1992. I couldn't go back there.

One thing we can be sure of. When President Clinton asks the audience if they are better off than they were four years ago, no one is making the calculation I have just described. What are people in the audience thinking about when they answer, clapping their hands, stamping their feet, and shouting hooray? In my opinion they are not thinking about anything. They are just giving the expected response.

At the student pep rally at Siwash U., the night before the big game, the cheerleader shouts, "Are we going to beat Woonsocki?" And the students all yell, "Yea!" No one is thinking about whether they really will beat Woonsocki. Across the state, at Woonsocki, the cheerleader is shouting, "Are we going to beat Siwash?" And the Woonsocki students yell, "Yea!"

Not much evidentiary value there.

16

A Primer on Pay and Productivity

There has been a lot of talk about wages and productivity lately. Of course, when I say a lot, I mean a lot for that kind of thing. It's not a lot compared with the talk about Whitewater or Gingrich's escapades or O. J. Simpson, for example. But for the kind of stuff I work with, the talk about wages and productivity has been exceptionally abundant.

Stagnant Wages, Rising Productivity?

The usual burden of this talk is that real wages have been stagnant or actually declining in recent years, whereas the productivity of labor has been rising sharply.

Looking into the available information on the subject, however, leads to the usual conclusion, to wit: first, the "truth" of the matter is not easy to come by and, second, the "truth" is probably not what it seems.

To get a picture of what is going on, one must answer a number of questions:

- Are we talking about cash wages only or about total compensation, including fringe benefits?
- Are we talking about production and nonsupervisory workers only or about all employees?
- Are we talking about employees only or about self-employed persons also?

• Are we talking about the average compensation of a labor force of fixed distribution among occupations and industries, or are we talking about the average compensation of the actual labor force whose distribution among occupations and industries is changing as it actually does?

• Are we talking about how much the compensation for an hour's work will buy of the product the worker produces or of the product the worker buys for his consumption?

• If we are talking about the real value of the worker's compensation in terms of what he buys for his consumption, shall we calculate that by reference to the official index of consumers' prices (CPI), or shall we make an adjustment for the overstatement of that index that is now commonly believed to exist?

• For what period is the observation to be made?

By giving different answers to these questions, people can get different answers about what has been happening to workers' pay absolutely and in relation to productivity. I hope I am not being too cynical to suggest that they not only can but also do get the answer they prefer.

Broad Measures

I suggest that primary or initial attention should be paid to the broadest available measures of both compensation and the work force. There are reasons for some purposes to look at more limited definitions, but for the kind of generalization now being commonly made, we should start with the most inclusive measures. Even more important, if there is to be a comparison of compensation with productivity, it is essential that the definitions of labor input be the same. We are comparing compensation per worker hour with output per worker hour, and the comparison is meaningless if the worker hours are not the same in the two cases.

The most comprehensive and internally consistent set of statistics we have is the series produced by the Bureau of Labor Statistics and published with the title "Productivity and Related Data, Business Sector." These statistics cover the hours of work of all persons engaged in the business sector, including the hours of proprietors and unpaid family workers. Compensation in the BLS report includes fringe benefits and an estimate of wages, salaries, and supplemental payments for the self-employed.

Deflating the hourly compensation reported in this series by the official CPI, we find that "real" hourly compensation rose by 5.9 percent from 1982 to 1996. (I use 1996 as "the present" throughout this chapter.) That is a measure of how much more of the kinds of things the worker buys for his own consumption he can get for his pay for an hour's work, according to the official estimate of consumers' prices. If, as some suggest, the official CPI has overstated the annual rate of increase of consumers' prices by 0.5 percent, the rise of "real" hourly compensation has been more than twice as much—13.9 percent. Little differences do add up.

The uncertainty of the CPI measurement is not, however, the most interesting point. We have a different way of looking at the whole thing. We can ask how much of his own product the worker can buy with the compensation for an hour's work. To answer that, we must adjust the compensation not for the price of consumers' goods but for the price of the totality of things the business sector produces.

Workers' compensation can come only out of the value of their product. If the value of their product rises little, because the price of their product rises little the workers' compensation cannot rise rapidly, however much the prices of the things they buy may go up. Since 1982, the prices of what business produces have risen by about 50 percent, while the CPI has risen by about 63 percent. While the real value of hourly compensation in terms of what workers consume has risen by 5.9 percent since 1982, it has risen by 14.7 percent in terms of what workers produce (see figure 16–1).

How can this be—how can the price of what workers consume (presumably, according to the official CPI) rise so much more than the price of what workers produce? The answer, of course, is that workers produce much more than the things they consume. Most important, they produce things that go into investment. Between 1982 and today when the prices of consumer goods and services rose by 63 percent (CPI), the prices of output going into nonresidential investment rose by only about 7 percent. In part, this is a reflection of the radical decline in the prices of computers.

All this is relevant, of course, to the question why "real" wages have risen less since 1982 than productivity—5.9 percent as conventionally computed against 19.6 percent for productivity.

FIGURE 16-1
Two Measures of Real Hourly Compensation, 1950–1995

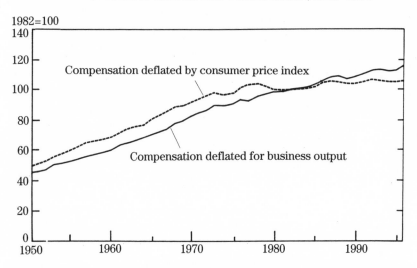

SOURCE: Bureau of Labor Statistics, "Productivity and Related Data, Business Sector."

One part of the answer is that the productivity of workers in producing the things they consume has increased much less rapidly than their productivity in producing the things they don't buy.

Congruence of Pay and Productivity?

Even when we measure real wages in terms of the prices of the things workers produce, we find that since 1982 they have risen less than productivity. Much of the recent discussion has run in terms of the change since 1982, perhaps because that was the year the Bureau of Labor Statistics used as the base for its index number. But 1982 was a highly unrepresentative year for the purpose of these calculations. The ratio of wages to productivity in 1982 was higher than in any other postwar year, except for 1980 when it was slightly higher. Between 1982 and 1996, the ratio of wages to productivity was declining from a quite unusual peak to about the relationship that has been common throughout the postwar period. In fact, if we take 1950 as a base, rather than 1982, we see that real compensation—in terms of the workers' product—has risen by 167 percent and that productivity has risen by 161 percent, which is surely an insignificant difference. The congruence of the index of compensation and the index of productivity is nearly perfect, except in the few years around 1982 that are now used as a standard of comparison for much current discussion (see figure 16–2).

As far as we can measure such things, the rate of growth of productivity has slowed down. The rate of growth of real wages has slowed down with it. Beyond that, there is not much to say about the relation of wages to productivity.

FIGURE 16–2

COMPENSATION AND PRODUCTIVITY, 1950–1995

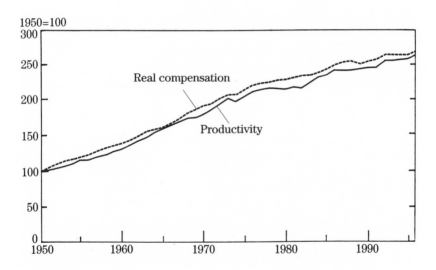

NOTE: Real compensation adjusted by the deflator for business output.
SOURCE: Bureau of Labor Statistics, "Productivity and Related Data, Business Sector."

17

The CPI: Servant or Master?

C hiseled in stone over the entrance to the Social Science Building at the University of Chicago, breeding place of so many winners of the Nobel Prize in economics, is an abbreviated version of a quotation from Lord Kelvin, who said: "When you cannot measure it, when you cannot express it in numbers, your knowledge is of a meager and unsatisfactory kind."

My great professor, Jacob Viner, commented: "Even when you can measure a thing, our knowledge will be meager and unsatisfactory." And my other great professor, Frank H. Knight, said that what Kelvin's dictum came down to, at least in the social sciences, was "If you cannot measure, measure anyhow."

I am reminded of these sages by the current search for a perfect, or at least much improved, measure of the consumer price index and the attendant implications for the indexing of social security benefits, other federal retirement benefits, and brackets in the individual income tax. The idea that revising the CPI would enable politicians to cut benefits and raise taxes without seeming to do so explains their sudden interest in the theory and practice of index numbers.

Three Propositions

I would like to stipulate three propositions without argument:

1. The CPI, calculated by the Bureau of Labor Statistics, provides valuable information. Its value is attested by its use in many

private agreements, such as labor contracts and long-term lease arrangements, as well as by its use in economic analysis. The process of calculating the index should continue to be as scientific and nonpolitical as possible.

2. There is good reason to believe that the present methods of calculation overstate the rate at which the costs of things we now buy have been rising and are continuing to rise. The amount of this overstatement is not known and should be carefully studied.

3. However improved, the CPI will not be an adequate measure of the cost of living or of the cost of maintaining a constant degree of "well-offness." That is simply because "living" is not a measurable quantity, except in coffee spoons, and therefore its cost cannot be measured. The same is true of well-offness.

I do not regard these propositions as debatable; this is not to deny that some people will come forth to debate them. I want to call attention to a more difficult question.

What to Do about Indexing?

What should we do about indexing retirement benefits and tax brackets? Let us leave all questions of measurement aside and assume that the change in the CPI accurately or adequately measures the change in a person's income from one year to the next that will hold him harmless, leaving him just as well off in the second year as in the first. Should we therefore increase social security benefits each year by the percentage increase in the CPI? Of course, it would be "nice" to do that. But it would be even nicer to increase benefits by the CPI plus 1 percent and nicer still to increase them by the CPI plus 2 percent. So niceness is not a sufficient reason.

Increasing benefits by the CPI seems, intuitively, to be fair. But there are other methods of indexing that also seem, intuitively, to be fair. Why not index social security benefits by worker compensation per hour, so that retired people could keep up with working people? Why not index benefits by personal disposable income per capita, so that retired people could keep up with the population at large? These measures would give more rapid increase in benefits than the CPI. But an argument could be made that benefits should be indexed by average prices of business product, which is the source from which benefits can be paid. That would, at least in recent years, have given slower increases in benefits than the CPI. Perhaps the benefits should be indexed to the Dow-Jones average. Wouldn't it be fair for the social security beneficiary to earn as good a return on his accumulated retirement fund as a private investor can get?

The first-blush intuitive response is not a good guide to fairness. The problem is that fairness is a two-sided thing. It is a relation between people who get and people who give, and looking only at what it is fair to give social security beneficiaries leaves out the other half of the equation, which is what it is fair to ask other people to pay. The more we index social security benefits the more someone—current workers, other taxpayers, or beneficiaries of other programs—has to pay. The more we index income tax brackets, the higher the rates of tax have to be, or more has to be collected in other ways or less spent. (In the following discussion, I concentrate on social security benefits, but much of the argument applies to tax brackets also.)

Limiting Escalation of Benefits

The crux of the present situation is not the possible errors in the CPI. It is that as we look out into the future, we do not see the people who are willing to pay the costs of benefits indexed on the present scale, and we do not know whether they can be fairly asked to do so. Proposals to limit the escalation were common ten or fifteen years ago, before the possible overstatement of the CPI received much attention. These proposals were made because it had become clear that unless something changed, the Social Security Trust Fund, or the budget as a whole, was going to run out of money. Some restraint on social security benefits seemed necessary, if additional sources of revenue were not to be found. Limiting the escalation was not the only possible way to restrain the growth of benefits—the retirement age could be postponed or the initial payment to be made upon retirement could be reduced—but limiting escalation was one way.

A graduated benefit not only has a different shape through time than a flat benefit but also is a bigger benefit if the initial payments are the same. For example, an annuity of $10,000 a year for twenty years has a present value of $114,699 if the interest rate is 6 percent. The present value of an annuity that starts at $10,000 and rises by 3 percent a year is $145,615, which is 27 percent more. Reducing or eliminating the graduation is a way to reduce the benefit. This suggests that the beneficiary could be given a choice of the time path on which he wants to receive his benefit and could have escalation if he were willing to pay for it. In the example I have just given, the beneficiary could receive $10,000 a year or $7,877 in the first year increasing by 3 percent a year. Some private annuities, such as Teachers Insurance and Annuity plans, offer that option.

Social security beneficiaries could also be given the option of having their benefits increased along with the change of some specified index—which might be the CPI—if they were willing to pay the cost of that escalation. The cost would come in the form of a reduction of the initial benefit as compared with what would be paid if the benefit were not indexed. The government would have to specify that cost on the basis of an estimate of the future behavior of the index. (If the government sold an indexed bond in the market, as has often been suggested, it would have a market determination of the value of indexing.) The beneficiary could take that option or not, depending on how his estimate of the future of the index compared with the estimate implicit in the cost. There would be no implication that the index was a true measure of anything. The beneficiary would simply be making a bet on the future behavior of the specified index. The benefit would be a kind of "derivative."

The basic point is that the government, as representative of both those who pay and those who receive the benefits, and as arbitrator between them, has to decide how much benefit is to be paid. Once that is decided, whether the benefits should be paid at a flat rate, or on a graduated scale, or indexed to something, and, if so, what, are questions of convenience. These questions will not be answered by revisions of the CPI and should be kept separate from the process of scientific, objective revision of the index. We should, in my opinion, face openly the fact that sometime in the next couple of decades we will have to reduce the benefits and should take the responsibility now for deciding how to do that.

18

Beware of Corporate Responsibility

C orporate responsibility is in fashion again. That happens every once in a while. People become aware of some social problem that they do not want the government to deal with, or think the government can't deal with, and they turn to that rich, powerful institution, the corporation, and call upon it to do something. We are surely in such a situation today. We think of job insecurity, pornography, deficient education, and environmental degradation, among other ills, and at the same time we have a strong aversion to more government. What is more natural than to declare that corporations have a responsibility to come to the rescue?

"Corporate Citizenship"

President Clinton recently blessed this idea by calling a meeting in Washington with about one hundred business executives to discuss their responsibility to help solve the nation's problems. He praised them for what they had done and urged them to do more. He announced the establishment of an award, named for the late Ronald Brown, to honor "corporate citizenship."

I have no desire to rain on this parade, but I have been around that track more than once and would like to offer some advice. For twenty-two years, from 1945 to 1967, I worked for the Committee for Economic Development, an organization mainly of executives of large corporations. They were wonderful people—at least, most of them were—and they had a strong hankering to be socially responsible. It was my lot, as a pious product of the University of Chicago Department of Economics, to tell them that social responsibility was not their business. I tried to tell them that they discharged their social responsibility if they maximized profits. But I could not dissuade them.

The case that sticks most in my mind occurred in 1958. The annual rate of price increase had risen from $1\frac{1}{2}$ percent in 1956 to $3\frac{1}{2}$ percent in 1957, and the committee decided to publish a statement about how to check inflation. (As it turned out, the inflation rate receded and didn't get up to $3\frac{1}{2}$ percent again for almost ten years, during the Vietnam War.) I wrote a draft policy statement containing the usual boilerplate about fiscal and monetary policy—which was not less valid because it was boilerplate. But while this was going on, some of our trustees, CEOs of large corporations, went to a meeting of the Business Council in Hot Springs, Virginia. There they hobnobbed with cabinet secretaries who, this being the Eisenhower administration, were also former executives of large corporations. They came back from the meeting with the idea that the statement should call upon the private sector to meet its social responsibility by not behaving in an inflationary way. What they mainly had in mind, of course, was a lecture to the unions not to demand large wage increases. But they were realistic enough to know that they could not credibly give such a lecture without also saying something about the responsibility of businesses in setting prices. The proposal was to include in the policy statement some guideposts for responsible union and business behavior.

I resisted this idea. For the only time in my twenty-two years at the CED, the chairman of the Board of Trustees and the chairman of the Research and Policy Committee, both eminences in the business world, came to my office in Washington to talk to me. I told them that if they said that they knew standards of proper wage and price behavior other than what emerged in the market, it would not be long before the government would say that it also knew such standards. Then some union or business would be found to violate those standards conspicuously. The government would not be able to stand by and watch its standards violated, so it would have to try to obtain conformity, by moral suasion if possible and by threats and sanctions if necessary. So the government would be accustoming the public to the idea that there were standards of wage and price behavior that the government had a responsibility to enforce. And since ad hoc, piecemeal enforcement was unlikely to work, the ground would be laid for comprehensive price and wage controls. The officers of the CED were not frightened by my ghost story, however. They were going to sign the statement, I was only the draftsman, and they had their way.

I don't have to say what happened. Ironically, I was at the bottom of the hill waiting to greet the sled when it came to the bottom of the slippery slope and we got the price and wage controls. Of course, I do not think that the conversation in my office in 1958 determined that we would have price controls in 1971. But it was part, surely a small part, of a way of thinking that led to that end.

I deduce from this one law about the social responsibility of corporations. Corporations should not accept responsibility for doing anything the government asks them to do. More specifically, they should not accept responsibility for doing something they would not want the government to do in the hope of thereby preventing the government from doing it.

Maximizing Profits

The talk about social responsibility tends to be slippery. Some well-meaning person says it is the social responsibility of corporations to do something—say, keep on the payroll old employees whose wage exceeds the value of their product. Then the CEO or, more likely, a dismal economist says that the corporation cannot afford to do that. And the well-meaning person says, "Well, if the corporation will only do that, the morale of all the workers will be so stimulated that their productivity will rise and profits will increase." Then we are no longer talking about social responsibility. We are talking about how to run a corporation efficiently to maximize profits. Surely business executives can learn more about that. But they are unlikely to learn anything about that from the president of the United States, any president of the United States.

Another source of confusion is connected with the fashionable word *stakeholders*. We are reminded that the stakeholders of a corporation—those with an interest in its performance—include not only the shareholders but also the workers, the customers, the community, and others. Corporation executives are held to be narrow-minded if they pay attention only to maximizing profits for the benefit of the shareholders and ignore the other stakeholders. Of course, the behavior of the executives is understandable, since it is the shareholders who, through the directors representing them, hire the executives and pay their salaries. But it is not out of any special love for shareholders that economists say that it is the business of business to try to maximize profits. Maximizing profits is the guide for attaining a certain kind of efficiency in the use of the nation's resources. It means that a corporation tries to use the labor and capital available to it to maximize the excess of the value of their product over the value the same resources would produce if used elsewhere—the value in each case being measured by markets. We don't know any other way of getting the nation's resources used efficiently.

Efficiency in maximizing the nation's product, as that product is valued in markets, is not the only objective of life. But it is the one that private corporations are best qualified to serve. I don't want to be a purist about this. I don't object to corporations' contributing to the United Givers Fund or to the American Enterprise Institute. But to rely on corporate responsibility to solve major social problems other than the efficiency problem would be a wasteful diversion from their most important function. Our other objectives can be better served in other ways, by individuals and other institutions.

PART FOUR
Budget and Taxes

19

Wanted: A Fiscal Policy

F or at least thirty years, the United States has had, or at least professed, one fiscal policy: reduce the deficit, ideally to zero, preferably within five years, and, recently and most preferably, by the year 2002.

I was never crazy about this policy. I never attached significance to the number zero. As far as I could see, the only thing one could say about zero was that it was $100 billion less than $100 billion and $100 billion more than minus $100 billion. This becomes obvious if you think of all the different plausible ways there are to define and measure the budget surplus or deficit.

In the early Reagan years, when the deficit was large, I was not among those most eager to reduce it. Although I believed that the deficit was retarding growth by absorbing private saving that would have been productively invested, I thought that we were a very rich country and had more important things to do than speed up growth. I was a strong supporter of the defense buildup and feared that the deficit argument would be used to restrain that.

Wisdom about Surpluses

More recently, as the deficit declined and the grand goal of zero was at hand, I changed my mind. I came to believe that just balancing the budget was not enough and that we needed to get to a surplus. What changed my mind was the prospect, which was becoming clearer and clearer, that we would run into huge deficits in the twenty-first century, as the baby boomers claimed their retirement and Medicare benefits. Although I was not one who wanted to maximize future growth, I would not like to see the growth of per capita income turn negative, and I was afraid that would happen if the federal deficit was large enough to absorb all private saving. So I thought we ought to be running a surplus in the years before the impact of the baby boomers on the budget, to reduce the debt and future interest charges, and that we ought to avoid making commitments now that would reduce future taxes and increase future expenditures. Although I did not myself think in those terms, one could say to the budget balancers that we still had very large deficits for the next fifty years taken as a whole, despite being in balance in 1998 or even in the next decade. One could still invoke antipathy to deficits as a guide to fiscal policy.

During the first half of 1998, the picture *seems* to have changed radically. Whereas previous estimates, from the Office of Management and Budget, the Congressional Budget Office, and the General Accounting Office, all showed large deficits running through the first half of the twenty-first century, we now have estimates from the OMB (February 1998) showing large surpluses for that period, if present tax and spending policies continue. Estimates from the CBO (May 1998) still show deficits for the first half of the twenty-first century, although they are much smaller than those estimated a year earlier, and the CBO shows surpluses continuing until about 2015.

If these estimates are correct, we have to face the problem of what to do about surpluses. We had an agreed-upon answer for what to do about deficits: reduce them! If that did not always appeal to economists, it was homely wisdom or, as Walter Heller once incautiously said, "the Puritan ethic." Even if it was homely, it was wisdom; and even if it was Puritan, it was an ethic. But we have no wisdom or ethic about surpluses.

Some people want to reduce taxes, and some people want to raise expenditures. There have always been such people. But in recent years, they have been constrained by the consensus on reducing the deficit and reaching a surplus. Now no one knows what the constraint is. We are at sea.

We have not had a policy about surpluses for almost seventy years. After World War I, we followed a policy of using surpluses to retire the war debt, and regular payments on the debt were included in the budget. But policy on surpluses was swept away by the depression, by World War II, and by Keynesian economics. At the end of World War II, the federal debt was a little over 100 percent of the gross domestic product. That was too big for anyone to think of paying it off. The accepted policy was to grow up to it, by avoiding deficits that would add to the debt while the economy expanded. We did not avoid the deficits, but we did grow up to the debt, by inflation as well as real economic growth, so that the debt is now less than 50 percent of GDP.

In principle, Keynesian economics provided some guidance on the proper timing and size of surpluses. Deficits should be large enough to yield high employment, and surpluses should be big enough to avoid overheating of the economy. But while much was heard from Keynesians about the need for deficits I can't remember any argument for a surplus on Keynesian grounds.

Consensus on Surpluses

The current arguments about cutting taxes or raising expenditures proceed without reference to any principle guiding how big a surplus ought to be. We need to discuss that question and try to reach some consensus on it.

President Clinton has said that we should not do anything with the surplus until we have dealt with the social security "problem," whatever that is. Saying that is only an excuse to defer thinking seriously about what our long-run surplus policy ought to be. And I don't believe we can come to any sensible decision about the expected cash deficit in the social security funds without at the same time, not later, coming to a decision about the long-run policy for the surplus. We can bring the social security funds into balance by measures internal to the system, such as cutting the promised benefits, or by a contribution from the general funds of the federal government. Which we do will affect the size of the unified budget surplus, and we should decide our policy about that surplus before, or at the same time as, the decision about social security.

I don't know what our long-range surplus policy should be, but I think I know how I would start thinking about it. I would think about it as a problem of choice between the present generation and the future generations. The more surplus we retain and use to retire debt, the larger the supply of private saving available for private investment will be, the larger the stock of productive capital will be, and the higher future incomes will be. In contrast, we can provide benefits for the present generation by cutting taxes or increasing expenditures.

When we seemed to be facing the large deficits in the next century that would seriously slow down the growth of the capital stock and injure the next generation, I leaned heavily in the direction of retaining the surplus while we had it and retiring debt. But if the estimates of the OMB that we may have surpluses running into the middle of the next century are correct, I am not so sure. Even if we rely on the CBO estimates, with surpluses running "only" until 2015, the answer is less obvious than it was.

The Need to Recognize Uncertainty

We have learned one thing about budgets in the past year. We have learned how unreliable forecasts of the budget deficit or surplus can be. In February 1997, the president submitted a budget with a deficit of $121 billion for fiscal 1998. In March 1997, the Congressional Budget Office reestimated the effects of the president's policies and concluded that they would yield a deficit of $145 billion. As I am writing this, in June 1998, it looks as if there may be a *surplus* of about $40 billion. If there can be so much error about a year we are going through, we have to be very cautious about attaching weight to a forecast of how big the surplus will be twenty or thirty years from now. That is, in my opinion, a reason for not committing ourselves to tax cuts or expenditure increases that will be hard to undo later. One thing we should certainly do for our children and grandchildren is to leave them room for decisions when the facts become clearer.

I don't know any substitute for the good judgment and responsibility of our elected representatives in deciding on a long-run policy about surpluses. They are the ones who have to make the choice between the present and the future, since the future is not here to participate in making the choice. I am only trying to call attention to the need for considering the problem as explicitly as possible, rather than leaving the outcome to bubble up from fragmented and shortsighted decisions about taxing and spending.

20

Chairman Bill's Big Blue Book

When President Clinton's budget came out, on February 2, 1998, we were all engrossed in the *affaire* Lewinsky and the spin the White House was putting on it—right-wing conspiracy, executive privilege, Talmudic definitions of adultery, and so on. Perhaps interest in that subject has now abated sufficiently to allow us to turn our attention to the budget. I propose here to comment not on the policy in the budget but on the rhetoric of the budget—on the spin the administration puts on its policy. I shall concentrate on the book called *Budget* and not on the other five volumes that come with it.

The Cult of Presidential Personality

What is most striking to a person who has been reading budgets for a long time is how far the cult of presidential personality has gone. In the past, the budget typically had two parts. One was the budget message of the president. This was written in the first person and signed by the president. Readers knew that that section would contain a fair measure of boasting and self-serving. But then most of the book consisted of chapters about the functions of government with prosaic titles like "National Defense" or "Agriculture." These chapters were written in the third person, they were probably boring, they had lots of facts, and one could learn a lot from them. Of course, they reflected the point of view of the administration, but the reader didn't have the feeling that he was constantly being urged to buy the Brooklyn Bridge. The word *president* hardly ever appeared. These chapters were about the government, not about the president.

The budget still has the president's message and a section organized according to the functions of government. But now inserted between these two parts is a long section—132 pages in the new budget—also pretending to explain the whole thing but now explaining it as having sprung full-blown from the brow of the president. This section has inspirational chapter heads like "Preparing the Nation for a New American Century" and "Creating a Bright American Future."

Each chapter and subchapter in this section starts with a quotation from previous utterances of President Clinton, in italics enclosed in a box. These quotations are of a banality that is hard to believe. For example, we have this:

> Americans want the best for our children. We want them to live out their dreams, empowered with the tools they need to make the most of their lives and to build a future where America remains the world's beacon of hope and freedom and opportunity. To do this, we must all make improving the quality of education in America one of our highest priorities.

There is an irresistible reminder here of Chairman Mao's little red book, except that Mao's dicta were more pointed.

In these 132 pages there are, by my count, 113 uses of the word *President.* (I include nine cases of the word *his* used in close proximity to and referring to the president.) And what is the president doing on these occasions? Of course, he is working and proposing and having visions and making commitments. But not only is he working: he is, in some instances, working "hard"—to expand health care coverage and improve the nation's health, to help families improve education, to improve the lives of working families, to eliminate fraud in Medicare and Medicaid, and to crack down on violent youth gangs. He also has initiatives:

- the brownfields initiative
- the water quality initiative
- the presidential initiative to increase seat belt use nationwide
- the president's initiative on drugs, driving, and youth
- the president's education technology initiative

- the president's 1997 antiterrorism/counterterrorism/security initiative
- the president's America reads initiative
- the president's initiative on landmines

This is truly a president whose eye is on the sparrow and who will look after us. This is all irritating or laughable, depending on your mood. But I cannot believe that it is helpful to the president. Its incredibility infects and pollutes everything else in the budget.

These pages are filled to overflowing with the names of programs that are to be increased or introduced for the first time. Of course, the federal government is an enormous enterprise; it has many, many programs; each of these programs has to have a name with capital letters; and every capital letter has to be part of an acronym. (My favorite is NEXTEA. Anyone who knows what that is should win money on Ben Stein's quiz show. Actually, it stands for National Economic Crossroads Transportation Efficiency Act.) Still, the budget could have spared us some of these programs. Reels the mind, reading all these programs. There seems to be little capacity for summarizing when describing the good things being done for us.

What Is Missing

What one would like to see is some listing of programs that are being reduced, or not being introduced. After all, to govern is to choose, and to budget especially is to choose. That means to choose to do some things and not to do some other things. We cannot appreciate the reason for the things that are to be done unless we can compare them with things that are not to be done. Why do we have a seat belt initiative and not a smoke detector initiative? (Maybe there is a smoke detector initiative and I missed it.) True, there are some cuts in expenditures and personnel. They are all the result of what we used to call minimizing waste, fraud, and abuse and what is now called the Vice President's Reinventing Government Program. There are no identifiable places where anyone is asked to give up anything or forgo getting anything.

Well, there are two exceptions to that. The American people, especially young people, are asked to give up smoking. By accounting maneuvers not worth describing here, this abstinence will enable the federal government to increase spending on a variety of programs, through an instrument modestly called the "Fund for America."

The second exception is that we are to forgo using the prospective budget surplus for tax cuts or expenditure increases "until we have a solution to the long-term financing challenge facing Social Security." It is at this point that we have the greatest mystery, the greatest need for more explanation, in the budget.

This formulation gives rise to the ridiculous table showing, for years beginning in 1999, an excess of receipts over outlays, exactly balanced by an item called "reserve pending social security reform," and a resulting surplus/deficit that is exactly zero. By that logic, we had a zero deficit every year for the past thirty years, except that the "reserve pending social security reform" was negative.

Although the proposal to reserve the surplus until we have a solution for the long-term financing challenge facing social security appears on page 3 of the budget, as far as I can see there is no clue to the nature of this challenge until we get to page 231. And an essential part of the story appears only in a chapter "Stewardship: Toward a Federal Balance Sheet" that is in the separate volume called *Analytical Perspectives*.

Moreover, the little word *until* contains a number of ambiguities. According to one interpretation, the surplus would be used to solve the financial problems of social security. That has now been denied by the Office of Management and Budget. That leaves open the question of the president's intention for the use of the surplus after some other solution has been found, such as cutting social security benefits or raising social security taxes. Would we then be free to spend whatever surplus there is in the unified budget, including the surplus that had been reserved until the solution had been found? Or would we still want to apply some of that surplus to reducing the federal debt that had been accumulated during the thirty years of deficits? Suppose that we "have" a solution for the long-run social security problem by December 1999 but that its financial impact does not begin to be felt for another twenty years. Will we then be immediately free to spend the surplus? In other words, is the surplus "reserved" to be part of any long-run fiscal program or only a carrot to be used to induce a solution to social security, after which the carrot can be eaten? I raise these questions not to disagree with what may be the president's program but to illustrate the inadequacy of the budget as an explanation of the program.

When I told a friend of my problems with the budget as an explanatory document, he replied, "But you're the only person who reads it." That may be true. But 15,000 copies were printed.

21

The Uneasy Case for the Flat Tax

About forty years ago, when all right-thinking people believed that the progressive income tax was the ideal form of taxation, two University of Chicago professors, Harry Kalven and Walter Blum, wrote an incisive article called "The Uneasy Case for Progressive Taxation." The article did not show that the progressive income tax was a bad tax. It showed only that many of the things said for it were unproved and probably unprovable.

What Kalven and Blum said about the progressive income tax could probably be said about any specific tax. In the rush to embrace the flat tax, it is time to remind ourselves that the case for it too is uneasy.

Introduction of the flat tax would change the present system of income taxation in two ways. First, it would change the base of the tax. Second, it would flatten the rate. These are two quite different things.

Changing the Tax Base

Presumably, changing the base will increase its size. That is what permits a "reduction" of the rate within a revenue-neutral policy. Actually, what happens is a reduction of the rate on what was previously included in the base and an increase in the rate on what was not previously included. Thus, the inclusion of employer-

provided health benefits in taxable income would permit a reduction of the rate on wage income that is paid in cash but entails an
increase of the rate on wage income that is paid in health benefits.
Not all of the base changes involved in moving to the flat tax would
be base broadening. At least one would reduce the base: the deduction of gross investment rather than depreciation from taxable
income. I will return to the question of the base later.

But even if the expansion of the base permits a reduction of
the effective rate on the base, and if that is considered a gain, that
is not an argument for a flat rate. While a rate schedule running
from 10 to 30 percent might clearly be better than one running
from 15 to 35 percent, it does not follow that a flat rate of 20 percent is better than one running from 10 to 30. The fairness question does not permit of an objective answer, and the economic
consequences are ambiguous.

Much of the argument for the flat tax is that it will greatly
simplify the preparation of tax returns. But that simplification results almost entirely from the redefinition of the base and hardly
at all from the flatness of the tax. If taxable income is calculated in
the manner that permits it to be reported entirely on a postcard,
applying a graduated tax rate to that income will not be a complicated matter. Anyone could read his or her tax liability then from
a tax schedule.

What seems to be the main practical reason for the proposed
flatness of the tax is that it simplifies the integration of the corporate tax and the individual tax. In the flat tax, all capital income
earned in corporations is taxed at the corporate level only and at
the same rate as all labor income is taxed at the individual level.
Then all income is presumably taxed at the same rate. If different
individuals paid different rates on their wage income, there would
be no way to apply the same rate to their corporate capital income
without allocating all the capital income to its individual beneficiaries, which is difficult in the case of undistributed corporate
profits.

But the flat tax does not really solve this problem. The flat tax
proposal involves a personal exemption from income tax for labor
income up to a specified level. Suppose, for ease of calculation,
that the exemption level for a family of four is $30,000 and the flat
tax rate is 20 percent. Then a family with $60,000 of labor income
would pay a tax of $6,000, and a family with $60,000 of capital

income would pay a tax of $12,000. That does not seem very "flat," and its fairness may not appeal to everyone. One may say that the marginal tax rate is the same for both, but we usually do not think of fairness in terms of marginal rates.

In fact, the marginal rates are not flat either. In the example given, a flat marginal rate of 20 percent of the excess of labor income over $30,000 applies *if the excess is positive.* But if the excess is negative, the marginal rate is zero. Thus, a family with a labor income of $25,000 pays no more tax than a family with a labor income of $15,000. The family with a capital income of $25,000 pays $2,000 more tax than one with a capital income of $15,000.

Within the logic of the flat tax, the reason for the two-rate system—a positive rate on the excess of wage income over the exemption if the excess is positive and a zero rate if the excess is negative—is hard to understand. Presumably, the reason for levying no tax on a family with labor income of $30,000 (in my example) is that a tax more than zero would be unfair—too much of a burden. If that is the case, a tax of zero on a family with labor income of $15,000 would be an even more excessive burden. Fairness would seem to require that the 20 percent rate be applied to the excess of the income over the exemption whether the excess was positive or negative. If the family had labor income of $15,000, their negative excess would be $15,000, and they would get a refund of $3,000. This system would also keep the marginal tax on labor income and on capital income equal at all income levels.

The Tax Base

Now I would like to turn to the question of the tax base. Proponents of the flat tax sometimes say (and sometimes admit) that it is really a tax on consumption. This is demonstrated in the following way. Suppose that all income is earned in the production of consumer goods and the production of investment goods. If we allow the deduction from income of all expenditures for the purchase of investment goods, what is left in the tax base is expenditure for the purchase of consumption goods. Net saving takes the form of the excess of gross capital investment over depreciation. That is now included in taxable income and would be excluded under the flat tax.

Whether consumption is a fairer tax base than income is another question to which there is no possible objective answer. Suppose there are two people who each spend $80,000 on consumption in a year, one of whom has a wage income of $100,000 and the other has a wage income of $1 million. Is it fair, or "equal treatment" as proponents of the flat tax like to say, that they each should pay $20,000 of tax? Would anyone but an economist, or the person with the $1 million income, say so? One might say that the person with the $1 million income is only deferring the payment of tax and that at infinity, when everyone has cashed in his chips, the amount of tax paid by each will be equal. But that seems a long time to wait.

Taxing income rather than consumption probably discourages the postponement of consumption—which is to say that it discourages saving. But not taxing saved income requires taxing something else more, and that also discourages some kind of economic behavior. It can discourage work in favor of leisure. It can encourage consumption in less-taxed forms, like the use of an owner-occupied home. Excluding the excess of gross investment over depreciation from the tax base distorts decisions in favor of long-lived assets. Excluding from the tax base investment in physical capital but not in human capital, as in education, also distorts economic decisions. We know very little about the magnitude of any of these effects, and so we know very little about the contribution that would be made to economic efficiency or growth by the shift to a flat tax of the kind now being proposed. That is to say, if the shift from an income tax to a consumption tax is not considered fair, one cannot be sure that the increase in efficiency and the growth in gains outweigh that objection.

But even if one wants a consumption tax, the flat tax route is a peculiar way to get there. It is not true that consumption is equal to income earned in domestic production minus gross private investment. Consumption equals income earned in domestic production minus gross private investment minus net exports minus government purchases of goods and services. Or the base of the flat tax, which is income earned in domestic production minus gross private investment, equals consumption plus net exports plus government purchases. Why net exports should be included in the base of a consumption tax is a mystery. It is also unclear whether government purchases should be considered consumption, and if so whose consumption it is.

Moreover, the preceding calculations apply to the aggregate national tax base. When we come to the base of the tax of the individual taxpayer, which is what counts, there is a further qualification. An individual's saving includes the purchase of assets from other individuals, but the individual gets no tax relief for that. Thus if A and B have equal labor incomes, they will pay equal taxes; but if A sells assets to B, he can consume more than B. Or if A sells assets in the national market, reducing his portfolio, he can increase his consumption without increasing his tax, and whoever buys the assets will be reducing his consumption but will get no tax credit for it.

An Elusive Interpretation

The flat tax has a "now you see it, now you don't" quality that makes its interpretation very elusive. In one light, it is a tax on income, with a deduction for saving. But, as noted, the deduction seems only partial. Moreover, the deduction is indirect and barely visible. The deduction is effected by grossing up the value of saving invested in business capital. Thus, omitting the personal exemption just for the sake of simplicity, we may take the case of a taxpayer with $100,000 of income. He pays a tax of $20,000, spends $20,000 on consumption, and invests $60,000 in the newly issued stock of a corporation. This permits the corporation to buy $75,000 of capital equipment, because the deduction of that much investment from its income will save it $15,000 of taxes. So the individual taxpayer ends up with $75,000 of assets, $20,000 of consumption and has paid $5,000 of taxes, which is 20 percent of his income minus his saving.

Alternatively, the flat tax can be regarded as a sales tax on consumption, or on the value of consumption goods produced in the domestic private sector. This implies that with the imposition of the flat tax all before-tax incomes earned in the private sector will rise by the amount of the tax, so that the imposition of the tax leaves after-tax income unchanged (and incomes below the exemption level increased). Then the prices of consumer goods rise by the amount of the tax, reducing the real income of individuals in proportion to their consumption.

Viewed in this way, the whole purpose of the tax at the individual level, which can be paid with a postcard, is to establish qualification for exemption from the sales tax. A somewhat similar result, even better, could be performed with a sales tax and a flat per capita refund for every resident. The required postcard return could be very simple, like this:

> Dear IRS:
> My name is John Doe, Social Security number 123-45-6789. I have a lovely wife and two fine children. Please send me $6,000. Having wonderful time, wish you were here.

John Doe would not have to report his income, only his existence.

Whether the markets would work to make these two processes, the sales tax and the income tax, come out the same way is not clear. But the two different possible pictures probably contribute to the salability of the plan—one picture appealing to those to whom income tax is a bad name and one to those to whom sales tax is a bad name. That is another way of saying that it is difficult for the citizen to tell on what the tax is and on whom it really falls.

From almost any standpoint, the present federal income tax is full of anomalies, distortions, and complexity. This is a good time to think seriously about how to correct it. Whereas the flat tax would correct it by eliminating it, we have other ways to correct it. Basically, we have three questions to consider:

- Do we want an income tax or a consumption tax?
- How graduated should the rates of either be?
- How comprehensive should either be?

The flat tax is a consumption tax with slight graduation of rates.

One proposal before Congress would set in place a consumption tax with rates more graduated than the flat tax. That is the Nunn-Domenici proposal.

The existing income tax could be made more comprehensive and less distortive by covering kinds of income now excluded, such as fringe benefits and the imputed rent of owner-occupied homes. This change would permit lowering of rates, and the rates could be either more or less graduated than at present. One possibility would be to eliminate or reduce substantially the taxation of corporate profits.

A radical version of the foregoing would be the Henry Simons style of income tax, eliminating the corporate tax entirely and taxing comprehensively all personal income, including capital gains at the same rate as other income. The rate of the income tax could be flat, on income above a personal exemption, as proposed by Friedman in 1962, or graduated.

A still more radical reform would be to combine two Friedman proposals—a flat positive tax rate on personal income, comprehensively defined, on income above the exemption level and a flat negative rate on income below the exemption level. This would have the incidental advantage of straightening out the taxation of capital gains by providing a refund for net capital losses in excess of ordinary income.

There is plenty of room for tax reform. Proponents of reform have no reason to allow flat taxers to monopolize the stage.

22

Straightening Out the Flat Tax

The current discussion of tax reform—centering on the flat tax—is a scene of utter confusion. The result, if there is one, will be a source of surprise and disappointment to many taxpayers. I have no hope of single-handedly unsnarling this tangled web. But perhaps if I make a start, some of the politicians may be induced to figure out and tell us what they are talking about.

There are at least four ideas mixed up in the flat tax proposal:

- equal taxation of equal amounts of income without differentiation by the source or use of the income
- equal treatment of taxpayers with different amounts of income
- lower tax rates
- lower tax burdens, meaning lower tax payments relative to income for the average taxpayer or for most taxpayers

Equal Taxation of Equal Income

The first of these ideas—equal taxation of equal income regardless of source or use—has been the standard idea of economist tax reformers for at least sixty years and probably much longer. It has appealed to economists as equitable. It is also supported on grounds of economic efficiency. The tax system would not divert people from earning income or using income in the ways on which the market placed the highest value. This idea also has most to contribute to simplification by getting rid of the itemized deductions or exclusions that taxpayers complain of having to deal with.

But the popular appeal of the equal treatment idea has, I believe, another basis. It is the feeling that rich people with high-priced lawyers are able to use the complexity of the tax system to avoid paying their fair share of taxes. Discussion of the flat tax idea has already revealed one major flaw in this argument. Some of the biggest changes that would have to be made to treat all income alike would not be mainly at the expense of the rich but mainly at the expense of the middle class. The exclusion of employer-provided fringe benefits from taxable income is one case. Even touchier is the deductibility of mortgage interest on owner-occupied homes, which is a rough approximation for treating the rental value of owner-occupied homes as taxable income. When these and similar cases are exposed, cracks begin to appear in the support for the idea of a flat tax.

An even greater difficulty, which has received little attention so far, is the taxation of corporate income—probably the biggest departure from equal treatment of all kinds of income in the present system. The profits of corporations, that is, the income of stockholders, are taxed twice, once at the corporate level and once at the personal level when dividends are received or capital gains realized. Equal treatment would call for abolishing the corporate profits tax and taxing all corporate profits at the personal level at the rate imposed on each person's income. But I doubt that most people now waving the flag for the flat tax have in mind the consequences of that for the distribution of the tax burden between rich and poor. Moreover, if the corporate tax were abolished, the rates of individual income tax would have to rise significantly to produce any desired amount of revenue.

In the sense of wanting to tax all equal incomes equally, I have always been a flat taxer. In a 1944 essay that won a national contest for plans to achieve high employment, I said: "Existing loopholes should be closed to permit the desired revenues to be secured with lower, less repressive tax rates. . . . Taxation of corporate profits as stockholders' income should be substituted for the corporate excess profits [which we had in 1944] and income taxes." My point is that I think most people other than economists do not have all its implications in mind when they talk about the flat tax and are surprised to learn that they are the beneficiaries of many loopholes.

Same Tax Rate for All Taxpayers

The second notion of flatness is that people with different incomes should pay equal taxes. Although this notion is smuggled in under cover of the first kind of flatness, there is no necessary connection between the two ideas. We could have a tax that treated all kinds of income equally and still differentiated among amounts of income.

Of course, no one means literally that persons with different amounts of income should pay the same amount of tax. They do not mean that Steve Forbes and his secretary—to take a name at random—should pay the same dollar amount of taxes. They mean that people should pay about the same proportion of their income in taxes. But no one really means that either. As the Kemp Commission put it, "For taxable income above the personal exemption, if one taxpayer earns ten times as much as his neighbor, he should pay ten times as much in taxes. . . . Ten times as much income, ten times as much taxes. That's the deal."

But the kicker is in the phrase, *taxable income above the personal exemption.* That already means that the proportions of income paid in tax will differ and be higher the higher the income. If the tax rate is 20 percent, a taxpayer at the exemption level pays nothing; a taxpayer at twice the income level pays 10 percent of his income; at ten times the exemption level, he pays 18 percent of his income; and at 100 times the exemption level, he pays 19.8 percent.

So we are already in a system of increasing proportions. And who is to say that these proportions are just right? If the progression from 0 to 10 to 18 to 19.8 is acceptable, why not 0 to 10 to 20 to 30? You cannot determine what is fair by simple arithmetic. The American people will have to decide what they think is fair. I am personally rather indifferent to the steepness of the tax rate schedule, as long as the poorest people are exempt and the revenue is adequate to pay for the important functions of government. But the people should not be brainwashed into thinking that to have a simpler tax, without loopholes, they can have only one rate of tax.

Lower Tax Rate

I believe that much of the attraction of the flat tax idea, aside from the appeal of simplification, is the belief that the rate would be not only flat but also low. No one is stumping New Hampshire peddling a 30 percent flat tax. In principle, it should be possible to lower the income tax rate. If the tax base is broadened by eliminating the mortgage interest deduction and the charitable contribution deduction and the exclusion of fringe benefits and so on, the revenue now yielded by the present system will be obtainable with lower rates. The problem arises with the corporate profits tax. If "flatness" means eliminating the corporate profits tax, as I believe it does, the substantial revenue now obtained from that tax will have to be obtained from the individual income tax. In that case, reduction of the rates of individual income tax may not be possible, although the combined rates of the individual and corporate taxes would be reduced.

Lower Tax Burden

A lowering of tax rates, even if that is achieved, would not per se mean a reduction of tax burdens or of the proportion of income paid in tax, if the plan is to be revenue neutral, as the reformers generally promise. There would be a redistribution of the burden, from the people who had the fewest exclusions from taxable income to the people who had the most. If the system is to be revenue neutral, it will reduce tax burdens only to the extent that it will raise incomes. That, of course, is what proponents promise. The tax reform would alter incentives. It would reduce the incentives to own one's own home, to make charitable contributions, and to take earnings in the form of fringe benefits. It would increase the incentives to work and invest, because it would reduce the tax rates on earnings from working and investing. This brings us back to the land of deep voodoo, where, by saying the magic words *lower taxes,* the politician can conjure up whatever rate of economic growth he likes.

With the proposed radical tax reform, the society would be different in several respects—the national income would be somewhat larger, it would be somewhat differently distributed among persons, and it would be used somewhat differently. How big any of these *somewhats* is, no one knows. At least, I don't know. Whether the society would be better, even if richer, I don't know either. And I don't think the politicians have made even a start of telling us.

23

Confessions of a Tax Lover

The costs and difficulties imposed on taxpayers in complying with the federal income tax are commonly used as reasons for a radical change in the federal tax system. They lead Congressman Archer, chairman of the House Ways and Means Committee, to say that we need to tear the income tax out by its roots. We are offered as simpler replacements the Armey flat tax, the Gephardt 10 percent tax, the value-added tax, or a national sales tax.

I believe that all this discussion is seriously mistaken, and possibly intentionally misleading, for two reasons. First, it implies an erroneous notion of what the purpose of the tax system is, and, second, it reflects an exaggerated impression of the costs of compliance.

One can ask whether a pencil is a simpler writing instrument than a word processor. The answer obviously depends on the purpose for which the instrument is to be used. If the object is to do a cross-word puzzle, the pencil is simpler. If the object is to write a long document, revise it along the way, check the spelling, insert charts and footnotes, make a clean copy, and store the work in a small space, the computer is much the simpler instrument, even though it comes with a thick instruction manual.

Complexity

Moaning about the complexity of the income tax assumes that the object is simply to raise about $600 billion of annual revenue. If that is the object, there are surely simpler systems than the federal income tax. But suppose that the object is to raise that much money in such a way that the higher the taxpayer's income is, the higher the proportion of it he pays in tax. The radical alternatives to the income tax that are now being proposed gain much of their simplicity by giving up the attempt to do that, or to do it to the degree that it can be done by the present tax system.

The difficulty of filing an individual income tax return does not result from the existence of a schedule of five different tax rates. The IRS provides a table that relieves most taxpayers of doing the simple arithmetic involved in that. The difficulty arises from requiring the taxpayer to list all his deductions and sources of income. The deductions problem can be solved by eliminating deductions—for taxes paid, for charitable contributions, for medical expenses, for mortgage interest, and so on. Congressman Gephardt's proposal would do that, except for that most sacred of sacred cows—the mortgage interest deduction. The idea of eliminating the deductions raises howls from the expectable sources, but it is a route to simplification, if that is the main objective. The desire for that kind of simplification is not, however, the main source of the drive for simplification.

The basic issue is the requirement that individuals list all their sources of income—not only wages and salaries but also interest, dividends, capital gains, self-employment income, business income, rental income, pension distributions, and anything else they have. That is where the difficulties enter.

A sales tax would bypass this problem by making it unnecessary for individual taxpayers to file any returns at all. But that would also eliminate any possibility of progressivity except in a crude and limited form by exempting from the sales tax some kinds of purchases believed to bulk largest in low-income budgets. The Nunn-Domenici proposal shows that taxing consumption is not a way to achieve simplification. The taxation of consumption at a progressive rate—that is, at a higher rate the more the consumption—requires a more complicated return from the taxpayer than the taxation of income does, because it requires a calculation of income and also a calculation of saving that can be deducted from income to arrive at consumption.

The Armey flat tax achieves a high degree of simplification by not requiring the individual taxpayer to report and pay tax on any income other than wages and salaries. All other income, which is essentially the quarter of the national income that is a return to capital, would be taxed only at the business level and at a flat rate. That is, the tax on corporate profits, other business earnings, and rental income would be at the same rate regardless of the income of the individual to whom that income belonged. Thus, a dollar of dividends would be taxed at the same rate whether the dollar accrued to a person with $10,000 of income or to a person with $1,000,000 of income. Mr. Gephardt cannot achieve the same degree of simplification because he wants the individual to pay tax on that kind of income at the same rate as on wages and salaries, which requires that he report all that income.

Progressivity versus Simplicity

The question before the American people is not whether they would like a simpler tax system. Of course, they would. The question is how much of the ability to levy taxes progressively are they willing to give up to achieve greater simplicity. Or, to put the question more crassly, how much additional tax are middle-income people willing to pay to achieve greater simplicity for themselves and, especially, for the higher-income taxpayers who have more complex tax returns.

So, how complicated is compliance with the federal individual income tax? Some people like to frighten us by pointing to a ten-foot shelf of impenetrable language that constitutes the federal tax code. But, in fact, few taxpayers have anything to do with that.

In 1993, 114 million individual income tax returns were filed. Of these, 21 million were filed on 1040EZ and 28 million on form 1040A, both very simple forms. The basic form, 1040, was filed by 65 million taxpayers, but of these half took the standard deduction rather than itemizing their deductions. These were probably also very simple returns.

Almost two-thirds of all the taxpayers filing the basic return—1040—used the assistance of a paid tax preparer. This fact is sometimes cited as evidence that the tax must be very complicated because so many people have to get paid assistance. But that argument is backward. Specialization is an aspect of a highly developed economy. We no longer grind our own flour, cut our own hair, or repair our own automobiles. Each of us does what he does best and relies on specialists to do other things for him. We have no more reason to expect that everyone should do his own tax return than that everyone should be his own cardiologist.

Of the 35 million people who file form 1040 and do not take the standard deduction, probably about 10 million do not have the help of a paid tax preparer. If anyone is struggling with the complexity of the individual income tax, they are. What do we know about them? Even though they itemize their deductions, they may still have a simple form, perhaps having to report some mortgage interest and contributions to their church. In any case, we know that they do not find the reporting process so burdensome that they want to pay someone to help them.

I will give myself as an example. My return for 1994 came to thirty-four pages of schedules, not because my income is so large but because I have a large variety of income sources, expenses, and deductions. I encountered some problems in filling out the forms, but I found the answers in a few paragraphs of a book that I bought for under $15 and that is smaller and clearer than the manual for my computer. Then I used a computer program costing around $30 that guided me step-by-step through my entries, called attention to any discrepancies, did all the calculations, and printed out the results. When I was through, I felt that I had met a challenge and had learned something about my own finances as well as about the income tax.

I may be unusual, but not extremely so. (People think that because I am an economist, I have exceptional ability to forecast interest rates and the stock market and to understand the income tax. Unfortunately, that is not so.) More than one-fourth of all households now have computers, and the proportion must be higher in households with complex tax returns. We are raising a generation of children who have been using computers since kindergarten and who will wonder why we found the income tax difficult. By their time, the postcard, of which the flat-taxers are so proud, will be obsolete, as will the post office.

The flat taxers have come along too late. In another generation, in Newt Gingrich's brave new world of high technology, all economic transactions will be electronically recorded in financial institutions, whence they will be electronically transmitted to the IRS computer that will calculate the tax liability of each individual taxpayer and instantly debit his or her bank account. Some people will miss the fun of doing their own income tax, but I suppose they will find other amusement.

For the present, compliance with the income tax is burdensome to some. But so are other responsibilities of membership in this society, like jury duty, voting, and, in case of need, serving in the armed forces. If, as I think, progressive taxation is a feature of a good society, the compliance costs are not too great.

24

Death and Taxes

N ow that Congress seems on the verge of doing something about the estate tax, it might be interesting, although probably not productive of any result, to speculate a little about what that tax is for. I have always thought that a good tax system would involve "some kind" of reckoning with the tax collector on the occasion of death. But I do not think that the present kind of reckoning is the right kind. And I don't think that the changes now being contemplated will get us any closer to the right kind of reckoning. (Students of public finance will recognize that the thoughts set down here are not original but are derived from what Henry Simons wrote sixty years ago. I operate in the belief that old wisdom is better than original folly.)

Qualities of a Good Tax System

To get to the subject of taxation at death, we must start with the ABCs. And the A of a good tax system is that persons who are similarly situated with respect to some relevant criterion should be taxed similarly. Of course, other qualities of the tax system need to be considered, including the amount of revenue yielded, the effects on the economy, and the distribution of tax burdens among persons who are not similarly situated. But these qualities of the tax system result mainly from the *rates* of tax. To a large degree, we can achieve what we want of these qualities by the appropriate choice of the rate schedule, once we have decided on the tax base, which is the criterion by which we classify persons for the purpose of levying tax.

So I focus on the question of the relevant criterion. It could be anything—the taxpayer's height, or his IQ, or merely the fact of his existence. But centuries of experience and discussion have narrowed the list of criteria that might be acceptable in a fair tax system to three—wealth, income, and consumption.

Certain exceptions to this trio are recognized. Taxes on some other basis are accepted as payment for particular services the government renders, as the gasoline tax is a loose payment for the provision of highways. Some taxes are accepted as ways of discouraging behavior that is considered undesirable, like smoking or drinking alcohol.

But these exceptions do not provide much rationale for the estate tax. The estate tax might be regarded as payment to the government by the propertied classes for the government's services in protecting them against the sans-culottes. But this is not a very plausible theory, especially when the propertyless sans-culottes are so few.

Wealth and Power

It used to be said, and perhaps it still is, that the estate tax is required to prevent an undesirable concentration of power resulting from the passing down of large and growing estates from one generation to the next. But that can hardly explain levying a tax on estates of one, ten, or even fifty million dollars in America. It takes a lot of money to generate power in America today. I can think of only two families that acquired power in America in this century by having a lot of money—the Rockefellers and the Kennedys. Time will tell whether the Forbes family will be another. But here we are talking about, say, $500 million. And if power comes with money, it doesn't have to be inherited money. Ross Perot got a run at power with the money he had made himself. And there is power around that is not associated with money. Even if we exclude political figures, I suppose that William Safire, George Will, and Oprah Winfrey have more power than any rich person today. (Well, I understand that Oprah is very rich, but that is not where her power comes from.)

I return to the three comprehensive tax bases—wealth, income, and consumption—and ask how a tax at death would comport with any of them.

If we had a wealth tax, death might be a convenient occasion for valuing the decedent's assets and levying a tax on them or on the part that had not been previously taxed. But we have learned that even for people who are very rich a large part of wealth consists of human capital—personal skills and position—that we have no way of valuing except by reference to the income they yield. The income tax is the only possible version of a comprehensive wealth tax.

We are left with the choice between a consumption-based system and an income-based system. What we should do about taxes at death depends on two questions. One is whether we want a consumption-based system or an income-based system. The other is whether we consider bequests and gifts to be consumption of the decedent or the donor. The intuitive answer to the second question, I suppose, is negative. But that may not be the right answer. A person may be assumed to make a decision about the uses of his income in terms of the benefit they yield to him. If he decides to give away some of his income rather than consume it in some other way, we might suppose that giving it away yields as much satisfaction as other ways of consuming it. Moreover, the distinction between giving and spending on consumption is hard to make in some cases. If Mr. A gives $100,000 to his mistress, is that a gift or a consumption expenditure? (I am making that up. I have no idea of what the going rate is.)

How to Tax an Inheritance

It seems to me hard to deny that funds received as a gift should be taxed as income to the recipient. There is no reason why a person who receives X dollars as a gift should pay less tax than a person who received it in compensation for work. One may say that the donor has already paid tax on the income that he gave. But that is a question about the taxation of the donor, not of the donee. If we treat the donor's gift as consumption, it should be included in his tax base, whether we are taxing him on his income or on his consumption. That is obvious in the case of a consumption tax. But it is also clear in the case of an income tax, if we define income, as we should, as consumption plus the increase in the value of assets. (If gifts and bequests are consumption, then lifetime income equals lifetime consumption, since you can't take it with you and any assets you have not consumed otherwise in your life are consumed by the bequest at the end of it.) By the same logic, if we do not treat the gift as the donor's consumption, it should be excluded from his tax base, whether that is defined as consumption or income. Thus, we have four possibilities:

A. Income tax: gift considered donor's consumption; gift included in taxable income of both donor and donee

B. Income tax: gift not considered donor's consumption; gift included in taxable income of donee but excluded from taxable income of donor

C. Consumption tax: gift considered donor's consumption; no tax on donee; gift included in donor's tax base

D. Consumption tax: gift not considered donor's consumption; no tax on donee; gift not included in donor's tax base

My own preference is for case A. But I do not propose to argue that here. I want only to point out the questions that, in my opinion, need to be considered in a logical approach to taxation at death.

This argument leaves no room for an estate tax, as distinguished from a comprehensive income or consumption tax. Since I mentioned the name of Henry Simons at the outset, I should say that although he supported what I call case A, he also wanted a supplementary, graduated inheritance tax in addition to the comprehensive income tax. He was greatly concerned about the possible concentration of power that could result from the accumulation of inheritances over several generations. I do not find this idea of a supplemental tax very attractive today. Income taxes are heavier than when he wrote, sixty years ago, and the association of power with wealth is weaker, in my opinion, than he thought. I would not, however, object to a supplementary tax on very large bequests, exceeding, say, $500 million, although I would not care very much one way or the other.

25

I'll Be All Right

I see by the papers that my Republican friends want to give us a big tax cut. I have been haranguing against this kind of thing since 1978 because I thought, and still think, a big tax cut is bad for the country. But now I believe I have paid my dues on this subject and it is time to think about ME.

A Delightful Prospect

A cut of 15 percent in the income tax, which some are proposing, would mean a lot of money to me—a lot by my standards, of course, not by Steve Forbes's standards. What makes the prospect particularly delightful is that almost all my taxable income consists of withdrawals from IRAs, Keoghs, and pension plans. That is money I saved tax-free when tax rates were high. Now I will pay income tax on it when tax rates are low—made even lower than they now are by the proposed tax cut.

What will I do with the money I am relieved of paying in taxes? A younger person might spend it on riotous living. But I don't have the energy to spend it—shopping for a new car or flying to Europe is too tedious. Expensive restaurants are always disappointing, and, anyway, how much can you eat? So I guess I will save my tax cut. That won't be bad because the increase of the budget deficit resulting from the tax cut will raise interest rates, so I will make more on my saving.

Of course, when interest rates go up, the value of the assets in my retirement accounts will go down. I better sell some of them before everybody gets wise to this, before this article is published. Then I can accumulate cash and buy the assets back after interest rates have risen.

I still have to think about the estate tax. But I suppose a seventy-three-year-old president will have the estate tax on his mind also. In fact, Bob Dole has said that he wants to reduce the estate tax on small businesses, farmers, and ranchers. I wonder whether he would consider being a free-lance economist a small business. It is certainly small enough, but is it a business? I'll have to see what I can do about that.

When I have said that a big tax cut would be bad for the country, I meant for the future of the country. The deficit will reduce the funds available for private investment, slow down economic growth, and reduce the incomes of future generations. What will that mean for my children?

The Next Generation

The bad effect on growth will not be suffered equally by everyone in the next generation. The slowdown of growth will result from the shortage of capital. It will hurt those people in the next generation who either work with a lot of capital or whose consumption preferences require a lot of capital. Employment in manufacturing, construction, transportation, and even in modern agriculture requires a lot of capital per worker. People in those industries will suffer from the shortage of capital. Their productivity and consequently their incomes will be limited by lack of capital.

But my children and their spouses are lawyers, writers, and, to a small extent, actors. The capital they work with consists essentially of pencil and paper plus what is in their heads. Their incomes will not suffer from the shortage of capital.

The story on the consumption side is a little different. The main problem is housing. People whose pattern of living involves relatively large expenditures for housing will find their cost of living increased by the shortage and high cost of capital. I don't think that my daughter's family falls in that category. But my son's does. Even if he owns the houses he lives in, the cost of living in them will be increased because the interest he will lose by being invested in houses rather than in some other asset will increase as interest rates rise. But he can protect himself. I will advise him to sell his houses, get as much cash out as he can, hole up in a rented bungalow for a while, and then buy his houses back after the rise of interest rates drives their prices down. He will have some money left over that he can invest in something else. And, of course, he and my daughter will both be enjoying the lower tax rates.

So, it looks as if the Stein family will be OK. And that's what counts, isn't it?

26

Who Pays for Privatizing Social Security?

Two important points are commonly missed in the current discussion of social security reform. Both these points are, I believe, recognized in the report of the Social Security Advisory Commission. But they are not highlighted there and have been ignored in the subsequent debate. The points are these:

- Privatizing the social security funds does not add to national saving, private investment, or the national income and does not allow the system to earn more income without anyone's earning less.

- If the purpose of social security is to provide a *certain* benefit on retirement, an investment policy that yields a probable, even though possibly higher, benefit is not appropriate.

No Increase in National Saving

The first point may be easily seen. Suppose there are no federal government and no social security system. Then national saving is equal to private saving, in which I include, for simplicity, state and local government saving and the net inflow of capital from abroad. Total investment will equal national saving, which, in this case, equals private saving.

Then, suppose we introduce a federal government that has two parts, social security and the rest of government, which I will call ROG. ROG, let us assume, has a balanced budget and social security has a surplus—takes in currently more than it pays out. National saving will equal private saving plus the social security surplus and so will total investment. Now, and this is the key point, the amount of saving and investment will not depend on how the social security surplus is invested. If the social security surplus is invested in private assets—businesses, houses, and the like—total investment will obviously equal private saving plus the social security surplus. But what if the social security surplus is invested in federal bonds? Since there is no ROG deficit, social security must buy the bonds from private holders of existing bonds. Then the private holders have available for private investment, and do invest, their private savings plus the money they get from selling their federal bonds to the social security system.

This is simply an application, in reverse, of the proposition that a government deficit crowds out private investment by absorbing private saving to finance the deficit.

Now, suppose that the ROG has a deficit and social security has a surplus. There are two possibilities. One is that the ROG borrows the social security surplus, and the other is that the ROG borrows its entire deficit from private savers and the social security surplus is invested entirely in private assets. In either case, private investment will equal private saving plus the social security surplus minus the ROG deficit.

Some very rough figures will illustrate the situation. Suppose that private saving, as I have defined it, is $500 billion a year, social security has a surplus of $100 billion, and ROG has a deficit of $200 billion. If ROG borrows $100 billion from social security, it has to borrow $100 billion from private savers, so that of their $500 billion of saving, they have $400 billion to invest in private assets. If social security, however, invests its surplus in private assets, that raises the amount available for investment in private assets but equally increases the amount that the federal government has to extract by borrowing from private savers. Again, there is $400 billion available for private investment.

I will consider some possible qualifications to the argument below. But up to this point, privatizing social security investment has not added to private saving. Therefore, it has not added to total investment and has not added to the national income generated by the stock of productive capital. But still, everyone will say, the social security accounts will be invested in assets with a higher yield than government bonds and will earn a higher income. How can this be? Where will this higher income come from if there has been no addition to saving, investment, and national income? Since there are only three players in this game—the social security accounts, the ROG, and private savers—the gain to social security must come from one or both of the two others. Private savers will have a portfolio more heavily weighted with low-yield assets—government bonds—and less heavily weighted with private high-yielding assets. They will have a lower-yielding portfolio than if the social security accounts had bought the government bonds and left the private investments to private savers. But to induce private savers to make this shift in their portfolios—to surrender some of the private assets to the social security accounts and take on more of the government bonds—there will have to be some change in prices and yields. The yield of government bonds will have to rise or the yield of private assets will have to fall, or both. One element of this shift will probably be a rise in the yield of government bonds, which means a rise in the interest rates paid by the government, and that means, sooner or later, a rise in the burden on taxpayers.

So, it seems to me that the additional earnings that the social security accounts will get as a result of privatization will come from private savers and from taxpayers, in some combination that I don't know. I can imagine some qualifications to this conclusion, but they are hard to evaluate and are probably rather small on balance. Some people think that if workers are given the management of their social security accounts, they will learn to love finance and will save more. It seems to me equally likely that promised a larger social security benefit, they will decide to save less in other forms. It may be that if workers see a larger and more secure social security benefit deriving from their work, they will work more. If the government has to impose higher taxes to pay the costs of higher interest rates on its borrowing, though, that may inhibit work and other income-earning activity. Possibly, if the government does not have a captive market for its bonds in the social security accounts but has to borrow entirely in the open market, it will be more cautious about deficit spending. Possibly, but I wouldn't bet on a very large effect.

Some aspects of the proposals made by the Social Security

Advisory Commission would almost certainly add to national saving, to private investment, and to the national income. That is true of the proposed increases in the payroll taxes, changes in the treatment of social security benefits in the income tax, deferring the age of eligibility for benefits, covering state and local employees in the system, and reducing escalation of benefits for inflation. My only point is that privatization per se does not add to the national saving and should not be justified on the ground that it will. There may be other arguments for privatization. One could argue that workers should not be required to subsidize other savers and taxpayers by being excluded from higher-yielding assets if they are appropriate to the social security system. That is, one could argue for a redistribution of income from other savers and taxpayers to workers. But one should not think that there is any free lunch here.

Investment of Social Security Funds

That brings me to my second question, which is the proper criterion for investment of social security funds, funds collected by a tax on wage income. To put the question in extreme form, suppose there are two kinds of investment. One will yield at retirement a *certain* 50 percent of the retiree's final salary. The other will yield a *probable* 60 percent, with a fifty-fifty chance of yielding zero and a fifty-fifty chance of yielding 120 percent of the final salary. Which of these is suitable for a social security system? The example, to be sure, is extreme. But even if on the average over long periods of time investments will all yield the productivity of capital, we do know that the returns earned by particular investors in particular portfolios over particular periods differ enormously. Even the returns earned by professional fund managers differ greatly.

We can say that the workers are consenting adults and if they choose investments that will make some of them very rich and some very poor, that is up to them. But if we say that, we have to ask why we have a social security system, with mandatory contributions, at all. Why not just leave the workers free to save or not and to invest whatever they save in the way they like? The answer, in my opinion, must be that there is some social interest in the amount of income that people have in retirement. If there is no such interest, there is no justification for the social security tax. If there is such an interest, there is a need for policies that will ensure that the intended amount of income is forthcoming, not just on the average of all persons and all periods but for each person in each period. It is not sufficient to say that some people who are very smart or very lucky in the management of their funds will have high incomes and those who are not will have low incomes and that everything will average out just as the return to all stocks over all time averages out to be more than the return to government bonds.

I find it helpful to think of the social security system as having two parts. One provides an ensured equal minimum retirement benefit to all workers. (One group in the Advisory Commission suggests a benefit of $410 a month.) The investment for this part of the system would have to be in very secure form, probably involving some government guarantee. But this part of the system would be much smaller than the total system we now have and could be financed by a much smaller payroll tax.

What are the rest of the system and the rest of the payroll tax for? One possibility is that there is some national interest in the size of the retirement benefits that individual workers receive, beyond the flat minimum just mentioned. For example, it might be public policy that every worker should receive a benefit equal to X percent of his final salary, up to some maximum. In that case, it would be necessary to control the investment and use of the funds generated by each worker's mandatory contribution to ensure that the desired retirement benefit is forthcoming. It would not be satisfactory to say that the worker can invest "his" fund however he likes and, upon retirement, spend it as he likes.

We could say, though, that there is no public interest in the retirement benefits workers get beyond the flat minimum already mentioned. In that case, workers should be allowed to manage their savings as they like. But in that case it is unclear why there is any mandatory contribution to social security, beyond that needed to finance the flat minimum. Let the worker decide not only how to manage his savings but also how much to save or whether to save at all. The case for mandating a contribution to social security and then allowing the individual to manage the funds eludes me.

PART FIVE
Politics

27

A Cautionary Memo for JFK Republicans

To many Republicans, the name of Nelson Rockefeller is anathema, while the name of John Fitzgerald Kennedy is revered. That may seem peculiar at first glance, but it really is not. President Kennedy *cut taxes*. For many Republicans, that is sufficient reason to cite him as a model. He now ranks up there with Andrew Mellon in the pantheon of tax cutters. JFK is now to taxes what G. Washington was to cherry trees.

Of course, to say that President Kennedy cut taxes is something of a stretch. He proposed the tax cut formally in December 1962, he was assassinated in November 1963, and Congress passed the tax cut, which was signed by President Johnson, in February 1964. (How's that for *post hoc ergo propter hoc?*) But let us call it Kennedy's tax cut.

The Facts

Before we wrap ourselves too tightly in Kennedy's mantle, though, we should recall a few facts:

• When Kennedy came into office in 1961, the top marginal rate of individual income tax was 91 percent, compared with 39.6 percent today. The corporate rate was 52 percent, compared with 35 percent today with much more ample depreciation allowances.

• When Kennedy came into office, the unemployment rate was

6.7 percent. The Kennedy economists thought that "full employment" was 4 percent. That is, they thought they were far below full employment. They thought that the economy was operating at about 9 percent below its potential total output, that is, the output the economy was capable of producing at full employment with the existing tax rates and other structural conditions. They thought that the economy was operating below potential because total demand was too low. Today, we seem to be close to full employment, if not there.

• In fiscal 1961, when Kennedy came into office, the federal deficit was about 0.6 percent of gross national product. But the administration believed that the budget would be in surplus, with the existing tax rates and expenditure programs, if the economy were at full employment. It believed that even with lower taxes or higher expenditures the budget would be in balance if the economy were at high employment.

• The administration believed that fiscal drag would be a long-run problem. They thought that the potential long-run growth of total output was 4 percent a year, without counting on addition to the growth rate from tax reduction or any other structural reforms. But this potential growth rate would not be achieved with the existing tax and expenditure policies because they would yield surpluses that were too big, which would depress demand. So, the long-run growth problem was to get rid of these troublesome budget surpluses.

• With some exceptions, the administration did not care much about balancing the budget, except as a useful political slogan. Walter Heller, Kennedy's chief economist, referred to balancing the budget as "the Puritan ethic," at a time when that epithet was considered dismissive.

• Cutting taxes was not Kennedy's first choice for getting rid of those troublesome surpluses. He had plans for many expenditure increases—for defense, federal aid to education, urban renewal, regional economic development, manpower training, and the provision of medical care for the aged. Congress did not approve any of that, except for an increase in defense spending after the Soviets put up the Berlin Wall.

• The Kennedy administration would have liked to "get the economy moving again" by easing monetary policy. But the administration did not control monetary policy, and in any case the balance-of-payments deficit combined with the commitment to support the dollar exchange rate inhibited monetary policy.

• In the summer of 1962, the stock market fell sharply. That was commonly attributed to anxieties in the financial and business community caused by the administration's heavy-handed pressure on the steel companies to roll back a price increase. The administration feared that the economy was entering another recession, which would be *its* recession. It felt the need to stimulate the economy but was blocked by Congress on the expenditure-increasing front. Moreover, it wanted to restore confidence in the business community. So it came up with the proposal of a big tax cut.

• The administration did not propose to couple the tax cut with an expenditure cut. It wanted to stimulate demand and reduce the troublesome full-employment surplus. It was the congressional leadership, notably Senator Harry Byrd and Congressman Wilbur Mills, who insisted on expenditure restraint along with the tax cut. This led to President Johnson's classic fiscal policy pronouncement to Walter Heller: "If you don't get this budget down around 100 billion dollars you won't pee one drop."

• The administration recognized that tax reduction would have some beneficial incentive effects, which we would now call supply-side effects, but it insisted that the main objective was the surplus-reducing, demand-side effect.

The Expansion of the 1960s

So we got the tax cut, signed in February 1964. And we got a prolonged economic expansion. But the connection between the cut and the expansion is unclear. By current measurements, the expansion began in February 1961 and continued until December 1969. That is, it began well before the tax cut and was prolonged at the end by the expenditures for the Vietnam War. There were "lulls" but no recessions in 1962 and 1966. In the middle of 1963, when the tax cut was being debated, the economic recovery became so obvious that some questioned whether the cut was really needed. That was an embarrassment to the administration, which wanted the tax cut to relieve the long-run fiscal drag and not just the immediate economic lull. Anyway, having offered the baby the candy, it could not take it away. Heller rationalized the policy by saying that the improving economic prospects "offer a solid launching pad" for the tax cut. (We were big on space-age meta-phors in those days.) A change in monetary policy probably had a good deal to do with the expansion. From the end of 1959 to the end of 1962, the money supply (M1, which seemed the significant measure at the time) increased at the annual rate of 1.8 percent. From 1962 to 1969, the annual rate of increase was 4.7 percent.

The Kennedy administration estimates of the long-run eco-nomic and fiscal position turned out to be seriously in error. The economy did not grow by 4 percent per annum. It grew from 1963 to 1997 by 3 percent per annum—which is a 25 percent error, not a 1 percent error. We did not face the problem of mounting full-employment surpluses that would be a drag on the economy be-cause they would depress demand. Instead, we faced the problem of large persistent deficits that depressed the economy by depriv-ing it of savings for investment.

No doubt a determined econometrician can "prove" that the Kennedy-Johnson tax cut was a great success. He will have to be pretty determined. But even so, that would not make the Kennedy-Johnson tax cut a model for us. We start with a much lower tax rate. We are much closer to full employment than we were, or thought we were, when Kennedy proposed the cut. And, most im-portant, we face the possibility of frighteningly large deficits in the next generation, whereas they thought they faced frighteningly large surpluses.[1]

---

1. The story of the Kennedy-Johnson tax cut can be found in more detail in my book *The Fiscal Revolution in America: Policy in Pursuit of Reality,* 2d. rev. ed. (Washington, D.C.: AEI Press, 1996).

28

On Presidential Republicans

I don't know what Colin Powell meant by saying that he is a "Rockefeller Republican." The words have caused some stir in Republican ranks, as if he had said he was a "Leon Trotsky Republican." As one of the few people who still remember Nelson Rockefeller, let me try to explain.

In fact, all the Republican presidents of the past sixty-six years have been Rockefeller Republicans, if not when they entered office, at least before they left it. That is true of three of the four Republican candidates for the presidency who did not get elected—Landon, Willkie, and Dewey. The probable exception is Goldwater, but in recent years he did not seem to be a Goldwater Republican any more.

What Is a Rockefeller Republican?

What I mean by a Rockefeller Republican is a moderate, activist, internationalist, progressive, compassionate, and pragmatic Republican—one who exemplifies these traits in contrast to many in the congressional wing of the party, including its leaders. He is a person with principles, but they are very general, and he realizes that most issues of public policy are between a little more and a little less, but not between good and evil or between freedom and slavery.

When I go back sixty-six years, I go back to Herbert Hoover. (I really do not remember Coolidge or Harding.) Today's readers may be surprised to learn that Hoover was nominated as a representative of the liberal wing of the party in 1928. He shared the modern, enlightened views of his time. He was overwhelmed by the depression, and his name became a synonym for indifference and ignorance. The reputation is unjustified. He was overwhelmed because the modern enlightenment of his times was inadequate to the problems of his times.

I skip to Eisenhower, the next Republican president. He obviously was the candidate of the liberal wing of the party, as distinguished from the conservative wing led by Robert Taft. (On examination, Taft turns out to have been less conservative than he sounded. Perhaps it is true of all conservatives, or even of all politicians, that—as Mark Twain said of Wagner's music—they are better than they sound.)

Eisenhower came into office after twenty years of Republican complaining about the New Deal. But he did not roll back the New Deal. He promoted the expansion of social security and unemployment compensation, created the Department of Health, Education and Welfare, inaugurated what was probably the biggest civil works program in our history—the Interstate Highway System— and established an agency to eliminate racial discrimination in federal contracting. He resisted tax cuts but also said that he did not make a fetish of balancing the budget. He maintained a strong defense against the Soviets but carefully avoided confrontation. (At least, he tried. The U-2 incident was a great disappointment to him.) He warned against the "military-industrial complex."

Rockefeller Republicanism came onto the national scene in 1960, when Rockefeller contested Nixon for the Republican nomination. From today's vantage, the difference in their 1960 statements seems small. In 1968 the two were again rivals. I thought that I was a Rockefeller Republican, and wanting a little hands-on experience with politics, I offered my services to Rockefeller. He ignored my offer, and I wound up spending six years with Nixon.

Nixon turned out to be as Rockefellerish as I could wish. He put forward expansive welfare and health reform programs; created the Environmental Protection Agency declared, with pride, "Now I am a Keynesian"; took America off the gold standard; and, alas, instituted price and wage controls. He was, and took pleasure in being, a "conservative man with liberal ideas."

Nixon chose as his successor Gerald Ford, the epitome of

centrism. And who did President Ford choose as his vice president? You got it—Nelson Rockefeller.

The story of George Bush is too recent to require any elaboration. He was the man who recognized "voodoo economics" when he first saw it, who wanted a "kinder, gentler society," and who infuriated the true believers by agreeing to a tax increase in 1990—the very model of a modern Rockefeller Republican.

Ronald Reagan is a harder case for my argument. His rhetoric was so attractive, it is hard to pay attention to his record. But in almost every year after 1981, he acceded to a tax increase. He stopped the rise of federal spending relative to gross domestic product but did not reverse it. He ran up big deficits. He was a disappointment to the more thorough-going deregulators. His most ardent admirers complained that his entourage had not allowed Reagan to be Reagan. But his entourage consisted of the people he wanted around him.

Different from Party Activists

There are, I believe, three reasons why Republican presidents turn out to be so different from the mainstream of party activists.

First, to be elected as president and to govern as president, a person must be responsive to a much wider range of opinions and interests than is required for a congressman or even a newspaper pundit.

Second, a president has a group of advisers who are diverse and are selected with more attention to special competence than to partisanship. They expose the president to a range of options that most other people do not have to think about.

Third, and I know this will sound sentimental, I think that living in the White House induces contemplation, responsibility, and prudence. The president lives in the shadow of men who have been adjudged great by history. He dreams of being among them and knows that the history will not be written by—to take a name at random—Rush Limbaugh.

The White House Effect

I am not making a case for Colin Powell. I am not in that business. I am suggesting only that if he is a Rockefeller Republican, that does not put him outside the Republican presidential mainstream. But the record also suggests that some of the candidates who are now sounding like a cross between Elmer Gantry and Attila the Hun might be presidents we could live with if they ever got into the White House.

Of course, to say that one is a Rockefeller Republican today is not to say that he now favors the policies of Rockefeller Republicans of 1960 or 1970. The world is different, and different policies are needed.

29

Tips on Political Economics

We typically hear a lot of economics stemming from the political campaigns—assertions about economic growth, interest rates, the export of jobs, and many other things. We can expect to hear more.

Economics, though, is not an exact and finished science. Many things are possible. But not everything is possible, and all the things that are possible are not equally probable. We do not have an Academy of Economics to certify which propositions are impossible and what the relative probabilities are of those that are possible. The citizen must form his own opinion. But although I am not licensed to certify what is true and what is false, I can offer some tips that may help.

1. Start with the presumption that what the candidate says about the economy has a fifty-fifty chance of being true. I don't believe that candidates ordinarily lie in the sense of saying what they know to be untrue. But distinguishing between what is true and what is false is not their highest priority, or the highest priority of their "experts."

2. Do not believe assertions that the candidate's program will cause the economy to perform outside the range of its past experience. Do not believe that the candidate can make the economy grow at the rate of 5 percent per annum if it has never grown at such a rate for any five-year period except when recovering from a deep depression. Economic performance changes, and it will sometimes depart from its past tracks. But that is not predictable.

The epigraph of one of the great economic classics, Marshall's *Principles of Economics,* is *"Natura non facit saltum."* A rough translation is that the Wizards may beat the Bulls but don't bet on it.

3. Beware of stubborn consistency. There are people who always say that the deficit is too small or that monetary growth is too slow or that taxes are too high. The world is not like that, and analysis and prescription shouldn't be either.

4. Beware of self-serving paradoxes. If someone with a safe-deposit box full of Berkshire-Hathaway stock that he has held for ten years tells you that cutting the capital gains tax will mainly help poor people who own no capital—watch out.

5. Beware of simple international comparisons. The fact, if it is a fact, that the flat tax did wonders for Hong Kong does not mean that it will do wonders for the United States. Homeownership in Israel is high even though mortgage interest is not deductible there. That does not mean that eliminating the deductibility in the United States would not reduce homeownership here. There are big differences between Hong Kong and the United States and between Israel and the United States.

6. Be very skeptical of television "debates" between opposing economists. On the Lehrer *NewsHour,* for example, you may see one economist who says that the moon is made of green cheese and one who says that it is not. Do not therefore conclude that the profession is divided and that the two answers are equally probable, or that the moon is half made of green cheese. You will have to form a judgment. It is a good bet that the one who talks most fluently, has the most apt statistics, and who occupies most of the time is wrong.

7. Do not give high marks for novelty. As the great economist Frank Knight once said, "Anything very original in economics would be wrong anyway."

8. Place more faith in old think tanks than in young ones. Almost all think tanks are founded and staffed by persons with an axe to grind, and they initially turn out studies tailored to that purpose. But as time passes, the original founders and staff leave the scene. The goal of the institution and its new staff becomes the survival and prosperity of the institution, the original intent having been forgotten. The new staff has more personal motives— their self-esteem and the esteem of their peers in the economics

profession. This moves them toward objectivity and scholarship, or at least in the direction of variety, which is some protection against being always wrong.

9. Place more faith in old economists than in young ones. Of course, this is not an invariable rule. But if you could choose at random ten economists who are seventy-five years of age and ten who are forty years of age, you would be better off listening to the old ones. They have fewer political ambitions and are more aware of their own fallibility. The old ones may not know as much as the young ones, but they don't know so much that isn't so, either.

10. Place more faith in economists who recognize the uncertainties to which the science is subject and who say, "on the one hand and on the other hand." They are being either very subtle or very honest.

11. Remember that all economists, including this old one, have their personal interests and biases.

PART SIX
Life

30

Golden Days

I do not propose to enter the debate about who caused the golden age America is now said to be enjoying. The subject baffles me. I don't see the chain of causation by which the specific acts of specific politicians are supposed to have led to the results noted today. If I don't know what caused the baby's death, I can't begin to think about whether the au pair (Reagan? Clinton?) did it.

Private Golden Days

I would like to offer some musings on another kind of "golden" condition. I refer to the golden days of private individuals. Between the golden days of individuals and the golden ages of nations, the connection is, I believe, quite loose. For most people most of the time, the possibility of enjoying a golden day does not much depend on the state of the nation. In saying that, I mean to exclude the Holocaust, the Great Depression, and total war, as well as people who are exceptionally vulnerable. But within the usual range of variation of the national condition, the difference between a golden national age and a not-golden national age is for most people not important for achieving a personal golden day.

If I had to describe a personal golden day in one word, I would say *peace*. That is the ultimate blessing in the key Judeo-Christian benediction: "May the Lord bless you and keep you, may He lift up the light of His countenance upon you and give you peace." I understand *peace* in this context to mean not the absence of international violence, or not only that, but a person's peace with himself, with his idea of how he should behave, and it includes loving and being loved and accepting and appreciating the universe and what man has created in it.

I cannot give a general prescription for achieving golden days, but I can give two examples from my own experience to suggest what some of the ingredients of a prescription might be.

About two months ago, I was sitting on the bench at my usual bus stop, at Connecticut Avenue and K Street, when a policeman escorted a girl or young woman (I couldn't tell which) across the street and seated her next to me. She was obviously blind, carrying a long white cane and keeping her eyes screwed shut. She could hear the buses coming up to the stop but didn't know which buses they were, so I began telling her which they were. It turned out that she was waiting for the bus that I was waiting for, the Number 80. Since she was so anxious about the coming of our bus, I asked her whether she had an appointment. She said that she was going to a class at George Washington University and the professor had warned the students not to come in late.

I thought of putting her in a taxi or taking her to her class in a taxi. It would not have cost much. But I was afraid that she would think I was trying to kidnap or molest her. (There's a comment on our golden age!)

At last our bus came, and I helped her up the steps. She indicated that I should sit next to her and tell her when we came to her stop. At the stop I helped her down the steps, and the driver kept the door open for me to get back. But it was clear that once she was on the sidewalk, she had no idea of where to go. I motioned to the bus driver to close the doors, took her by the hand, and led her along G Street to the university building she wanted. Along the way, she told me that she had just graduated from Smith College and was taking postgraduate work in international relations. When I left her at her building, she thanked me, but I said that it was I who had to thank her, because she had given me the great feeling of being needed.

That little incident made my day, and several days to follow, golden. I had done a deed of "lovingkindness." Lovingkindness is different from charity; charity can be done with money, but lovingkindness requires personal involvement. Lovingkindness yields a greater reward to the giver. "Sow according to your charity, but reap according to your lovingkindness" (Hosea 10:12). Writing tax-deductible checks to charitable institutions does not make my day golden the way holding that young girl's hand did.

Receptivity to Beauty

On my other example of a golden day, I had been out for a walk in the sunshine, an article of mine had been published in the morning paper, and a stranger on the street had complimented me on it. Returning home, a little tired but pleased that I had been able to do the walk, I lay down and turned on the radio, which just happened to be playing Mozart's flute and harp concerto. I was elated and knew that there were a few people to whom I could tell of this feeling with confidence that they would understand and share my joy. That was a golden day, brought about by the beauty of nature and of art, the feeling of achievement and of physical well-being relative to my age, and the connection with a few—one may be enough—sympathetic people.

Golden days do not necessarily result from extraordinary events. They can result from ordinary events happening to people who are receptive, appreciative, attuned to what is happening around them. A person's psychological and emotional stance, not the external events, is what mainly determines his possibility of enjoying a golden day.

In my own case, I think that three years ago I would not have experienced the golden days I have described here. I would have been too shy, or "buttoned down," to take that young girl's hand, and I would have been too absorbed with trivia to appreciate the things that made me so happy a few weeks ago. I suppose it is aging that has changed my attitude. To resume my economist's hat, scarcity confers value, and the realization that one's days are few increases one's appreciation of their value. But one doesn't have to be old to appreciate that. Even for the young, the remaining days are few.

Every day will not be a golden day. Golden days will not be captured by a steely pursuit of them. Appreciation and receptivity are the keys.

31

A Tourist at Home

O bserving America from a seat in the bus: when the weather is good, I often take the bus to my office. I suppose that is partly because the bus trip costs six dollars less than the taxi trip and I am of the depression generation that still thinks six dollars is a lot of money. I tell myself that it is only sixty cents in real 1933 dollars, but that doesn't stick in my mind. Also, I really like the bus. I like to observe the other passengers. And I get a better view of the people on the sidewalk and of the city from my seat in the bus than I do from the back seat of the taxi, especially if I am closing my eyes to blot out the dangers of the wild taxi ride.

Watergate

The bus stop is across the street from the Watergate apartment in which I live. Twenty years ago, possibly even fifteen years ago, when I came out of the building there would be knots of tourists, often Japanese, standing around, looking to take pictures of the building where it happened. They are all gone now. *Watergate* has become an abstraction, a symbol for something bad done by a president, but there are fewer and fewer people who remember just what the president did. Hardly anyone now remembers why Alexander Hamilton and Aaron Burr fought a duel or why the Congress almost impeached Andrew Johnson. So it is becoming with Watergate.

How accommodating it is of history to locate the break-in of the Democratic National Committee in a building with a distinctive architectural style and name! Suppose the break-in had been at one of those identical cubical office buildings that fill downtown Washington, with names like 1150 Seventeenth Street. Would tourists have come to take its picture? And what would we have instead of Iran-contragate and Whitewatergate and Filegate? Journalists would have been cliché-less.

But back to my bus. The driver is always an African American and often an African American woman. I can't get used to saying *African American.* Her ancestors came here long before mine— probably well over a century before mine. If she is an African American, what am I, a Russian American? But whatever we call her, I am glad to see her. She has overcome centuries of race and gender prejudice to get where she is. I am pleased to see the competence with which she wrestles that big bus around the corners, hands out transfers, and answers passengers' questions about stops and connections. Not long ago such competence would not have been expected of her.

After snaking around eight blocks, we arrive at a corner on Virginia Avenue where one can see, separated by a narrow street, the buildings of the Federal Reserve and the State Department. What a concentration of worldwide power! But more impressive than the power is the concentration of homeless men lounging on the grates and the grass.

The Fountain

Two blocks down on Virginia Avenue, we come to the site of my epiphany. Looking out of the bus window one day, I saw a tall, graceful fountain in the garden behind a building that fronted on Constitution Avenue. I had passed it dozens of times without noticing it, perhaps because the water had not been playing before. I suddenly had the thought that if I had been in a tour bus in Rome or Vienna, the guide would have called our attention to that fountain, explained its history, and we would all have marveled at it. From that moment, at least for a while, I looked at my surroundings with fresh eyes—the eyes of a tourist.

Going up Eighteenth Street

We turn up Eighteenth Street and pass the rear entrance of Constitution Hall, the property of the Daughters of the American Revolution. I wondered how many other buildings are famous for something that didn't happen in them. Marian Anderson didn't sing here in 1939. I have recently seen assertions that the DAR excluded Marian Anderson from Constitution Hall because she wanted to sing on Easter Sunday and not because she was "colored," as we used to say. I don't know the truth of that, but it really doesn't matter. The truth is that conditions in America in 1939 were such that a Marian Anderson *could* be excluded because of her race and that conditions today are such that she could not.

A little further up Eighteenth Street, we see the huge building of the Department of the Interior that houses, among other things, the Bureau of Indian Affairs. That is the locus of one of Ronald Reagan's favorite stories, about the bureaucrat who was found with his head down on his desk, sobbing, because his Indian had died. That is a funny story, but it should not be told by a president of the United States, who should realize that the historic relation between the federal government and the American Indians is no laughing matter.

As we proceed up Eighteenth Street, we take on more passengers, almost all African Americans and Hispanics. Often I am the only "white" person in the bus. In my new stance as a tourist, I think to myself: "How exotic. I could be on a bus in Tokyo and all the other passengers could be Japanese. I know so little about them, about their lives and thoughts and feelings." But then I realize how superficial that attitude is. Fundamentally, the African Americans and Hispanics and I are pretty much alike, riding on the same bus to the same destination over the same potholes. (And we have reached a degree of liberation that permits me to think of them as Mayor Barry's potholes without feeling guilty of racism.)

The word *fundamentally* in the previous paragraph carries a lot of weight, but it is important to think of what is fundamental. I mean having the experience of love and loneliness, illness and health, the joy of children, the satisfaction of work, and the inevitability of death. That is the sense in which we are all alike. That is the sense in which we are all in the same bus. Perhaps it is being eighty years of age that makes me think that these are the overwhelmingly important and overwhelmingly common aspects of life. But many people much wiser than I have thought that at a much earlier age than mine.

Nearing the end of my trip, I realize that a large part of my observations has been about race. That is not surprising. Race is the great American problem. From the standpoint of human history, race is not the distinctive American condition. That is freedom and prosperity. But even this pretend tourist takes that for granted. It is the race problem—that tangled web of history, hostility, demands, frustrations, injustice, and lawlessness—that gets, and deserves, attention. And yet, as I think about Marian Anderson and about my fellow passengers and about the female bus-driver, I feel hopeful.

At my destination, she pulls the handle to open the door for me. I say, "Thank you." She says, "Have a nice day."

32

Gertrude Stein—Republican

G ertrude Stein was not really my aunt. I sometimes like to
pretend to think that I was her nephew, but that is a long
way from being her nephew or even from thinking I was.
I suppose many people like to indulge in the occasional fantasy of
being a different person in a different life, and being her nephew
and a member of her charmed circle would certainly have been
different for me. Of course, the fantasy is 100 percent crazy, but it
is not 200 percent crazy. It isn't as if I had adopted Anastasia as
my imaginary aunt. Gertrude and I share the name, Stein, and we
are both Jewish. And I have recently discovered another affinity.
We are both Republicans.

A Coolidge Republican

The idea that this revolutionary in literary style—this patron of
Bohemians and radicals, this most famous lesbian since Sappho—
was a Republican is staggering, and delicious. I wonder what Jesse
Helms, Pat Buchanan, and Jerry Falwell think about that. Some
other avant-garde writers have been conservatives but not of her
type. Ezra Pound was a Fascist conservative. T. S. Eliot was a high-
church, elitist conservative. William Faulkner was an antique
Southern gentleman conservative. Gertrude Stein, whom I will call
GS for brevity, was not only a Republican but a mainstream, mid-

I thank Professor Catherine Stimpson, a real expert on Gertrude Stein, for
her guidance to an amateur but absolve her of all responsibility.

dle-America, small government Republican. She would not have been a Rockefeller Republican, even though Rockefeller endowed the Museum of Modern Art, celebrating the artists she was among the first to recognize. She was more like a Coolidge Republican. In fact, even Coolidge's literary style had traces of hers. When he said, "When people are out of work there is unemployment," it sounded like her—superficially so simple-minded that one thinks there must be some deeper meaning beneath it.

GS once said, in January 1934, that Republicans "are the only natural rulers" in the United States. That was because of something special about the United States, which is that individuals are free and government is small. She said that Theodore and Franklin Roosevelt did not understand that. "When I say Theodore and Franklin Roosevelt are not American I mean they do not feel America to be a very large country around which anybody can wander and so although a government is there it is not always anywhere near but they feel it to be a little country which they can govern, and so it is European and not American."

It is interesting that she applied that argument to Theodore Roosevelt, who, after all, was a Republican. But she did not consider him an authentic Republican. She said, "It is not that Theodore Roosevelt destroyed the republican party that might have happened anyway." It was Franklin Roosevelt that she most consistently disliked. In the talk where she said that the Republican Party was the only natural ruler of the United States, she also said that Democrats were elected president only if they had a "singular seductiveness." "Roosevelt [Franklin] was honestly elected, but he is not half as seductive as his predecessors, so I don't think he will be elected a second time."

GS's Economics

Her dislike of FDR was based partly on economic policy. She asked, "Is Franklin Roosevelt trying to make money be so that it has no existence that it ceases to be a thing that anybody could count, so that nobody can any longer believe in it or is it all electioneering." If he were really trying to get rid of the belief in money so that people would no longer believe in it, GS thought that might be a good thing, but she thought that FDR just wanted to have a lot of money at his disposal so that he could control everything.

GS gave the most extensive view of her thoughts on economics in a series of articles published in 1936 in—where else?—the *Saturday Evening Post,* the house organ of Main Street Republicanism. The main theme of these articles was that governments spend too much money. Although he is not mentioned, one can tell by the time and place of this publication as well as by her remarks elsewhere that the main culprit was Franklin Roosevelt. The articles had two minor themes—that the unemployed did not want to work and that if there were fewer rich people, there would be more poor people. She thus plucked all the strings of the mainstream Republican harp.

The first of these articles, entitled "MONEY," illustrates the style of rhetoric and argument. She starts with a simple, "brass tacks" statement: "Everybody just has to make up their mind. Is money money or isn't money money. Everybody who earns it and spends it every day in order to live knows that money is money, everybody who votes it to be gathered in as taxes knows money is not money. That is what makes everybody go crazy."

GS is saying that the people in government who tax and spend do not realize what money is to the people who earn it. But money really is money, and the people who tax and spend should treat it the way that the earners treat it, and they don't. There is trickery or confusion in this argument. Of course, money is money, but there are different kinds of money and they need to be regarded and managed differently. Apples and oranges are both fruit, but that does not make them the same thing or indicate that they should be handled in the same way. The soldiers in an army division are all someone's sons, but we do not expect the commanding general to regard and manage them in the same way that their mothers would.

Governments may be wasteful in their management of money—probably are. But to say that they don't act as if they were sitting around the cliché kitchen table is no evidence. The only evidence GS provides is in the story of Louis XV, who, when accused of spending too much, said, "After me the deluge." But the story was singularly inappropriate in 1936. The deluge had come after Coolidge and Hoover. Roosevelt's spending was an effort to stem the deluge or at least to keep some people from drowning in it.

These 1936 articles by GS contain eerie suggestions of words we were to hear fifty or sixty years later. The Louis XV story reminds me of one of Ronald Reagan's favorites, about the Muslim philosopher who said that the king came to the throne with high taxes and departed with low revenue. Her asking "Is money money" presages Bob Dole in the 1996 campaign repeating, "It's your money! It's your money! It's your money!" And I can imagine her testifying before Senator Hatch on the balanced budget amendment when she asks: "Who is to stop congress from spending too much money. They will not stop themselves, that is certain."

Speculations on GS

How did GS, this unconventional woman, get to these conventional ideas? I never spoke to my aunt, and I am not a student of the large literature by and about her. But if she could write about fiscal policy, perhaps I can speculate a little about her.

She may have been either terribly ignorant about economic affairs or terribly foresighted. She was away from the United States continuously from 1904 to 1934, when she returned for a lecture tour and left again, never to come back. She missed the worst part of the Great Depression. She did receive American newspapers in Paris, which we know because of the story of her giving the comic pages to Picasso, but we, or I at least, don't know what she read. If she had been more aware of the depth and despair of the depression, she might have been more understanding of Franklin Roosevelt.

One might say, though, that she had such great understanding of human nature that she could see beyond the depression, beyond World War II, beyond the cold war, to the fiscal problems we would have in the last years of the century. One could say that, but I don't believe it. She was not a woman of great foresight about public events. Living in France in the summer of 1939, she rejected the opinion of well-informed people that war was imminent.

However ignorant of economics she may have been, there is one economic fact that she must have known, as all Americans living abroad do know, and that is the exchange rate. Before FDR devalued the dollar, she could get 25.6 francs for each dollar of her income from America. After the devaluation, she could get only 15.2 francs. The value of her dollar income in francs fell by 40 percent. I can easily imagine her being greatly annoyed at FDR by that.

GS, however unconventional, was not the stereotypical intellectual who is poor, alienated, and therefore an enemy of capitalism. She was not terribly rich, but she always had a comfortable income, derived for most of her life from her inheritance and supplemented after she was sixty years old by royalties on her writings. She had great investments—in Picassos, Matisses, and other paintings. She was far from alienated. She was an internationally recognized grande dame of a group of rising geniuses.

And she was not an intellectual. She had little interest in general ideas about economics or politics. "The real ideas," she said, "are not the relation of human beings as groups but a human being to himself inside him and that is an idea that is more interesting than humanity in groups."

It seems to me that her view of society was "cubist" like the paintings she was early to appreciate and the literature she wrote. A cubist painter tried to decompose an object into the atoms that were its real essence. He could paint a violin as a number of superimposed geometrical shapes of varying shades of brown. GS tried to reveal the essence of communication by stringing together heavy words without the punctuation, connectives, adjectives, adverbs, and allusions we are accustomed to. She understood society, or was interested in society, only as a collection of individual human beings not bound together by any political or economic system.

This attitude has its merits, but it also has its drawbacks. No one can play music with the cubist's idea of a violin. Very few people could understand what GS was writing. Her atomistic view of society nourished her assignment of a high value to individual freedom, but it limited her ability to understand much that was going on in the world.

As GS might ask, What is the question to which this essay is the answer? Perhaps there is none. Every answer doesn't have a question. But one lesson of this essay is that the Stein family, like every other family, contains some surprises.

33

An Old Couch Potato's Lament

I watch lots of television. If you are as long in years and short in energy as I am, watching TV is the second-best occupation. The first-best, of course, is sleeping, but you can't sleep all the time. I watch many kinds of TV, but some kinds I don't watch. I don't watch cop shows. If I wanted all that violence, I would watch the 10 or 11 o'clock local news. I do not watch sitcoms. They seem to me all juvenile leering about sex. I am weaning myself from the talk shows about public policy that I used to think it was my duty to watch. I have concluded that they are all games of Pin the Tail on the Donkey—blindfolded journalists trying to stick pins in evasive politicians.

What's on TV?

I watch the evening news because it comes at dinner time and serves as background music to which we—my wife and I—don't have to pay much attention. I think I could do with about three minutes of news a day. I watch some sports, especially Sunday afternoon professional football. I love to see something done extremely well, and I think that throwing a pass twenty yards down the field to a precise point where the receiver catches it amid a forest of defenders is doing something extremely well. I like to watch with the sound off, because the sports pundits are no better than the policy pundits, and if I fall asleep during the game, that's fine.

I watch the occasional symphony concert broadcast on TV. I

can hear better sound on the radio or on a CD, but there is something special about the TV performance that is connected with doing something extremely well. When I only listen, I can hear Mozart or Haydn doing something extremely well, but on TV I can see 100 musicians doing something extremely well. In the course of an hour, they play—I don't know how many—say, 100,000 notes, and they all come out right. I look at the second clarinet player. He's no genius. He probably makes his living by giving lessons. But he always comes in with his "duh" at the right time. As the former second clarinet in the Schenectady High School orchestra, I appreciate that.

The heart of our TV meal is the detective story. Properly done, with little violence and much detection, a TV detective story is the ideal, nonirritating, guilt-free interactive program. I am not sitting passively on the couch while gales of canned laughter blow over me or waves of fake blood wash over me. I am doing something. I am helping the detective find or prove who did it. If I don't find the answer—and I never do—I don't feel stupid about it. And if I do find a little piece of the answer—noting a clue or narrowing down the list of possible perpetrators—I am pleased with myself. But here is my lament: the detective story is disappearing from the TV screen.

TV Detectives

For many years, Britain has been the source of TV detective stories. I am grateful to the British for that, but their stories have never been entirely satisfactory. Sherlock is, of course, the father of the British detectives, and when he began to appear on PBS in the 1980s, we watched him regularly. But he does not stand repetition. As played by Jeremy Brett, Holmes was so eccentric, so mannered that all attention was drawn to him rather than to the story, and after you had seen him several times, he elicited giggles rather than puzzlement.

Hercule Poirot was my favorite among the British detectives who made their American TV debut on PBS. Perhaps that is a connection formed fifty years ago when I used to pass the time on the train between Washington and New York reading his adventures. Anyway, in his TV incarnation, the stories were the right length—one hour—Poirot spoke clearly, and the clues were not too obscure to be occasionally recognized by the viewer. But there have been no new Poirot stories for a long time, and although we still watch the reruns, I have the feeling that his shiny mustache is getting shinier and his mincing steps even more mincing.

The two British detectives now appearing in new series on PBS are Inspector Morse and Commander Dalgliesh. We appreciate and watch them but are not entirely happy with them. Their stories run for two to four hours, in two installments separated by a week. That is too long for even a couch potato to sit still. The detectives mumble. Surprisingly, an English actor speaking with what he thinks is a Belgian accent speaks more clearly than an English actor speaking in his own accent. The clues are too faint— too understated. I don't feel that I am coming closer to the solution, even after three hours. Maybe I am just not smart enough for a modern British TV detective story, as I am not smart enough for an English crossword puzzle. But I often think that even Morse and Dalgliesh don't have a clue until the whole thing is revealed in the last fifteen minutes.

My favorite detective stories are American, and the best of all is CBS's *Murder, She Wrote,* starring Angela Lansbury as Jessica Fletcher. They are almost always one hour in length. Everyone speaks clear English—whether he is a French detective, an Indian chief, or a Chinese banker. The clues are not obvious but not too hard to get either, especially after a second or third rerun. The "production values" are high. Wherever the setting is around the world, you feel that the setting is authentic, not a Hollywood back lot.

The stories are set in different walks of life—a TV studio, a rodeo, a bank, an advertising agency, a toy factory—and each one seems to reflect the setting accurately. (Having seen so many episodes and observed the formula, I have thought it would be amusing to write an episode set in a think tank. But I have been unable to visualize one think tank scholar killing another. For what— citation in a newspaper column?)

But best of all, there's Angela. She always says the right thing, does the right thing, wears the right clothes. She is an example of doing something extremely well. She does not rely on eccentricities to create a recognizable character, and that is why you can watch her over and over again. Time cannot wither nor custom stale her infinite normality. Alas, no new episodes of *Mur-*

der, She Wrote have been made for several years. We are living on reruns. That is all right for now. A true fan can enjoy seeing the same episode four or five times. He will discover something new each time. But that cannot go on much longer. I fear that when we reach the sixth or seventh repeat, it will have become boring. And what shall we do then?

When CBS gave up programming new episodes of *Murder, She Wrote,* it was allegedly because of the "demographics." We fans of Jessica Fletcher are too old to be a good market for advertisers. It is not because we are old that we like the polite, civilized detective story. My generation liked that when we were young; we liked Nick and Nora Charles in the movies and Ellery Queen on the radio. In our middle years, we liked Perry Mason on TV. We are of the generation that likes to have its intellect teased. Later generations like to have their emotions aroused. But it is true that we are not a good market for advertisers. We have money and spend it or invest it. But we have been around too long, and have had too much experience, to buy something or invest in something just because we see it advertised on television.

Perhaps in the era of 500 TV channels there will be one devoted to new episodes of *Murder, She Wrote, Columbo, Perry Mason,* and other, newly conceived, civilized detective stories. But for many fans of that genre, time is running out. For the present we have to try to learn to understand the British detectives. And we have to nurse the supply of old *Murder, She Wrote*s, rationing ourselves to not more than one viewing a week, hoping to preserve the fascination until the need for such entertainment has passed.

34

On Families and Values

O Family Values, what wonders are performed in your name! In your name, some political leaders propose to give a tax credit of $500 dollars per child to every income-tax–paying unit except the very richest. I use the expression *income-tax–paying unit* because no particular family relationship is required. There may be a couple, married or unmarried, or there may be a single taxpayer, male or female, and the children may have a biological relationship to both adults, to one, or to neither. At the same time, also in the name of family values, it is proposed to reduce federal benefits to mother-children units if the mother is young and poor.

A Children Problem

We do not have a family problem in America, or at least that is not one of our major problems. We have a children problem. Too many of our children are growing up uncivilized. The family deserves attention today mainly because it is the best institution for civilizing children. We shouldn't get too sentimental about that, however. Through most of history, the family that reared children was not our idealized poppy-mommy-kiddies group but a much more inclusive relationship. The first family was the scene of a fratricide. The most famous families in literature, the Montagues and Capulets, were obsessed with fighting each other, with fatal consequences for their children. Long before Freud, we knew that the family could be a nest of vipers.

Despite its blemishes, perhaps exaggerated in literature because they are exceptional, the family is the best institution we
know for rearing children. It is the best because it is most likely
to be governed by certain values—love, responsibility, voluntary
commitment to the welfare of others, including those least able to
fend for themselves, who are, of course, the children. That is what
family values are.

In the rearing of children, there is no satisfactory substitute
for the well-functioning family. We should try to strengthen such
families by private example, public policy, and any other way we
can. But even families that function well need supplementation by
other institutions. Some families do not function well, for economic or psychological reasons, and they need even more assistance. In modern societies, it is recognized that other institutions
have a responsibility and capacity to contribute to the raising of
children. These institutions include government, whose wide-
ranging functions, from education to the prevention of child abuse,
are generally accepted.

Human Values

Moreover, there are really no such things as "family values." What
we call "family values" are simply "human values" that also exist
and are desired in relationships outside the family, although they
are probably less dominant there.

Our need now is to bring what institutions, resources, and
values we can to bear on the problem of our children. From that
standpoint, the current trend of policy seems perverse. The "child
credit" has little to do with the welfare of children. Very few of the
children in the tax-paying units that would receive the credit are
part of the children problem in America, or if they are, it is not
because the after-tax incomes in the units are too small. Little of
the income that would be provided would go to the benefit of children. Presumably, the additional income would be used for the
purposes that the taxpayer had previously thought were of lowest
priority. Any need of a child that a taxpayer with an income of, say,
$60,000 would meet only upon receipt of a tax credit of $500 could
not be a very important need.

Neither is it reasonable to think that reducing government
cash and food benefits to poor children who are themselves the

children of poor child-mothers will help to civilize our children, although it may reduce somewhat the number of them born in the future. More care, nurturing, counseling, and education will be needed in the home, in a foster home, in a school, or perhaps even in an orphanage. The drive to cut costs in the name of family values provides none of that.

When I say that "our" children need to be civilized, I do not refer to my biological children and grandchildren, or yours either, dear reader. I refer to America's children. When the bomb exploded in Oklahoma City we all wept and prayed for the children. We did not say that they were only their parents' children or Oklahoma's children. They were America's children.

The children growing up in wretched families, in unsafe schools, and in vicious streets are also "our" children. A decent respect for family values calls for more concern with them and more commitment to them than is shown by most of those who now wave the flag of family values.

35

The Watergun Hearings—Excerpts from the Testimony of Herbert Stein before the House Select Committee on Domestic Disarmament

CHAIRMAN: Counsel, have you read the witness his rights?

COUNSEL: Yes, I have, sir.

CHAIRMAN: Then we will proceed in the usual way. Each member of the committee in turn will get to fire thirty rounds at the witness. I mean, each member will have five minutes for questioning. I will start.

Mr. Stein, we have here a report saying that you do not own a gun. Is that correct?

STEIN: Yes, sir.

CHAIRMAN: Do you mean that you do not own an assault rifle, or do you mean that you do not own a gun of any kind?

STEIN: I do not own a gun of any kind.

CHAIRMAN: Mr. Stein, or should I call you *Doctor Stein*?

STEIN: *Mister* is fine.

CHAIRMAN: You are an educated man. I suppose that you are familiar with the Second Amendment to the Constitution.

STEIN: I am not a lawyer, but I know of the amendment.

CHAIRMAN: Do you not think that you are in violation of the Second Amendment?

STEIN: I do not think that the amendment requires me to bear arms.

CHAIRMAN: The amendment clearly says that a well-regulated militia is necessary to the security of a free state. How do you think we can have a well-regulated militia to protect our rights if people like you do not bear arms?

STEIN: We have the National Guard.

CHAIRMAN: But the National Guard is subject to being federalized. Who will protect your rights against the federal government after the federal government has taken control of the National Guard?

STEIN: I guess that I would appeal to my congressman to protect my rights.

CHAIRMAN: And who is your congressman?

STEIN: You are, sir.

CHAIRMAN: Really! And did you contribute to my campaign?

STEIN: No, I did not, sir.

CHAIRMAN: So why do you think that I would try to protect your rights?

I see my time has expired. The ranking member will inquire.

RANKING MEMBER: Dr. Stein, have you ever fired a gun?

STEIN: Yes, I have, sir.

RANKING MEMBER: Tell us the circumstances.

STEIN: Well, it was during World War II. I was an ensign in the navy, stationed in Washington, working on economic plans. The navy sent me down to Quantico so that a Marine could teach me to use a revolver.

RANKING MEMBER: Didn't it feel good, having all that power in your hand?

STEIN: No, sir, it didn't. I couldn't hit the target, and my thumb got sore.

RANKING MEMBER: Did the navy issue you a side arm?

STEIN: No, they didn't.

RANKING MEMBER: Why not? You were an officer, and it was a time of war.

STEIN: I believe they thought that they would win the war even if I was unarmed. I believe they were also afraid that I might shoot a flag officer—accidentally.

NONRANKING MEMBER: In the fifty years since World War II, haven't you ever thought that you ought to have a gun?

STEIN: No, I haven't.

NONRANKING MEMBER: Suppose you were walking down the street and a tough guy came up to you and demanded your watch. What would you do?

STEIN: Well, I guess I would give it to him.

NONRANKING MEMBER: But if you had a gun, you wouldn't have to give him your watch.

STEIN: I don't want to shoot someone just because he doesn't have a watch.

NONRANKING MEMBER: You wouldn't have to shoot him. You could just point the gun at him.

STEIN: If I did that, he would probably take the gun away from me, and a gun costs more than a watch.

NONRANKING MEMBER: Your witness.

LEAST-RANKING MEMBER: Dr. Stein, I believe you are an economist. Is that correct?

STEIN: Yes, it is.

LEAST-RANKING MEMBER: I want to look at the question from an economic point of view. Suppose there was a great drought, and the corn crop failed. Then the price of meat would become terribly high, wouldn't it?

STEIN: Yes, after a little while it would.

LEAST-RANKING MEMBER: But if you had a gun, you could go out and shoot a cow and keep some beef on the table to feed your family.

STEIN: In the conditions you postulate, cows would be very scarce, and I don't know where I would find one to shoot. Anyway, we don't eat beef.

LEAST-RANKING MEMBER: You could shoot a rabbit.

STEIN: We don't eat rabbit, either.

LEAST-RANKING MEMBER: Well, what do you eat?

STEIN: We eat chicken and fish.

LEAST-RANKING MEMBER: So you could shoot a chicken.

STEIN: I don't think I could eat a chicken I had shot myself.

CHAIRMAN: Take the witness out and shoot him. I mean, thank you, Dr. Stein. You are excused.

36

Talk, Talk, Talk . . .

Having reached an advanced age, I am retiring from my duty as regular moderator of *Slate*'s Committee of Correspondence. On this occasion, I am moved to reflect on half a century—fifty-one years, actually—of producing talk about economic policy. What is such talk for, and, especially, does it influence policy? Economic policy talk runs a wide gamut, from unintelligible articles in learned journals to unbelievable TV spots in political campaigns. I confine my remarks here to the part of the gamut in which I have been active—which, I trust, has been the more intelligible and believable part of the range.

For twenty years I have been writing little essays about economic policy, about eight a year, in the *Wall Street Journal*; for six years I wrote a weekly syndicated column; and for six months I have been conducting a panel on policy issues for *Slate* magazine. Such writing, opinion pieces, editorials, and news analyses in papers and magazines of general circulation are the most common form of policy talk in America. But I do not think of it as mainly part of the process of determining economic policy. I think of it as an exercise in "economic policy appreciation."

Economics Appreciation

I use the analogy of the courses in music appreciation given in colleges. The students in these courses will not become musicians or composers. What goes on in the courses will not affect the output of actual composers—most of whom are already dead, anyway.

And yet the courses are useful. They help interested students understand and appreciate an element of the world they live in and thereby enrich their lives forever. A less high-flown analogy is the sports columns in the newspapers. I read those columns about games I have never played and will never play, about games I will never see in person, and mostly about games I have not seen on TV. And yet I like to know what is going on in that world and to be able to discuss it with my barber and my economist colleagues.

So it is with journalistic writing about economic policy. Some people, not as many as are interested in sports but still a large number, are interested in economic policy as a major part of life in America. They see it as an arena in which there is conflict among ideas and among identifiable personalities, and so they like to read about it. At least, there are enough such people to make publishers willing to pay (a little) to get such writing.

Journalistic Economics

I think that within the past fifty years the quality of journalistic writing about the economy and about economic policy has greatly improved. Fifty years ago newspaper writing about the economy was mainly in the hands of either the people who covered Wall Street or the people who covered politics. Then we began to get some reporters who, although without any formal training in economics, tried to learn about it and to write about the economy from that standpoint. I used to complain that such writers worked by telephoning and getting short quotations from a little list of economists who all had visible political identifications. This situation has changed. More journalists have studied economics, and they consult a wider range of sources. In addition, more papers regularly publish articles by professional economists. So I think that journalistic writing about economic policy has improved, as journalistic writing about sports probably has as well.

But whether this talk influences policy is another question. I don't have any statistics about this, but I am sure that many fewer people read editorials or columns about economic policy in the *Washington Post* than read Ann Landers's advice on life's human problems. The evidence on what Americans know about economics does not suggest very close reading. The number of people in Washington who know the Redskins' win-loss record must be enormously larger than the number who could come within hailing distance of knowing the unemployment rate.

The talk on the Op-Ed or editorial pages hardly adds up to discussion, if discussion means the confrontation of differing views, disciplined by rules of logic and evidence, and leading either to a conclusion or to agreement that no conclusion is possible. Some papers have representatives of different views—generally labeled "liberals" or "conservatives"—on their Op-Ed pages, but these representatives rarely confront each other or even write about the same subject. The TV talk shows make a point of confrontation, but those confrontations are too brief and superficial to be significant. I think that the exchanges on *Slate's* Committee of Correspondence have come closer to being discussions, with fairly extensive presentation of facts and arguments from different sides. But at the end of each week, I have usually felt that we are only beginning to get to the heart of the matter. Sometimes I think that instead of a week-long discussion of an issue, we should have a year-long discussion of it—but I would not want to be the moderator of that.

I think that most people—even those who read the editorial and Op-Ed pages—do not want to encounter opposing views. They want a good expression and confirmation of the views they have, or the views they would have if they thought about the subject. I can see that tendency in myself. I rarely read the columnists I know I am going to disagree with. Life is too short. I don't know anyone who reads the *Washington Times* who is not a conservative. Probably almost all readers of magazines with pronounced ideological or partisan slants share those slants. They want to be massaged, not informed.

In all my years of writing opinion pieces, I don't think that I have ever received a letter from a reader who said that I had changed his mind. I get some letters—a few—from readers who say they agree with me. Many of them say not only that they agree with me but also that they had had the same thought ten years ago and had written a fifty-page essay about it that they would like my help in getting published. Some write to disagree with me, often violently. But I don't remember any saying that I had changed his mind.

When I was in the administration as economic adviser to President Nixon, I, of course, read a good deal of journalistic writing about economic policy. I don't think that I felt that I learned anything about the facts or about the analysis from that reading. And yet, I believe that this journalistic talk had some effect on policy. The decision to impose price and wage controls in 1971 is an example. In the months before August 1971, the leading newspapers, magazines, and TV news shows were full of pleas for "some kind" of controls. That did not convince me that the controls were desirable. But it did create the impression that the people "out there" wanted controls. And if I got that impression, it must have come more strongly to the president who read such talk every morning in his daily news summary and for whom opposition to the controls was not quite so much a religion as it was to me.

Think Tank Publications

A different kind of talk, more purposeful and persistent than newspaper articles, may have a greater influence on policy. That is the talk in the form of pamphlets and books emanating from what are loosely described as "think tanks." One distinguishing feature of a think tank is that, unlike a newspaper or a magazine, it makes little attempt to sell its product but is happy to give it away free or at a greatly subsidized price.

For twenty-two years, from 1945 to 1967, I was a researcher and draftsman for a group of businessmen, the Committee for Economic Development. Each year the committee issued four or five pamphlets giving its view on current issues of policy. A statement on budget policy issued in 1947 exemplifies how such talk can influence policy. I shall not elaborate that policy here but identify it only as proposing that the condition of the budget should be judged by a calculation of what the surplus or deficit would be if the economy were at full employment. That idea gained a considerable currency in the twenty years after it was put forward by the CED; and although now much diluted, it still plays a part in thinking about budget policy. How did this influence come about? It was not simply because the basic idea was sound—as I believe it was. Several other factors were important. The proposal met a need—to bridge the gap between the naive Keynesianism with which the economics profession was infected and the balanced-budget fetishism of the business community. The fact that the proposal came from a group of businessmen lent it credibility. People are always willing to believe you if you say something that seems to be against your own interest or your own conventional dogma. Moreover, after the initial statement in 1947, the committee issued a statement almost every year for about twenty years applying the principle to the conditions of that year, creating a cumulative educational effect.

I could give other examples of influence flowing from the work of policy-studying institutions. The series of studies of taxation produced by the Brookings Institution in the 1960s and 1970s and the studies of regulation produced by the American Enterprise Institute in the 1980s and 1990s seem to me to have been effective.

Government by Trial and Error

Two qualifications have to be noted, however. Each year when I was at the CED, the president of that organization would report to the Board of Trustees on how influential that year's statements had been on that year's government policy. But when I was in the government, I never found the committee's recommendations on that year's problems valuable or effective. I thought, and I still think correctly, that we inside the government knew more about the issue of the day than any outsiders did, not because we were smarter but because we got information earlier and worked on it more intensively. The contribution of the think tank, when it is at its best, is not in solving the day's problems but in developing and promulgating a set of enduring principles for thinking about those problems.

In recent years, the number of think tanks has greatly increased. We are a rich country and can afford many think tanks. Many of these institutions are highly specialized, not only in the questions they study but also in the answers they give to those questions. I fear that they will depreciate the value of think tanks in general, conforming to Frank Knight's Law of Talk: Bad talk drives out good.

My sainted professor Knight also said that democracy is government by discussion. I would amend that to say that democracy is government by trial and error. The contribution of discussion—of talk—is to expand the range of options from which trials may be selected and to speed up the detection and correction of errors. I think talk has done that. But, anyway, talk about public policy is one of the pleasures of a democracy, and that's a good thing.

37

Microwaveconomics

S ince I have been living alone, many people have recommended that I should get a microwave oven. That would
make it easy for me to prepare a meal for myself and would
save a lot of time. So, earlier this year, during the post-Christmas
sales, I bought myself one. Ever since, I have been wondering
how to figure out what it does for me—how to do a cost-benefit
analysis.

Saving Time

The time-saving business is very tricky. I can buy a frozen chicken
potpie, for example, that would require sixty minutes to heat up in
the conventional oven but could be heated in twelve minutes in
the microwave, a saving of forty-eight minutes. But the saving is
for my kitchen appliances, not for me. If I use the conventional
oven, I am not going to spend sixty minutes of my time standing
next to the oven and waiting for it to finish. I might spend a few
minutes—say, five—putting the potpie in the oven. Then I have
fifty-five minutes for myself—to read the paper, or write the Great
American Novel, or do whatever I do with my time—while waiting
for the cooking to finish.

Paradoxically, the time saving is more real the smaller the
amount of time to be saved. Heating up a frozen pizza in the conventional oven, for example, takes twelve minutes, whereas doing
it in the microwave takes only four minutes. The eight extra minutes that I spend waiting for the conventional oven are too few for

me to use outside the kitchen. If I use the conventional method, I am likely to spend eight more minutes in the kitchen than if I use the microwave. So, by using the microwave, I gain eight minutes outside the kitchen.

What is the value to me of those eight minutes? I suppose the conventional answer is to divide my annual earned income by the number of minutes I spend working and so arrive at the income I could gain by having another minute at my disposal. In my case, this would be a difficult calculation. The time I spend "working" is not only the time I spend sitting at my word processor and writing these essays. It also includes all the time I spend musing about these essays, while in the shower, or on the bus, or trying to fall asleep, and I have no idea how much time that is in a year. Anyway, the eight minutes I don't spend in the kitchen will probably not be used to earn more income. It will probably be used to lie down listening to music.

The eight minutes I would have had to spend in the kitchen if I didn't have a microwave, though, would not have been entirely valueless. I can listen to music there or simply muse about an essay like this or about something else. The basic fact is that at my advanced age the important use of time is simply being alive. Still, the time spent outside the kitchen is probably more valuable than the time spent in the kitchen.

Thus, one benefit of the microwave is the excess of the value of the time spent outside the kitchen over the value of the time spent in the kitchen. If I make two pizzas a week and "save" eight minutes per pizza, it is the excess value of almost fourteen hours a year spent outside the kitchen.

High-Tech Benefits

There is, for me at least, another benefit. That is the pleasure of owning, operating, and observing a high-tech instrument. That pleasure is independent of any service delivered; it is pure enjoyment of the miracle of technology. I first observed this with television. I, like many others of my generation, was fascinated by TV even though almost everything we saw on TV was terrible. We were fascinated by the fact that it worked at all. To a large extent, the Internet is like that. We enjoy surfing the net just because it is so amazing and not because what we learn on it is so valuable.

There is some of the same satisfaction in watching a microwave at work.

What is the cost of acquiring these benefits? My microwave cost $150. If it will last for ten years, and the interest I could earn on my money is 5 percent, when I bought it I was facing a cost of about $19 a year. But once I have bought the microwave, the cost of keeping it is much less. One of the basic lessons of economics is "Bygones are forever bygones." What I paid for it is a bygone. Now the cost of keeping it depends on what I could sell it for. The nuisance of trying to sell it would probably make that not worthwhile. The best alternative would be to give it to some charitable organization like the Salvation Army. Suppose I could donate it and take a charitable deduction of $100. That might reduce my taxes by around $50. The cost of keeping my microwave, rather than giving it away, is the sacrifice of about $6.50 a year (including the interest I could have obtained on the $50) plus the sacrifice of the good feeling of having performed a charitable act. Then, as this calculation might be summarized in the microeconomics text-book,

X is the value per hour of time spent outside the kitchen
Y is the value per hour of time spent in the kitchen
Z is the value of the satisfaction of having given a $100 gift to charity
W is the annual value of the satisfaction of owning and operating this amazing instrument
$6.50 is the monetary cost of keeping the microwave for a year
14 is the number of hours per year of release from the kitchen as a result of using the microwave.

The question is whether 14 times (X minus Y) plus W exceeds $6.50 plus Z. Of course, I can't answer this question, because I can't measure W, X, Y, or Z in dollars or any other quantity that is common to them all. (I leave out the further complication of the cost of electricity for the microwave compared with the cost of gas for the oven. I live in an apartment building where most of these costs are borne by about 200 other families, just as I bear their costs. That is what economists call an "externality.")

Nevertheless, despite all these imponderables, I do make a decision. I decide to keep and use the microwave. In the end, if you ask me why I bought a microwave, why I keep it, and why I use it, I can't give a better answer than "I like it."

This is, of course, an exceedingly trivial case of decision making. But much of life is like that—personal life, business life, government life. Perhaps it is most like that in government. We cannot compare the incomparables and weigh the imponderables. We do what we like, and when we stop liking it, we change.

About the Author

Herbert Stein earned his B.A. from Williams College and his Ph.D. from the University of Chicago. He was a member of the President's Council of Economic Advisers from 1969 to 1974 and was chairman from 1972. He is the A. Willis Robertson Professor of Economics Emeritus of the University of Virginia and a senior fellow of the American Enterprise Institute (AEI). He writes regularly for *Slate,* on the Internet. He is also a member of the board of contributors of the *Wall Street Journal,* for which he writes frequently.

Among his publications are *Presidential Economics: The Making of Economic Policy from Roosevelt to Clinton* (1994), *The New Illustrated Guide to the American Economy* (1995, with Murray Foss), *On the Other Hand . . . : Essays on Economics, Economists, and Politics* (1995), *The Fiscal Revolution in America: Policy in Pursuit of Reality* (rev. ed. 1996), *Washington Bedtime Stories* (1986), and *Governing the $5 Trillion Economy* (1989).

Acknowledgments

Most of the chapters of this volume were originally published elsewhere, in some cases in slightly different form. Listed below are the original sources, with the date of publication.

AEI Press
"The Uneasy Case for the Flat Tax, in *Fairness and Efficiency in the Flat Tax*, by Robert E. Hall, Alvin Rabushka, Dick Armey, Robert Eisner, and Herbert Stein (Washington, D.C., 1996)

Brookings Review
"On Families and Values" (Summer 1995)

Cosmos Journal
"Reflections on an Early Libertarian" (Summer 1996)

Journal of Economic Perspectives
(Reprinted with permission)
"Fifty Years of the Council of Economic Advisers" (vol. 10, no. 3, Summer 1996)

New York Times
"The Watergun Hearings" (September 15, 1995)

Slate
(First published in *Slate,* www.slate.com. Reprinted with permission.)
"Brave New World" (May 19, 1998)
"Chairman Bill's Big Blue Book" (March 19, 1998)
"Gertrude Stein—Republican" (February 6, 1997)

"Golden Days" (November 27, 1997)
"Herb Stein's Unfamiliar Quotations" (May 15, 1997)
"Microwaveconomics" (February 19, 1998)
"The Nixon I Knew" (January 1, 1998)
"An Old Couch Potato's Lament" (March 6, 1997)
"Reading the Inaugurals" (January 10, 1997)
"Talk, Talk, Talk" (December 20, 1996)
"A Tourist at Home" (April 3, 1997)

Wall Street Journal
(Reprinted with permission of the *Wall Street Journal* © 1995, 1996, 1997, 1998. Dow Jones & Company, Inc. All rights reserved.)
"The American Dream" (December 24, 1996)
"Am I Better Off?" (November 5, 1996)
"Beware of Corporate Responsibility" (July 15, 1996)
"A Cautionary Memo for JFK Republicans" (May 30, 1996)
"The CPI, Servant or Master" (November 1, 1995)
"Death and Taxes" (July 3, 1997)
"The Debate over Economic Inequality" (May 1, 1996)
"Eighty-One Years" (October 21, 1997)
"Looking Back to August 15, 1971" (August 15, 1996)
"On Presidential Republicans" (October 9, 1995)
"A Primer on Pay and Productivity" (August 23, 1995)
"Wanted: A Fiscal Policy" (May 19, 1998)
"Who Pays for Privatizing Social Security?" (February 5, 1997)

Washingtonian
"Inside Washington's Old Executive Office Building" (September 1997)
"Washington before the War" (December 1996)

Washington Post
"Confessions of a Tax Lover" (September 10, 1995)
"Tips on Political Economics" (February 18, 1996)

A NOTE ON THE BOOK

This book was edited by the staff of the AEI Press.
The text was set in Century Old Style.
Coghill Composition, of Richmond, Virginia, set the type,
and Edwards Brothers of Lillington, North Carolina,
printed and bound the book, using permanent acid-free paper.

The AEI PRESS is the publisher for the American Enterprise Institute for Public Policy Research, 1150 17th Street, N.W., Washington, D.C. 20036; *Christopher C. DeMuth,* publisher; *Ann Petty,* editor; *Leigh Tripoli,* editor; *Cheryl Weissman,* editor; *Alice Anne English,* managing editor.